From a Native Daughter

Haunani-Kay Trask addressing 15,000 people gathered at ʻIolani Palace in Honolulu on the centenary of the American military invasion of Hawaiʻi and overthrow of the Hawaiian government. January 17, 1993.

Haunani-Kay Trask

From a Native Daughter

Colonialism and Sovereignty in Hawai'i

Revised Edition

A Latitude 20 Book
University of Hawai'i Press
Honolulu

In Association with
the Kamakakūokalani Center for Hawaiian Studies,
University of Hawai'i at Mānoa

Published by Common Courage Press 1993
Revised edition published by University of Hawai'i Press 1999

Printed in the United States of America
13 12 11 10 09 08 10 9 8 7 6 5

Library of Congress Cataloging-in-Publication Data

Trask, Haunani-Kay.

From a native daughter; colonialism and sovereignty in Hawai'i / Haunani-Kay Trask.—Rev. ed.

p. cm.

"A Latitude 20 book."

"In association with the Center for Hawaiian Studies, University of Hawai'i."

Includes biographical references and index.

ISBN 978-0-8248-2059-6 (paper: alk. paper)

I. Title.

DU627.8.T73 1999

320.9969—dc21

98-47188

CIP

University of Hawai'i Press books are printed on acid-free paper and meet the guidelines for permanence and durability of the Council on Library Resources.

Designed by Nina Lisowski

Printed by The Maple-Vail Book Manufacturing Group

For my parents

Bernard Kauka'ohu Trask
and
Haunani Cooper Trask

who taught me to love
Hawai'i and to protect
her for our children to come

Despite American political and territorial control of Hawai'i since 1898, Hawaiians are not Americans. Nor are we Europeans or Asians. We are not from the Pacific Rim, nor are we immigrants to the Pacific. We are the children of Papa—earth mother—and Wākea—sky father—who created the sacred lands of Hawai'i Nei. From these lands came the taro, and from the taro, the Hawaiian people. As in all of Polynesia, so in Hawai'i: younger sibling must care for and honor elder sibling who, in return, will protect and provide for younger sibling. Thus, Hawaiians must nourish the land from whence we come. The relationship is more than reciprocal, however. It is familial. The land is our mother and we are her children. This is the lesson of our genealogy.

In Polynesian cultures, genealogy is paramount. Who we are is determined by our connection to our lands and to our families. Therefore, our bloodlines and birthplace tell our identity. When I meet another Hawaiian, I say I am descended of two genealogical lines: the Pi'ilani line through my mother, who is from Hāna, Maui, and the Kahakumakaliua line through my father's family from Kaua'i. I came of age on the Ko'olau side of the island of O'ahu. This is who I am and who my people are and where we come from.

Contents

Part III

The Colonial Front: Historians, Anthropologists, and the Tourist Industry

Part IV

Native Hawaiians in a White University

Appendixes

Acknowledgments

For the second edition of this book, I am indebted to Eiko Kosasa who contributed both technical and sisterly support to enable me to finish my revisions on time. For her, a sincere *mahalo nui.*

In Indian country, *mahalo nui* to Ward Churchill for his gracious support in the publication of the first edition of this work.

In Hawai'i, *aloha nui* to David Stannard who has accompanied me on all the journeys; political, intellectual, personal. To Anne Landgraf and Ed Greevy, photographers and political comrades, my deep respect and *aloha.*

The following articles were first published in these journals and books: "New World Order," appears as "Mālama 'Āina: Take Care of the Land," in *Global Visions: Beyond the New World Order* (Boston: South End Press, 1993), pp. 127–131; "Racism against Native Hawaiians at the University of Hawai'i: A Personal and Political View," in *Amerasia Journal* 18:3 (1992); "Kupa'a 'Āina: Native Hawaiian Nationalism in Hawai'i," in *Politics and Public Policy in Hawai'i* (New York: SUNY Press, 1992); "'Lovely Hula Hands': Corporate Tourism and the Prostitution of Hawaiian Culture," in *Border/Lines*, no. 23 (1991/1992), 22–34; "The Politics of Academic Freedom as the Politics of White Racism," in *Restructuring for Ethnic Peace* (Honolulu: University of Hawai'i Institute of Peace, 1991), pp. 11–22; "Politics in the Pacific Islands: Imperialism and Native Self-Determination," in *Amerasia Journal 16(*1990): 1–20; "From a Native Daughter," in *The American*

Indian and the Problem of History (New York: Oxford University Press, 1987), pp. 171–179.

The evolution of my thinking owes a great debt to some of the most creative intellectuals and revolutionaries of the twentieth century: Frantz Fanon, Malcolm X, and Ngũgĩ wa Thiong'o. Genealogically, I am indebted to those many chiefs of old, from the Pi'ilani and Kamehameha lines especially, who believed the dignity and inheritance of my Hawaiian people could only be taken in war. I am descended from these chiefs, in whose memory I have written these words.

Haunani-Kay Trask
He'eia, 1999

From a Native Daughter

Introduction

We protest against the movement in favor of doing away with the independence of our country; we protest against the effort to force annexation to the United States without consulting the people. . . .

Memorial to President Cleveland from the Hui Aloha ʻĀina (Hawaiian patriots) on the American overthrow of the Hawaiian government, 1893

I do not feel. . . we should forfeit the traditional rights and privileges of the natives of our islands for a mere thimbleful of votes in Congress; that we, the lovers of Hawaiʻi from long association with it should sacrifice our birthright for the greed of alien desires to remain on our shores. . . .

Kamokila Campbell before Congress on statehood for Hawaiʻi, 1946

Our country has been and is being plasticized, cheapened, and exploited. They're selling it in plastic leis, coconut ashtrays, and cans of "genuine, original Aloha." They've raped us, sold us,

> killed us, and still they expect us to behave. . . . Hawai'i is a colony of the imperialist United States.
>
> Kehau Lee on evictions of Hawaiians from Native lands, 1970

> The time has come to create a mechanism for self-government for the Hawaiian people. The question of Hawaiian sovereignty and self-determination needs to be dealt with now.
>
> Mililani Trask before Congress on Hawaiian sovereignty, 1990[1]

Spanning nearly a hundred years, these statements by Native Hawaiians stun most Americans who have come, over the course of their consumer society, First World lifetimes, to believe that Hawai'i is as American as hot dogs and CNN. Worse, Americans assume that if an opportunity arises, they too may make the trip to paradise, following along after the empire into the sweet and sunny land of palm trees and *"hulahula"* girls.

This predatory view of my Native land and culture is not only opposed by increasing numbers of us, it is angrily and resolutely defied: Hawaiians commemorated the centenary of the overthrow of our government with mass arrests and demonstrations against the denial of our human right to self-determination. For us, Hawaiian self-government has always been preferable to American foreign government. No matter what Americans believe, most of us in the colonies do not feel grateful that our country was stolen, along with our citizenship, our lands, and our independent place among the family of nations. We are not happy Natives.

On the ancient burial grounds of our ancestors, glass and steel shopping malls with layered parking lots stretch over what were once the most ingeniously irrigated taro lands, lands that fed millions of our people over thousands of years. Large bays, delicately ringed long ago with well-stocked fishponds, are now heavily silted and cluttered with jet skis, windsurfers, and sailboats. Multistory hotels disgorge over six million tourists a year onto stunningly beautiful (and easily polluted) beaches, closing off access to locals. On the major islands of Hawai'i, Maui, O'ahu, and Kaua'i, meanwhile, military airfields, training camps, weapons storage facilities, and exclusive housing and beach areas remind the Native Hawaiian who owns Hawai'i: the foreign, colonial country called the United States of America.

But American colonization has brought more than physical transformation to the lush and sacred islands of our ancestors. Visible in garish "Polynesian" revues, commercial ads using our dance and language to sell vacations and condominiums, and the trampling of sacred *heiau* (temples) and burial grounds as tourist recreation sites, a grotesque commercialization of everything Hawaiian has damaged Hawaiians psychologically, reducing our ability to control our lands and waters, our daily lives, and the expression and integrity of our culture. The cheapening of Hawaiian culture (for example, the traditional value of *aloha* as reciprocal love and generosity now used to sell everything from cars and plumbing to securities and air conditioning) is so complete that non-Hawaiians, at the urging of the tourist industry and the politicians, are transformed into "Hawaiians at heart," a phrase that speaks worlds about how grotesque the theft of things Hawaiian has become. Economically, the statistic of thirty tourists for every Native means that land and water, public policy, law, and the general political attitude are shaped by the ebb and flow of tourist industry demands. For our Native people, the inundation of foreigners decrees marginalization in our own land.

The state of Hawai'i, meanwhile, pours millions of dollars into the tourism industry, even to the extent of funding a booster club—the Hawai'i Visitors Bureau—whose television and radio propaganda tells locals, "the more you give" to tourism, "the more you get."

And what Hawaiians "get" is population densities like Hong Kong in some areas; a housing shortage owing to staggering numbers of migrants from the continental United States and Asia; a soaring crime rate, as impoverished locals prey on flauntingly rich tourists; and environmental crises, including water depletion, which threaten the entire archipelago. Rather than stem the flood, the state is projecting a tidal wave of twelve million tourists by the year 2010 and encouraging rocket launching facilities and battleship homeporting as added economic "security."

For my people, this latest degradation is but another stage in the agony that began with the first footfall of European explorers in 1778, shattering two millennia of Hawaiian civilization characterized by an indigenous way of caring for the land, called *mālama 'āina*.

History

Before there existed an England, an English language, or an Anglo-Saxon people, our Native culture was forming. And it was as antithetical to the European developments of Christianity, capitalism, and predatory individualism as any society could have been. But in several respects, Hawaiian society had remarkably much in common with indigenous societies throughout the world.

The economy of pre-*haole* Hawai'i depended primarily on a balanced use of the products of the land and sea.[2] Each of the eight inhabited islands was divided into separate districts (known as *'okana*), running from the mountains to the sea. Each *'okana* was then subdivided into *ahupua'a,* which themselves ran in wedge-shaped pieces from the mountains to the sea. Each *ahupua'a* was then fashioned into *'ili,* on which resided the *'ohana* (extended families), who cultivated the land. The *'ohana* was the core economic unit in Hawaiian society.

As in most indigenous societies, there was no money, no idea or practice of surplus appropriation, value storing, or payment deferral because there was no idea of financial profit from exchange. In other words, there was no basis for economic exploitation in pre-*haole* Hawai'i.

Exchange between *'ohana* who lived near the sea with *'ohana* who lived inland constituted the economic life of the multitudes of communities which densely populated the Hawaiian islands. *Ahupua'a* were economically independent. As local anthropologist Marion Kelly has written, "Under the Hawaiian system of land-use rights, the people living in each *ahupua'a* had access to all the necessities of life," thus establishing an independence founded upon the availability of "forest land, taro and sweet potato areas, and fishing grounds."[3]

If kinship formed the economic base of Hawaiian society, it also established the complex network of *ali'i* (chiefs), who competed in terms of rank (established by *mana,* or spiritual power derived from chiefly genealogies or from conquest in war) and ability to create order and prosperity on the land. The highest ranking *ali'i* were advised by a council of chiefs and a *kahuna* (priestly) class who were themselves quite powerful.

The *maka'āinana* (people of the land) made up the great bulk of the population and, although subordinate to their *ali'i* caretakers, were independent in many ways. Unlike feudal European economic and political arrangements—to which the ancient Hawaiian system has often been erroneously compared—the *maka'āinana* neither owed military service to the *ali'i* nor were they bound to the land.

The genius of the mutually beneficial political system of pre-*haole* Hawai'i was simply that an interdependence was created whereby the *maka'āinana* were free to move with their *'ohana* to live under an *ali'i* of their choosing while the *ali'i* increased their status and material prosperity by having more people living within their *moku*, or "domain." The result was an incentive for the society's leaders to provide for all their constituents' well-being and contentment. To fail to do so meant the loss of status and thus of *mana* for the *ali'i*.

Moral order, or the code upon which determinations of "right" and "wrong" were based, inhered in the *kapu*, or system of sacred law. It was the *kapu* that determined everything from the time for farming and war-making to correct mating behavior among *ali'i* and *maka-'āinana* alike. My people believed that all living things had spirit and, indeed, consciousness and that gods were many and not singular. Since the land was an ancestor, no living thing could be foreign. The cosmos, like the natural world, was a universe of familial relations. And human beings were but one constituent link in the larger family. Thus gods had human as well as animal form and human ancestors inhabited different physical forms after death. Nature was not objectified but personified, resulting in an extraordinary respect (when compared to Western ideas of nature) for the life of the sea, the heavens, and the earth. Our poetry and dance reveal this great depth of sensuous feeling—of love—for the beautiful world we inhabited.

When Captain James Cook stumbled upon this interdependent and wise society in 1778, he brought an entirely foreign system into the lives of my ancestors, a system based on a view of the world that could not coexist with that of Hawaiians. He brought capitalism, Western political ideas (such as predatory individualism), and Christianity. Most destructive of all, he brought diseases that ravaged my people until we were but a remnant of what we had been on contact with his pestilential crew.[4]

In less than a hundred years after Cook's arrival, my people had been dispossessed of our religion, our moral order, our form of chiefly government, many of our cultural practices, and our lands and waters. Introduced diseases, from syphilis and gonorrhea to tuberculosis, small pox, measles, leprosy, and typhoid fever, killed Hawaiians by the hundreds of thousands, reducing our Native population (from an estimated one million at contact) to less than 40,000 by 1890.[5]

Upon the heels of British explorers and their diseases, Americans came to dominate the sandalwood trade in the 1820s. Coincident with this early capitalism was the arrival of Calvinist missionaries who introduced a religious imperialism that was as devastating a scourge as any venereal pox. Conveniently for the missionaries, the Hawaiian universe had collapsed under the impact of mass death. The fertile field of conversion was littered with the remnants of holocaust, a holocaust created by white foreigners and celebrated by their later counterparts as the will of a Christian god. By the 1840s, Hawaiians numbered less than 100,000, a population collapse of nearly 90 percent in less than seventy years. Missionary imperialism had been successful in converting our dying people who believed that the Christian promise of everlasting life meant the everlasting *physical* life of our nation.

A combination of religious and economic forces enabled aggressive Americans to enter the government, where they pressured the chiefs and King unceasingly for private property land tenure. In the meantime, whaling had come briefly to control the economy, while in the United States, President John Tyler enunciated the infamous Tyler Doctrine of 1842, which asserted to European powers that Hawai'i was in the "U.S. sphere of influence" and therefore off-limits to European interventions. The U.S. House Committee on Foreign Affairs, meanwhile, replied to the Tyler Doctrine with a Manifest Destiny statement suggesting that "Americans should acknowledge their own interests" in Hawai'i as a "virtual right of conquest" over the "mind and heart" of the Hawaiian people.

Gunboat diplomacy by Western powers and missionary duplicity against the Hawaiian chiefs forced the transformation of Hawaiian land tenure from communal use to private property by the middle of the nineteenth century. After a five-month British takeover of the government in 1843, a weary and frightened King Kamehameha III gave in to *haole* advisers for a division of the lands, called the *Māhele*. This dispossession of the Hawaiians' birthright—our *one hānau*, or birthsands—allowed foreigners to own land. Through the unrelenting efforts of missionaries like Gerrit P. Judd, the *Māhele* was attained in 1848–1850.[6] Our disease-ridden ancestors, confused by Christianity and preyed upon by capitalists, were thereby dispossessed. Traditional lands were quickly transferred to foreign ownership and burgeoning sugar plantations. By 1888, three-quarters of all arable land was controlled by *haole*.[7] In this way, as one *haole* legal scholar has remarked, "Western imperialism had been accomplished without the usual bothersome wars and costly colonial administration."[8]

The decade of the 1850s witnessed a struggle between those planters seeking annexation to avoid U.S. sugar tariffs and a monarchy attempting to preserve its sovereignty while fending off military interventions and a growing foreign element in the Kingdom. The first annexation treaty was drafted by Americans in the King's government, and it sought Hawai'i's admission as a state in order to guarantee Native rights.[9] But Kamehameha III was opposed to annexation, and the treaty remained unsigned at his death. His successor, Prince Alexander Liholiho, ascended the throne in 1854. He terminated ongoing negotiations for annexation to the United States, substituting a policy of "sovereignty with reciprocity." Concerned that American sugar planters in Hawai'i would agitate for annexation to circumvent both the high U.S. sugar tariff and competition with sugar from the Philippines and other foreign markets, Liholiho attempted to ease their fears through a reciprocity treaty that would satisfy the planters' demand for profit. To protect Hawaiian independence, meanwhile, he coupled his reciprocity position with an independence policy. Under this plan, the United States, France, and Britain would agree to respect and maintain the independence of Hawai'i.

The Reciprocity Treaty died in the U.S. Senate, while all three Euro-American powers proclaimed their lack of interest in annexing Hawai'i. Of course, sugar planters were unhappy at the failure of the treaty, but the boom in sugar profits (1857–1867) caused by the ban on southern sugar in the northern states during the Civil War delayed the cries for another treaty. A post-Civil War depression, however, rekindled agitation for reciprocity in Hawai'i.

In the meantime, Liholiho died, quite suddenly, in 1863. His brother, Prince Lot, succeeded him as Kamehameha V. He, too, was a strong advocate of Hawaiian independence, and he continued his brother's policy of seeking a reciprocity treaty and a quadripartite treaty with France, Britain, and the United States ensuring the independence and neutrality of Hawai'i.

But while the King's government sought to protect Hawaiian sovereignty, the new U.S. Minister to Hawai'i, James McBride, was suggesting that cession of a port at Honolulu should be a condition of any reciprocity treaty. He also urged the permanent stationing of a U.S.

warship in Hawaiian waters to guard American interests. This became a reality in 1866 when the U.S.S. *Lackawanna* was assigned to the islands for an indefinite period.

Protecting economic interests with military might was but an extension of the Manifest Destiny policy that Americans had practiced on the continent. Indeed, after the American imperium had spread to the Pacific Coast (California and Oregon were part of the United States by 1848), bellwether newspapers like the *New York Times* stated on July 22, 1868, that the United States was "bound within a short time to become the great commercial, and controlling, and civilizing power of the Pacific." This sentiment accurately reflected the policy of the American government whose Secretary of State, William H. Seward, had been an advocate of annexation since before the Civil War and who had considered "purchasing" Hawai'i as Alaska had been "purchased" in 1867.

The biggest push toward annexation, however, did not come from the continent but from *haole* sugar planters in Hawai'i. Each downswing in the sugar industry resulted in familiar cries for closer union. Heated controversies broke out in the press and the legislature as Hawaiians responded to planter demands for "reciprocity or annexation" with intensely nationalistic statements opposed to American control and intervention. The feverish atmosphere was exacerbated when Henry Pierce assumed his post as Minister to Hawai'i in 1869 and immediately urged the cession of Pearl River Lagoon as a naval station in exchange for a reciprocity treaty. The *haole* newspapers, such as the *Pacific Commercial Advertiser,* supported cession of Pearl River as a quid pro quo for reciprocity. But they also supported annexation, as did Pierce, seeing in reciprocity the first step toward union.

The *Advertiser's* pronouncements coincided with a change in sovereign. Kamehameha V had died in 1872. His successor, William Lunalilo, was greatly loved by his people, who overwhelmingly elected him as sovereign. Once elected, however, Lunalilo gave in to his Ministers' urging and reluctantly agreed to negotiate a reciprocity treaty that included the cession of Pearl River Lagoon.

Lunalilo's position on cession had been encouraged by local *haole* banker and Cabinet Minister Charles Bishop who, with U.S. General Schofield, had discussed the American desire for a military base at Pearl River. Later, Schofield would tell Congress that the Hawaiian Islands constituted the only natural outpost to defenses of the Pacific Coast, implying support for annexation by the United States.

Both Bishop and Schofield were disappointed, however, when Lunalilo reversed himself. The Native public outcry against any cession of Hawaiian land convinced the King he would receive no support for his actions. To a person, Hawaiians viewed cession as a prelude to annexation, which they vigorously and vehemently opposed, arguing in the Hawaiian newspapers that annexation would be national death.

Keenly aware of American racism because of *haole* treatment of American Indians and enslaved African peoples on the continent, Hawaiians understood they would be classified with other "colored races," like Liholiho had been when, as Crown Prince, he had traveled by train through the United States and had been ejected, along with his brother Prince Lot, because of his skin color.

As their newspapers argued, Hawaiians would suffer "virtual enslavement under annexation," including further loss of lands and liberties. Understanding both the predatory designs of the sugar planters in Hawai'i and the *haole* politicians on the continent, Hawaiians supported their chiefs in resisting annexation.

Lunalilo had no sooner changed his mind, bowing to the wishes of his people, when he contracted tuberculosis and died in 1874. His reign had lasted less than thirteen months.

The King's death was but the most glaring example of the toll introduced diseases had been taking on the Native people since the arrival of Cook in 1778. The first "gifts" of venereal disease and tuberculosis brought by the British were followed by diseases introduced by Americans and Asians: typhoid fever, measles, smallpox, influenza, and leprosy. Lacking immunities and plagued by political and economic crises, the Hawaiian population continued its rapid decline. It was a vastly weakened nation that faced yet another political crisis following the death of their beloved sovereign.

While debates over the threat to Hawaiian sovereignty raged in the papers, an immediate menace to Native independence was posed by the constant interference of U.S. naval forces to quell civil disturbances in the city of Honolulu. Since the early eighteenth-century presence of whalers and merchants in the new towns, such as Lahaina and Honolulu, civil disturbances had increased. Alcohol and prostitution exacerbated the problem. The Kingdom was periodically inundated by foreigners, often rowdy and drunk, congregating at the ports and in city saloons.

But peacekeeping was a superficial excuse for the continuing American military presence. As every U.S. Minister after the Civil War had argued, warships were needed to protect American *economic* interests. Thus when political disturbances threatened to disrupt the sugar industry, the U.S. military intervened.

Just such an occurrence followed the untimely death of Lunalilo, when Kalākaua ran against Dowager Queen Emma for the throne. His supporters and those of the Queen engaged in a brief conflict that precipitated the landing of United States marines, ostensibly to maintain order but in reality to support the pro-American Kalākaua against the pro-British Emma. Kalākaua became King, but he was indebted to the Americans for his election.

After nearly forty years of negotiation, a Reciprocity Treaty was concluded under Kalākaua's administration in 1875. It brought immediate relief to the sugar industry, indeed, an unprecedented boom. Sugar exports to the U.S. went from 17 million pounds in 1875 to 115 million pounds in 1883. Of the 32 plantations that dominated the Hawaiian economy, 25 were American-owned.

But while the treaty brought a temporary boost to Hawai'i's economy, it also brought a flood of foreign immigrants to work the sugar plantations. Between 1877 and 1890, 55,000 new immigrants flooded Hawai'i, an increase of 33 percent in their numbers. During the same period, the Native population was halved, while the *haole* population soared. By 1890, Hawaiians made up less than half the population (45 percent) while *haole* and Asians were 55 percent of the population. This increase infuriated Hawaiians, who saw, correctly, that the decline of their own people coupled with the large-scale foreign influx would endanger Native control of their homeland.

American interests, meanwhile, grew larger by the day: plantation ownership was predominantly American, and Kalākaua's ministry was entirely American in sentiment. Henry Pierce, American Minister to Hawai'i, reflected this reality when he argued in 1877 that the islands were an American colony in all their material and political interests.

A predictable economic crisis in the 1880s left Kalākaua with a debt-ridden government and public agitation by both Natives and *haole* planters for a resolution. President Garfield's Secretary of State James G. Blaine had begun the decade by baldly stating that Hawai'i had become the key to the dominion of the Pacific. For him, and for most other arrogant politicians from the continent, American control of the commercial life of Hawai'i made it an outlying district of California.

Finally, American military and economic interests triumphed in the Reciprocity Treaty of 1887 when Pearl River Lagoon was ceded to the United States in exchange for duty-free sugar. The treaty had been accomplished as a result of the aptly named "Bayonet Constitution" forced upon Kalākaua by *haole* merchants and politicians. Impudently self-titled the "Hawaiian League," this group was in fact an all-white gang of businessmen, armed with guns from San Francisco, formed specifically to protect the interests of *haole* property owners. A subgroup, the Honolulu Rifles, was an all-*haole* annexation club. Unable to dominate the legislature, the Hawaiian League effectively seized power by forcing Kalākaua to agree to a new constitution in which the Ministry was no longer responsible to the King but to the legislature. To ensure *haole* domination of the legislature, the electorate was severely restricted by income qualifications of $600 or $3,000 worth of property. The intended and immediate result was that missionary descendants, whose parents had benefited from the land division of 1848, captured the legislature. The Cabinet and patronage went to the Hawaiian League. Predictably, what the *haole* capitalists could not achieve through their much-touted system of American-style democracy, they took through another time-honored American tradition of thuggery and armed intervention. The worst cut of all was the extension of suffrage to foreigners willing to swear allegiance to the new government.

Of the results of this usurper's constitution, U.S. Commissioner James Blount, sent years later to investigate the overthrow of the Hawaiian government, wrote:

> Power was taken from the King in the selection of nobles, not to be given to the masses but to the wealthy classes, a large majority of whom were not subjects of the Kingdom. Power to remove the Cabinet was taken away from the King not to be conferred on a popular body but on one designed to be ruled by foreign subjects. Power to do any act was taken from the King. . . . This instrument was never submitted to the people for approval or rejection, nor was this ever contemplated by its friends and promoters.[10]

Together with the cession of Pearl River Lagoon, the Bayonet Constitution effectively challenged the sovereignty of the Kingdom.

British Minister Wodehouse observed at the time, ". . . the Hawaiian Kingdom has relinquished its own territory to a foreign power." The United States, in collusion with white settlers in Hawai'i, moved inexorably to fulfill the prophecy of Manifest Destiny. Extending the American imperium into the Pacific seemed entirely natural to a people and a government seasoned by centuries of genocide against American Indians.

After the Bayonet Constitution, racist arguments about Native cultural inferiority and political and economic inability appeared daily in the *haole* newspapers of the times, justifying the seizure of power and the deafening calls for annexation. Enraged by the actions of the planter aristocracy, the Hawaiians revolted, seeking to revise the Bayonet Constitution in favor of the more equitable Constitution of 1864. Once again, American troops were landed to "restore order," prefiguring their role in the eventual overthrow of the Hawaiian government in 1893.

In that fateful year, the "missionary gang" of white planters and businessmen plotted with the United States Minister to Hawai'i, John L. Stevens, to overthrow the lawful Native government of our last ruling *ali'i,* Lili'uokalani. The Queen had succeeded her brother, Kalākaua, upon his death in San Francisco in 1891. Unlike him, she was determined to return her people to their rightful political place in their own land. Having received dozens of petitions signed by thousands of her subjects requesting a new constitution, and realizing that the deadlocked legislature would not call a constitutional convention, the Queen decided to give her people a new and more democratic constitution, one that removed the property requirement for voters and restricted the franchise to subjects of the Kingdom. Foreigners would not be allowed to vote.

But Lili'uokalani was thwarted by her Ministry, which betrayed her to the *haole* planters.

As they had rehearsed so many times before, the *haole* businessmen and their foreign supporters immediately organized themselves as a "Committee of Safety" to create a new, all-white regime and to seek immediate military help from Minister Stevens. Agreeing to land the marines and to recognize the *haole* "Provisional Government" (as they called themselves), Stevens played out his imperialist role.

Confronted by the American-recognized Provisional Government, and facing an occupying U.S. military force across from her palace, Lili'uokalani ceded her authority not to the Provisional Government but to the United States on January 17, 1893.

She wrote to Sanford B. Dole, descendant of missionaries and newly chosen head of the Provisional Government:

> I yield to the superior force of the United States of America, whose minister. . . has caused United States troops to be landed at Honolulu. . . .
>
> Now to avoid any collision of armed forces and perhaps the loss of life, I do under this protest, and impelled by said force, yield my authority until such time as the Government of the United States shall, upon the facts being presented to it, undo the action of its representatives and reinstate me in the authority which I claim as the constitutional sovereign of the Hawaiian Islands.[11]

On February 1, 1893, Minister Stevens proclaimed Hawai'i a U.S. protectorate and raised the American flag. But his dream for swift annexation was short-lived. President Cleveland, a mere five days after his inauguration on March 4, withdrew the pending annexation treaty from Congress.

On March 29, Cleveland's commissioner, James Blount, arrived in Hawai'i to investigate the overthrow. He sent the American troops back to their ship and lowered the American flag. For four months Blount conducted his investigation in an atmosphere of intimidation by the "missionary gang" and hopeful trust on the part of Hawaiians. When he returned to the United States on August 8, the *haole* government knew he was no friend to their party.

Blount's Report has justly come to be known among Hawaiians as the single most damaging document against the United States, the missionary descendants, and the arrogant Mr. Stevens. Thorough and scrupulously fair, Commissioner Blount found the United States and its Minister guilty on all counts. The overthrow, the landing of the marines, and the subsequent recognition of the provisional government pointed to clear conspiracy between Minister Stevens and the "missionary gang." President Cleveland, upon reading the lengthy and careful Blount report, explained to Congress why he would never again submit the annexation treaty to them:

> The lawful Government of Hawai'i was overthrown without the drawing of a sword or the firing of a shot by a process every step of which, it

> may safely be asserted, is directly traceable to and dependent for its success upon the agency of the United States acting through its diplomatic and naval representatives.
>
> But for the notorious predilections of the United States Minister for annexation, the Committee of Safety, which should be called the Committee for Annexation, would never have existed.
>
> But for the landing of the United States forces upon false pretexts respecting the danger to life and property the committee would never have exposed themselves to the pains and penalties of treason by undertaking the subversion of the Queen's Government.
>
> But for the presence of the United States forces in the immediate vicinity and in position to afford all needed protection and support, the committee would not have proclaimed the provisional government from the steps of the Government building.
>
> And finally, but for the lawless occupation of Honolulu under false pretexts by the United States forces, and but for Minister Stevens' recognition of the provisional government when the United States forces were its sole support and constituted its only military strength, the Queen and her Government would never have yielded to the provisional government, even for a time and for the sole purpose of submitting her case to the enlightened justice of the United States.
>
> Believing, therefore, that the United States could not, under the circumstances disclosed, annex the islands without justly incurring the imputation of acquiring them by unjustifiable methods, I shall not again submit the treaty of annexation to the Senate. . . .

If Cleveland had said only this, it would still be the clearest statement of American culpability, of American wrongdoing, of American injustice regarding the overthrow of our nation. But Cleveland did not stop here. He went on:

> By an act of war, committed with the participation of a diplomatic representative of the United States and without authority of Congress, the Government of a feeble but friendly and confiding people has been overthrown. A substantial wrong has thus been done which a due regard for our national character as well as the rights of the injured people requires we should endeavor to repair."[12]

Thus was the issue of reparation, of undoing the harm and the injury to the Hawaiian people first brought to the attention of the American government. It was an exquisite irony of history that an American president would be the first to argue for restitution, indeed to pursue restoration of our highest chief, the living heart of Hawaiian sovereignty.

Unfortunately, Cleveland left office after only four years. Lili'uokalani was never restored. Indeed, she was imprisoned for some five months by the *haole* planters after a failed effort by Hawaiians to reestablish their sovereignty. Because Cleveland had stalled annexation, the all-white Provisional Government became the all-white oligarchy renamed, euphemistically, the Republic of Hawai'i. Of course, the alleged "republic" was actually an oligarchy, with a franchise limited by property and language requirements and a loyalty oath that effectively excluded all Natives. Final annexation in 1898 had to wait for a real imperialist, William McKinley.

No vote was taken on a treaty of annexation, neither in the colony nor in the Congress. Both annexationists in Hawai'i and in America knew that a vote would go against them. The Natives, as Blount had repeatedly heard from *haole* and Hawaiians he interviewed, were against annexation to a person. They had seen and tasted American democracy: white gang rule supported by white military thugs. Hawaiians preferred their own Native government.

Asian immigrants would not have been allowed to vote, even if the *haole* planters had agreed to a referendum on annexation, which they did not. Since most immigrants owned no property and neither read nor wrote English or Hawaiian, this was a fitting ruse for excluding them, too.

On the continent, the large majority in Congress was opposed to annexation, if only because the "mongrel" population of Hawai'i meant that a predominantly "colored" people would enter a predominantly white nation.

Thus, it was by resolution (which only required a simple majority) rather than by treaty (which required a two-thirds majority) that Hawai'i was annexed. Once the empire spilled out into the vast Pacific, the Philippines and other Pacific Islands would follow Hawai'i in short order.

Because of the overthrow and annexation, Hawaiian control and Hawaiian citizenship were replaced with American control and American citizenship. We suffered a unilateral redefinition of our homeland and our people, a displacement and a dispossession in our own country. In familial terms, our mother (and thus our heritage and our inheritance) was taken from us. We were orphaned in our own land. Such brutal changes in a people's identity—their legal status, their government, their sense of belonging to a nation—are considered among the most serious human rights violations by the international community today.[13]

As a result of these actions, Hawaiians became a conquered people, our lands and culture subordinated to another nation. Made to feel and survive as inferiors when our sovereignty as a nation was forcibly ended, we were rendered politically and economically powerless by the turn of the century. Cultural imperialism had taken hold with conversion to Christianity in the middle of the nineteenth century, but it continued with the closing of all Hawaiian language schools and the elevation of English as the only official language in 1896. Once the Republic of Hawai'i declared itself on July 4, 1894, the "Americanization" of Hawai'i was sealed like a coffin.

Today, Hawaiians continue to suffer the effects of *haole* colonization. Under foreign control, we have been overrun by settlers: missionaries and capitalists (often the same people), adventurers and, of course, hordes of tourists, nearly seven million by 1998. Preyed upon by corporate tourism, caught in a political system where we have no separate legal status—unlike other Native peoples in the United States—to control our land base (over a million acres of so-called "trust" lands set aside by Congress for Native beneficiaries but leased by their alleged "trustee," the state of Hawai'i, to non-Natives), we are by every measure the most oppressed of all groups living in Hawai'i, our ancestral land.

Despite the presence of a small middle class, Hawaiians as a people register the same profile as other indigenous groups controlled by the United States: high unemployment, catastrophic health problems, low educational attainment, large numbers institutionalized in the military and prisons, occupational ghettoization in poorly paid jobs, and increasing outmigration that amounts to diaspora. Indeed, so great is the oppression caused outmigration of Hawaiians from their island homes that, despite the highest birthrate in Hawai'i, we remain only twenty percent of the resident population. Some estimates report that more Hawaiians now live on the West Coast of the United States than in their Native land.

The latest affliction of corporate tourism has meant a particularly insidious form of cultural prostitution. The *hula*, for example, an ancient form of dance with deep and complex religious meaning, has been made ornamental, a form of exotica for the gaping tourist. Far from encouraging a cultural revival, as tourist industry apologists contend, tourism has appropriated and prostituted the accomplishments of a resurgent interest in things Hawaiian (for example, the use of replicas of Hawaiian artifacts, such as fishing and food implements, capes, helmets, and other symbols of ancient power, to decorate hotels). Hawaiian women, meanwhile, are marketed on posters from Paris to Tokyo promising an unfettered "primitive" sexuality. Burdened with commodification of our culture and exploitation of our people, Hawaiians exist in an occupied country whose hostage people are forced to witness (and, for many, to participate in) our own collective humiliation as tourist artifacts for the First World.

In the meantime, shiploads and planeloads of American military forces continue to pass through Hawai'i on their way to imperialist wars in Asia and elsewhere. Throughout the Second World War and its aftermath, Hawai'i was under martial law for seven years, during which time over 600,000 acres of land was confiscated, civil rights were held in abeyance, and a general atmosphere of military intimidation reigned. Now, as we approach the American president's New World Order, Hawai'i is a militarized outpost of empire, deploying troops and nuclear ships to the south and east to prevent any nation's independence from American domination. Fully one-fifth of our resident population is military, causing intense friction between locals, who suffer from Hawai'i's astronomically high cost of housing and land, and the military, who enjoy housing and beaches for their exclusive use.[14]

In our subjugation to American control, we have suffered what other displaced, dislocated people, such as the Palestinians and the Irish of Northern Ireland, have suffered: We have been occupied by a colonial power whose every law, policy, cultural institution, and collective behavior entrench foreign ways of life in our land and on our people. From the banning of our language and the theft of our sovereignty to forcible territorial incorporation in 1959 as a state of the United States, we have lived as a subordinated Native people in our ancestral home.[15]

For visitors to Hawai'i, these statements are quite shocking because the Hollywood, tourist poster image of my homeland as a racial paradise with happy Natives waiting to share their culture with everyone and anyone is a familiar global commodity. No matter how false and predatory this image remains, hordes of tourists from both the Euro-American and Japanese First Worlds believe enough tourist propaganda to spend millions on a romanticized "Pacific Island" holiday. For these foreigners, any ugly truths about the real conditions of Native Hawaiians are an unwelcome irritation, and it is far simpler to ignore misery and injustice than to acknowledge and address their realities. [16]

Even for many residents of Hawai'i, the conditions and status of Native Hawaiians are little known and intentionally obscured by missionary descended landowners, the state and federal governments, local politicians and the media, as well as a complicitous university system ideologically and economically dependent on state agencies. Like many a colony, Hawai'i has a very centralized political system with the most powerful chief executive of all fifty American states. Of course, this sharp pyramidal structure is itself a product of our territorial period (1900-1959), when the all-white oligarchy feared (and therefore constrained) an organized majority "colored" population of Asian immigrants and Hawaiians.

Finally, there is always that particular variant of racism that fashions America's moral stupidity: vociferous denial of the presence, unique histories, and self-determination of America's conquered Natives. To Hawaiians, *haole* Americans seem to cherish their ignorance of other nations (especially conquered peoples who live wretched lives all around them) as a sign of American individualism. Americans have no cultural beliefs that connect them, as a people or nation, to other human beings or to the natural world as brothers and sisters in a familial cosmos. Therefore, peoples who suffer and die in the Third World, for example, or on Indian reservations, either deserve their fate or are unfortunate outcasts in an ordered world that finds white people at the top. From a Hawaiian perspective, this is not only incorrect, it is unbelievably cruel to family members.

In colony Hawai'i, not only the cruelty but the stench of colonialism is everywhere: at Pearl Harbor, so thoroughly polluted by the American military that it now ranks among the top priorities on the Environmental Protection Agency's superfund list; at Waikīkī, one of the most famous beaches in the world, where human excrement from the overloaded Honolulu sewer system floats just off shore; at Honolulu International Airport, where jet fuel from commercial, military, and private planes creates an eternal pall in the still hot air; in the magnificent valleys and plains of all major islands where heavy pesticide/herbicide use on sugar plantations and mammoth golf courses results in contaminated wetlands, rivers, estuaries, bays, and, of course, groundwater sources; on the gridlocked freeways, which swallow up more and more land as the American way of life carves its path toward destruction; in the schools and businesses and hotels and shops and government buildings and on the radio and television, where white Christian American values of capitalism, racism, and violent conflict are upheld, supported, and deployed against the Native people.

This is Hawai'i, once the most fragile and precious of sacred places, now transformed by the American behemoth into a dying land. Only a whispering spirit remains.

Notes

1. The first quotation is from Blount's Report, officially titled, *Report of the Commissioner to the Hawaiian Islands*, 53rd Congress, 2nd sess., 1893, p. 929. Exec. Doc. No. 47. The second quotation is from testimony by Kamokila Campbell, wealthy heir to the Campbell Estate, before the Larcade Committee, U.S. Congress, House Committee on Territories, *Statehood for Hawai'i Hearings*, 79th Congress, 2nd Sess., January 7–18, House Document 263, p. 482. The third quotation is from an interview with Kehau Lee in *Hawai'i Free People's Press* 1 (1971). The fourth quotation is from testimony by Kia'āina (Governor) of Ka Lāhui Hawai'i, Mililani Trask, before Senator Daniel Inouye's Senate Select Committee on Indian Affairs, Honolulu, Summer 1990.

2. The word *haole* means "white foreigner" in Hawaiian. "Pre-*haole*" refers to the period before contact with the white foreign world in 1778.

3. Marion Kelly, *Majestic Ka'ū* (Honolulu: Bishop Museum Press, 1980), p. vii.

4. For a discussion of the large Hawaiian population at contact with the West, and the subsequent catastrophic decline due to introduced diseases, see David Stannard, *Before the Horror: The Population of Hawai'i on the Eve of Western Contact* (Honolulu: Social Science Research Institute, University of Hawai'i, 1989).

5. See David Stannard, "Disease and Infertility: A New Look at the Demographic Collapse of Native Populations in the Wake of Western Contact," *Journal of American Studies* 24 (1990): 325–350.

6. For a pathbreaking account of the *Māhele* from a Hawaiian point of view, see Lilikalā Kame'eleihiwa, *Native Land and Foreign Desires* (Honolulu: Bishop Museum Press, 1992).

7. For an analysis of the dispossession of the Hawaiian people as a result of the imposition of capitalist accumulation for the purposes of export agriculture, see Noel Kent, *Hawai'i: Islands Under the Influence* (New York: Monthly Review Press, 1983), pp. 20–58.

8. Neil Levy, "Native Hawaiian Land Rights," *California Law Review*, 63 (July 1975): 857.

9. The following historical information is summarized from Ralph Kuykendall, *The Hawaiian Kingdom 1854–1874* (Honolulu: University of Hawai'i Press, 1966); and Merze Tate, *Hawai'i: Reciprocity or Annexation* (East Lansing, MI: Michigan State University Press, 1968).

10. James H. Blount to Mr. Gresham, report/letter, 17 July 1893, *The Executive Documents of the House of Representatives for the Third Session of the Fifty-Third Congress. 1894–1895.* 35 Volumes (Washington D.C.: Government Printing Office, 1895), p. 579.

11. Lili'uokalani to Sanford B. Dole. Cited in James H. Blount to Mr. Gresham, 17 July 1893, *The Executive Documents of the House of Representatives for the Third Session of the Fifty-Third Congress,* p. 586.

12. The president's message and Lili'uokalani's statement can be found in Blount's Report, pp. 445–461.

13. For a discussion of the rights of indigenous peoples in the context of international human rights, see the special issue of *Without Prejudice: The EAFORD International Review of Racial Discrimination* 2:2 (1989), which is devoted to an exploration of indigenous rights in the Canadian, U.S., and U.N. contexts and which includes the International Labor Organization Document 169 concerning indigenous and tribal peoples in independent countries.

14. For a detailed report on Hawaiian trust lands illegally taken and used by the military see the *Report of the Federal-State Task Force on the Hawaiian Homes Commission Act,* (Washingtion, D.C.: U.S. Department of the Interior, 1983). A good example of illegal use is the 4,000 acre valley Lualualei on O'ahu, which is designated for exclusive Hawaiian use but has been used continuously since World War II as a munitions magazine.

15. For a discussion of the banning of the Hawaiian language, see Larry Kimura, "Native Hawaiian Culture," in *Native Hawaiians Study Commission Report* (Washington, D.C.: U.S. Department of the Interior, 1983), Vol. 1, pp. 173–197.

16. For a statistical picture of the kinds of tourists who annually visit Hawai'i and how much they spend, see the financial report of the Bank of Hawai'i, *Hawai'i, 1990: Annual Economic Report*. On page 12, for example, the report graphs the origins of tourists in the following way: almost 4.3 million from the United States and nearly 2.4 million from foreign countries. The Japanese, who comprise about 1.3 million visitors a year, spend nearly 4.5 times what U.S. visitors spend. This explains why so many signs in major resort areas are written in Japanese, not only in English, and why so much propaganda in Hawai'i is focused on welcoming Japanese tourists.

Part I

Sovereignty: The International Context

Hawaiians and Human Rights

Modern Hawai'i, like its colonial parent the United States, is a settler society; that is, Hawai'i is a society in which the indigenous culture and people have been murdered, suppressed, or marginalized for the benefit of settlers who now dominate our islands. In settler societies, the issue of civil rights is primarily an issue about how to protect settlers against each other and against the state. Injustices done against Native people, such as genocide, land dispossession, language banning, family disintegration, and cultural exploitation, are not part of this intrasettler discussion and are therefore not within the parameters of civil rights. This is true whether we are speaking of French settler colonies like Tahiti, New Caledonia, and Algeria or British colonies like Australia, New Zealand, and India or Portuguese colonies like Brazil, Angola, and Mozambique or Dutch colonies like South Africa and Indonesia or the strange Spanish, French, British amalgam called the United States of America.

Indeed, for indigenous peoples, civil society is itself a creation of settler colonies. Before the coming of the colonizers, Native society was a familial relationship organized by tribes or chiefdoms in which the necessities of life—land, water, food, collective identity, and support—were available to everyone.

But colonialism changed all that. By definition, conquest is an extermination not a recognition of aboriginal peoples and their familial relationship with the earth.

The famed American Constitution, for example, does not address the protection of Native relationships to land, to language, to culture, to family, to self-government, indeed, to anything Natives value. In point of historical fact, the Constitution of the United States—that is, the document from which civil rights emanate within the boundaries of the United States—has nothing to say to Chamorros, Samoans, Hawaiians, Inuit, and American Indians.

As indigenous peoples, we are all outside the Constitution, the settler document that declares ownership over indigenous lands and peoples. Since the Constitution is an imposed colonial structure, nothing therein prevents the taking of Native lands or the incorporation of unwilling Native peoples into the United States. This explains why the American military invasion and occupation of Hawai'i in 1893, the resulting overthrow of the Hawaiian government, and the eventual forced annexation of Hawai'i to the United States in 1898 were not unconstitutional acts, nor were they a violation of civil rights. As intended, the single greatest injury to my people caused by the United States cannot be raised within the context of the U.S. Constitution.

Hawaiians, then, are absent from the most fundamental of American constructs, those "legal niceties," De Toqueville called them, that continue to allow every manner of war, removal, and genocide against Native people within and beyond U.S. boundaries.

This outsider situation is not unique. Most of the world's indigenous peoples are outside the legal systems of their colonial overseers. Indeed, colonialism has, as one of its goals, the obliteration rather than the incorporation of indigenous peoples. Exclusion from colonial legal systems is but part of the process of obliteration.

Our daily existence in the modern world is thus best described not as a struggle for civil rights but as a struggle against our planned disappearance. For example, in the United States, the "vanishing" Indian has steadfastly refused to vanish, resisting all manner of genocide, from Wounded Knee in the Lakota nation to the removal of Navaho and Shoshone peoples from their sacred lands.

The meaning of such resistance is not lost on the American government, which has created an entirely separate body of statutory and case law to confine and define Indians and other Native peoples. Over the years, Congress and the courts have reflected changing national moods, resulting in federal policies that shift from removal to termination to self-determination and back again.

This mercurial colonial legacy is longer and more detailed for American Indians than for Native Hawaiians. But the shape of our histories is similar: we are Natives at the mercy of federal, state, and county governments. In the case of Hawaiians, we are not even recognized as indigenous people, nor do we have any separate legal status, other than wardship, from which to command land and other rights that federally recognized Natives enjoy.

Because of this colonized condition, and in the face of increasing loss of control over our lives, Hawaiians have been agitating for federal recognition of the following:

1. our unique status as Native people;
2. the injury done by the United States at the overthrow, including the loss of lands and sovereignty;
3. the necessity for reparation of that injury through acknowledgment of our claim to sovereignty, recognition of some form of autonomous Native government, the return of traditional lands and waters, and a package of compensatory resources, including monies.

"Universal" Human Rights

The injury Hawaiians have suffered at the hands of the American government begins with those characteristic practices now commonplace in twentieth century international relations: invasion, occupation, and takeover. Although the United States gave many assurances of respect for Hawaiian sovereignty during the nineteenth century, the lure of empire was too great. The overthrow of the Hawaiian government with American military support in 1893, the subsequent diplomatic and military support given by America to the haole Provisional Government (1893–1894) and to the Republic of Hawai'i (1894–1898), and the eventual appropriation of Hawai'i by the United States through forced annexation in 1898 were the result of America's imperial desire to control lands and peoples not her own. Far from exporting democracy, the United States committed, through these acts, *undeniable violations* of the right of self-determination. Under international law, these violations include

1. an arbitrary deprivation of our nationality;
2. an arbitrary deprivation of our lands;
3. a denial of our rights to self-determination as a people, including aboriginal rights to our natural resources.

These deprivations, as a whole, comprise violations of Articles 15, 17, and 21 of the Universal Declaration of Human Rights. In addition, they are violations of Article 1 of both the International Covenant on Civil and Political Rights and the International Covenant on Economic, Social and Cultural Rights. And finally, they are violations of the American Convention on Human Rights. [1]

Article 15 of the Universal Declaration of Human Rights and Article 20 of the American Convention on Human Rights, respectively, state:

> Everyone has the right to a nationality.[2]
>
> No one shall be arbitrarily deprived of his nationality nor denied the right to change his nationality.[3]

In the Universal Declaration, Article 21 states:

> No one shall be arbitrarily deprived of property.[4]
>
> The will of the people shall be the basis of the authority of government; this will shall be expressed in periodic and genuine elections which shall be by universal and equal suffrage and shall be held by secret vote or by equivalent free voting procedures.[5]

In the International Covenants referred to above, the first article of each is identical:

> All peoples have the right of self-determination. By virtue of that right they freely determine their political status and freely pursue their economic, social and cultural development.[6]

In every one of these articles, nationality and free choice are central to the human rights under discussion. Regarding the Hawaiian case, it is clear that the human rights of Hawaiians have been and continue to be violated by the United States because:

> There is no historical doubt about American complicity in the overthrow, in the establishment of the provisional government and the Republic of

> Hawai'i, and in the forcible annexation of Hawai'i without referendum of any kind and against the expressed wishes of the Hawaiian people.
>
> Had Hawaiians been allowed to choose annexation or independence, they would have chosen their own sovereignty, according to estimates of all contemporary observers of the time, from annexationist leader Lorrin Thurston to Presidential Commissioner James Blount to Hawaiian leaders such as the Hui Aloha 'Āina.

The fact that the overthrow and annexation occurred before international covenants went into effect does not invalidate the Hawaiian case. The ideal of universal self-determination is a settled principle of peremptory international law, superseding customary rules and bilateral treaties. This means that the principle of universal self-determination is of sufficient importance to be applied retroactively to relationships among states and people before the adoption of the 1948 United Nations Charter.

Since Hawaiians never surrendered their political rights through treaties nor voted on annexation, they should fall under the United Nations category of a "non-self-governing people." This dependent status has been maintained through state (rather than Native) control of Hawaiian trust lands. These lands include Hawaiian home lands and ceded lands, nearly two million acres, or almost half of the state of Hawai'i. The first trust is controlled by the Department of Hawaiian Home Lands and the second by the Department of Land and Natural Resources, both state agencies. The Office of Hawaiian Affairs (created by the state of Hawai'i in 1978), which receives 20 percent of the revenues from ceded lands, is subject to the laws of the state and federal governments. None of these institutions can be said to constitute Hawaiian self-governance.

As a non-self-governing people, Hawaiians occupy a category recognized by the United Nations as eligible for the right of self-determination. But this right is continually denied Hawaiians for several reasons.

First, there is the claim that Hawaiians, the Native people of Hawai'i, are the same as settlers to Hawai'i. Apart from denying Hawaiians their 2,000-year-old *indigenous* history, this position also equates *voluntary* status (settlers) with *involuntary* status (a forced change in nationality resulting from colonization). This argument often underlies state and federal policy.

Unlike settlers in Hawai'i (*haole*, Asians, and others), who *voluntarily* gave up the nationality of their homelands when they became permanent residents of Hawai'i, Hawaiians had their nationality *forcibly changed in their own homeland.*

Second, there is the allegation that Hawaiians are "equal" to other Americans since Hawaiians have "their own state" and are American citizens. Both these points are irrelevant because Hawaiians *never were* members of the United States until we were forcibly annexed. When American citizenship was conferred on Hawaiians, it was done so unilaterally, that is, without Hawaiian consent. Statehood was a condition that came long *after* annexation, not prior to it. Moreover, the statehood vote was taken when Hawaiians were a minority in our own country. Settlers voted overwhelmingly for statehood, while Hawaiians did not, a fact conveniently overlooked by statehood promoters. Finally, the fiction of "equality as Americans" obscures the historical reality that the United States has no claim—except one based on military and economic aggression—to control the lands and Native people of Hawai'i.

A third argument for the continued denial of Hawaiian self-determination is the notion of "prescription." Here, a right peacefully exercised over a long period can no longer be questioned. Prescription has sometimes been advanced by colonial powers, such as the United States, as a source of legal title to overseas possessions, such as Hawai'i.

Contrary to popular opinion, however, Hawai'i has not been controlled by the United States for "a long time." It is, in 1998, but little more than a hundred years since Hawaiians governed their own country. When compared with Hawaiian self-governance for two millennia prior to the overthrow and annexation, the century of American control is paltry indeed.

In addition, while American occupation of Hawai'i certainly prevents colonizing attempts by other powers, it does not extinguish the rights of indigenous Hawaiians. On this point, the International Court of Justice has declared that the emerging principle of self-determination supersedes states' historical claims to territorial integrity.

Finally, there is the argument that America and the American way of life are superior to Native countries and Native ways of life. This argument is constantly advanced to justify the American annexation of Hawai'i and continued American control over Native resources and people. Interestingly, it is also an argument with a rich and revealing history: throughout the nineteenth century American proponents of slavery advanced it to claim that African-Americans were better off as slaves in "civilized" America than as free people in "primitive" Africa.

Similar to notions of white supremacy (and, ultimately, "The White Man's Burden") that accompanied European conquest of the Americas, Africa, Asia, and Oceania from the fifteenth through the nineteenth centuries, the idea that one culture is superior to another and should, thereby, dominate in all areas has been thoroughly repudiated by international law as a matter of imperial policy masquerading as historical fact.

The right of self-determination exists for all peoples regardless of race, creed, or culture and includes the right to territorial integrity. A legal theory of dispossession based on racial or cultural distinctions is not acceptable under international law.

Based on assumptions of Native Hawaiian inferiority and of white American superiority, the argument that American control of Hawaiian lands was, *and continues to be,* preferable to Native control is a *racist argument.*

As a racist argument, the position that the American way of life is somehow the "best" in the world, and therefore Hawaiians should be grateful for the "opportunity" to enjoy it, flies in the face of historical evidence to the contrary. After more than a century of American contact—including the "benefits" of disease and a 97 percent decline in the Hawaiian population; the "joy" of repressive Christianity; and the loss of lands through private property to the *haole*—Hawaiians at the turn of the century clearly preferred to be Hawaiian citizens. In international legal terms, they preferred self-determination to American control. It was the *haole* elite (missionaries and businessmen) who agitated for Hawai'i to become a possession of the United States without popular referendum. All this was done, of course, after American military invasion and occupation of Hawai'i.

In the context of international law, then, continued American claims to political and cultural superiority are seen as merely the ideology of a colonizing power. This ideology has been condemned by the United Nations as wholly unacceptable in relationships between peoples and states. Despite a 1993 apology by the American government for the overthrow, Hawaiian self-determination, including Native control of a Native land base, continues to be obstructed by the United States, and the State of Hawai'i.

Of course, American violations of human rights, especially the rights of American Indians, are both legion and well known, if also officially and categorically denied. Americans and their government are quite fond of blaming other countries, particularly in the Third World, for human rights violations while insisting that justice prevails in the United States. Even on those few occasions when the U.S. government acknowledges such violations, rarely, if ever, is the status of Natives within the American imperium addressed. The congressional apology by the United States in 1993 regarding the overthrow is a typical example. Not an acre of stolen Hawaiian land has been returned to Natives as a result of the apology.

"Indigenous" Human Rights

American recalcitrance on the issue of Native claims moved various Indian tribes to lobby the United Nations for the creation of a Working Group on Indigenous Populations under the auspices of the Human Rights Commission. After two decades of work and thousands of hours of testimony from indigenous people themselves, the Working Group concluded a Draft United Nations Declaration on the Rights of Indigenous Peoples at the Forty-Sixth Session of the Sub-Commission on Prevention of Discrimination and Protection of Minorities (see appendixes).

The survival of indigenous peoples and their habitats is a problem approaching global recognition. Even within the boundaries of the United States, there is a growing perception that indigenous peoples occupy a different status because of their First Nation history that cannot be addressed solely through existing legal constructs.

Along with many other indigenous peoples and organizations, some of us in the Hawaiian nationalist community believe the Draft United Nations Declaration on the Rights of Indigenous Peoples should become part of the framework within which future analyses, including legal discussions, regarding our special status should occur in Hawai'i and in the United States.

Of course, what I am suggesting flies in the face of nearly every assumption lawyers, courts, legislative bodies, and the general public accept regarding civil rights in the United States. To most Americans, including and most especially lawyers, the American Constitution is akin to the Christian Ten Commandments: a set of rules inscribed in stone given by a sacred authority and unchangeable for all time.

But as the family of nations comes increasingly to acknowledge the diverse nationalities of its members, the United States finds itself ever more isolated from the global movement for self-determination. By insisting that the American Constitution is the only instrument for the protection of rights and the assertion of obligations, the United States continues its suppression of the human rights of indigenous peoples within its borders. In the international community, if not among Americans, it is increasingly problematic for the U.S. government to raise issues of human rights violations regarding other nations while the United States systematically engages in such violations against its own indigenous peoples.

For those of us who have worked in the international arena for years, our major issues have been human rights rather than civil rights. And we have concentrated on the Draft United Nations Declaration on the Rights of Indigenous Peoples as a statement of principles and a guide to actions and policy.

A cursory overview of the declaration reveals that most of the protections included in it are not currently available under the U.S. Constitution.

Definition

Indigenous peoples are defined in terms of collective aboriginal occupation prior to colonial settlement. They are not to be confused with minorities or ethnic groups within states. Thus "indigenous rights" are strictly distinguished from "minority rights." The *numbers* of indigenous peoples, therefore, does not constitute a criterion in their definition.

Human Rights, Self-Determination, and Nationality

> Article 1: "Indigenous peoples have the right to the full and effective enjoyment of all human rights and fundamental free-

doms recognized in the Charter of the United Nations, the Universal Declaration of Human Rights. . . ."

Article 3: Indigenous peoples have the right of self-determination. By virtue of that right they freely determine their political status and freely pursue their economic, social and cultural development.

Article 5: "Every indigenous individual has the right to a nationality."

Security, Identity, and Liberty

Article 6: "Indigenous peoples have the right to live in freedom, peace and security. . . ."

Article 7: "Indigenous peoples have the collective and individual right not to be subjected to ethnocide and cultural genocide. . . ."

Article 8: "Indigenous peoples have . . . the right to identify themselves as indigenous and to be recognized as such."

Tradition and Customs, Labor and Media

Part III of the declaration states that "Indigenous peoples have rights to practice their cultural traditions and customs." These include spiritual practices; preservation of sacred places, including burials; oral traditions; and the right to transmit their histories and languages.

In Part IV, Article 17 declares that "Indigenous peoples have the right to establish their own media in their own languages." And in Article 18, they are accorded "all rights established under international labour law and national labor legislation."

In Part V, Articles 21 and 23 declare that "Indigenous peoples have the right to maintain and develop their political, economic, and social systems, to be secure in the enjoyment of their own means of subsistence and development, and to engage freely in all their traditional and other economic activities."

Land Rights

Part VI of the declaration is often thought to be the most controversial to existing nation-states because land rights and restitution are addressed.

> Terra Nullius (the "vacant land" argument of Europeans who colonized the Americas, Australia, and other lands) is an unacceptable legal doctrine.
>
> Article 26: "Indigenous peoples have the right to own, develop, control and use the lands and territories . . . they have traditionally owned or otherwise occupied or used. This includes the right to the full recognition of their laws, traditions and customs, land-tenure systems and institutions for the development and management of resources, and the right to effective measures by States to prevent any interference with, alienation of, or encroachment upon these rights."
>
> Article 27: "Indigenous peoples have the right to restitution of the lands, territories and resources which they have traditionally owned or otherwise occupied or used, and which have been confiscated, occupied, used or damaged without their free and informed consent. . . . Unless otherwise freely agreed upon by the peoples concerned, compensation shall take the form of lands, territories and resources equal in quality, size, and legal status."
>
> Article 28 speaks to military and other dangerous activities: "Military activities shall not take place in the lands and territories of indigenous peoples, unless otherwise freely agreed upon by the peoples concerned."
>
> Article 29: "Indigenous peoples are entitled to the recognition of the full ownership, control and protection of their cultural and intellectual property.
>
> They have the right to special measures to control, develop and protect their sciences, technologies and cultural manifestations, including human and other genetic resources, seeds, medicines, knowledge of the properties of fauna and flora, oral traditions, literatures, designs and visual and performing arts."

> Article 30 continues: "Indigenous peoples have the right to determine and develop priorities and strategies for the development or use of their lands, territories and other resources, including the right to require that States obtain their free and informed consent prior to the approval of any project affecting their lands, territories, and other resources. . . ."

These statements underscore both the uniqueness and the great significance of the declaration. Obviously different in focus and issues from other human rights instruments, the Draft United Nations Declaration on the Rights of Indigenous Peoples highlights the importance of specific indigenous problems: protection and transmission of the collective group or nation, of the specific indigenous culture, and of chosen forms of self-governance on traditional lands.

Of course, the meaning and practice of self-determination has been much debated and resisted by states, but the general understanding is that self-determination does not include, in the case of indigenous peoples, the right of secession. Some nations have suggested that the principle of "internal self-determination" might apply here.

In clarifying and codifying these rights, the Working Group and its indigenous participants understood full well that realization of these rights depends on nation-states and is thus fraught with difficulty and resistance. In giving guidance to states, the Working Group also suggested that states have the following duties: to respect the characteristics, traditions, and languages of indigenous peoples; to protect or to guarantee, for instance, the life and physical existence of indigenous peoples as groups; and to fulfill or provide, through appropriate legal frameworks of participation, social services, education, and development of indigenous peoples.

The Hawaiian Case

While the Draft United Nations Declaration on the Rights of Indigenous Peoples has been evolving, Native Hawaiians have been organizing politically to achieve an independent land base. Over the last twenty years, several suggestions have been put forward by various movement leaders and organizations that can be grouped under the following strategies: active education of Hawaiians about their history and Native rights and about the need for a land base; litigation against the state and federal governments for abuses of trust lands and for reparations; offensive political demonstrations such as land seizures, illegal protests at restricted places, including military sites, and disruptions of institutional activity; offensive cultural actions such as religious worship on sacred sites closed to such worship, the construction of fishing villages and taro patches on lands scheduled for other economic activity, and the disruption of tourist attractions that commodify and degrade Hawaiian culture. The purposes of offensive action are threefold: they awaken both Hawaiians and the general public to Hawaiian problems; they assert rights through direct actions against abuse or in support of cultural practices; and they reinforce the practice of self-determination.

Finally, practical enunciations of self-determination include the creation of different forms of self-government (for example, the formation of Ka Lāhui Hawai'i as a kind of government-in-exile), the Native alternative practice of *aloha 'āina* (love of the land) in opposition to resort development, industrial parks, upper-income residential subdivisions, and military use. Arguments for restitution and for international adjudication of the territorial conflict between Hawaiians and the state and federal governments are also examples of the sovereignty question in theoretical form.

At the largest level, discussions of Hawaiian sovereignty entail a choice among self-governing structures: a completely independent Hawai'i under the exclusive or predominating control of Hawaiians; "limited sovereignty" on a specified land base administered by a representative council but subject to U.S. federal regulations; legally incorporated land-based units within existing communities linked by a common elective council; a "nation-within-a-nation" on the model of American Indian nations.

Ka Lāhui Hawai'i, a Native initiative for self-government first created in 1987 and currently enrolling thousands of members, is the only organization whose structure, constitution, and political agenda approximate the "nation-within-a-nation" model. Headed by Mililani Trask, the elected Kia'āina, or Governor, Ka Lāhui currently poses an alternative to the Office of Hawaiian Affairs (OHA) and all other nonrepresentative structures as agencies of the State of Hawai'i. Beyond this, Ka Lāhui argues for federal recognition of Hawaiian sovereignty, including claims to self-government on an identifiable land base. Ka Lāhui opposes all efforts by the state legislature, OHA, and other state agencies, such as the Department of Hawaiian Homes, to settle sovereignty claims for money rather than land. Ka Lāhui also argues that Hawaiians should have standing to sue for breaches of trust in both state and federal courts. And finally, Ka Lāhui constantly asserts that the best way for Hawaiians to practice their culture and flourish in their Native land is by attaining sovereignty, not by continuing the wardship of Hawaiians under state and federal control. (See the Ka Lāhui Master Plan, or *Ho'okupu*, in the appendixes.)

This conflict over Native sovereignty is not unique to Hawaiians. It is repeated throughout the Pacific Islands, indeed, anywhere in the world where Native peoples suffer the yoke of oppression. Like Tahitians, Kanaks, Maori, Australian Aborigines, Palestinians, the Kurdish peoples, Tibetans, the Maya, Quechua, and many other indigenous peoples, Native Hawaiians continue to struggle for self-determination and self-preservation as a people.

The international issue of indigenous human rights has only now, and with great resistance, been included in the local Hawai'i discussions regarding Hawaiian sovereignty. Ignorance of human rights instruments is but part of the reason why so little attention has been focused on this issue. Refusal by various organizations to understand the human rights dimension and resistance by government agencies and political actors in Hawai'i to acknowledge that human rights is an issue in the case of Hawaiians has been very effective in limiting the local discussions to immediate land claims and other concerns.

The agenda for Hawaiians more than a century after the overthrow of our government by the agency of the United States must include the largest framework of indigenous human rights. Civil rights must be subsumed under human rights; land claims, language transmission, and monetary compensation must be understood and argued in terms of our human rights as indigenous people rather than merely as citizens of the United States or the state of Hawai'i. Given that Hawaiians were once self-governing under the Kingdom of Hawai'i and given that the United States, through its diplomatic and military offices, played a central role in the overthrow of that Kingdom, our historical injury involves violations of international law. Thus the context of the U.S. Constitution is too small a framework in which to argue for sovereignty. An international frame of reference, one that involves universal human rights, must be the context for discussion.

Today, in an age of rapacious transnational capitalism, Hawaiians are beginning to think beyond the habitual boundaries of the state of Hawai'i, even of the United States. We increasingly assert genealogical claims as children of our mother—Hawai'i—and therefore, as caretakers of our land. This relationship as indigenous people, as the first nation of Hawai'i, places us in a different category from all settlers in Hawai'i. It is our duty, as Native people, to ensure this status for generations to come.

Notes

1. *Universal Declaration of Human Rights.* Adopted by the U.N. General Assembly, Dec. 10, 1948. U.N.G.A. Res. 217 A (III), U.N. Doc. A/810, at 71 (1948). *International Covenant on Civil and Political Rights.* Adopted by the U.N. General Assembly, Dec. 16, 1966. U.N.G.A. Res. 2200 A(XXI), also in *Professional Training Series No. 4, National Human Rights Institutions: A Handbook on the Establishment and Strengthening of National Institutions for the Promotion and Protection of Human Rights* (New York: United Nations Publications, 1995), pp. 43–46. *International Covenant on Economic, Social and Cultural Rights.* Adopted by the U.N. General Assembly, Dec. 16, 1966. U.N.G.A. Res. 2200 A (XXI), also in *Professional Training Series No. 4, National Human Rights Institutions: A Handbook on the Establishment and Strengthening of National Institutions for the Promotion and Protection of Human Rights* (New York: United Nations Publications, 1995), pp. 46–52. *American Convention on Human Rights.* O.A.S. Treaty Series No. 36, 1144 U.N.T.S. 123 entered into force July 18, 1978, reprinted in Basic Documents Pertaining to Human Rights in the Inter-American System, OEA/Ser.L.V/II.82 doc. 6 rev 1 at 25 (1992), or in *Treaty Series: Treaties and international agreements registered or filed and recorded with the Secretariat of the United Nations,* Vol. 1144 (New York: United Nations, 1987), pp. 123–163.

2. Article 15, Section 1, of the *Universal Declaration of Human Rights.* Article 20, Section 1, of the *American Convention on Human Rights,* or in *Treaty Series: Treaties and international agreements registered or filed and recorded with the Secretariat of the United Nations,* Vol. 1144, p. 150.

3. Article 15, Section 2, of the *Universal Declaration of Human Rights.* Article 20, Section 3, of the *American Convention on Human Rights,* or in *Treaty Series: Treaties and international agreements registered or filed and recorded with the Secretariat of the United Nations,* Vol. 1144, p. 150.

4. Article 21, Section 1, of the *Universal Declaration of Human Rights.*

5. Article 21, Section 3, of the *Universal Declaration of Human Rights.*

6. Article 1 of the *International Covenant on Civil and Political Rights,* or in *Professional Training Series No. 4, National Human Rights Institutions: A Handbook*

on the Establishment and Strengthening of National Institutions for the Promotion and Protection of Human Rights, p. 43. Article 1 of the *International Covenant on Economic, Social and Cultural Rights,* or in *Professional Training Series No. 4, National Human Rights Institutions: A Handbook on the Establishment and Strengthening of National Institutions for the Promotion and Protection of Human Rights,* p. 52.

Politics in the Pacific Islands: Imperialism and Native Self-Determination

For a dozen millennia, the vast Pacific has been home to a diverse humanity only recently grouped by Western scholars as Micronesia, Polynesia, and Melanesia. Since the dawn of the nuclear age, however, the Pacific has come to be known primarily by its surrounding Rim countries (Asian, American, and the former Soviet states). For the First World, the Pacific archipelagoes are filled with tiny fantasy islands more reflective of a "state of mind" than an actual geographic and cultural place. This view, of course, is rejected by Pacific Islanders themselves, since the Pacific is their ancestral ocean but lately invaded by colonial powers. As indigenous peoples, Pacific Islanders have been struggling against imperialism for nearly 300 years. Indeed, imperialism is the key here. Since this word, like racism and genocide, appears to have passed from the scholarly canon, I want to underscore my definition and use of it.

For peoples who suffer the yoke of imperialism, it is a total system of foreign power in which another culture, people, and way of life penetrate, transform, and come to define the colonized society. The results are always destructive, no matter the praises sung by the colonizer. But the extent of the damage depends on the size of the colony, the power of the colonizing country, and the resistance of the colonized. In the Pacific, tiny islands, large predatory powers—such as the United States, France, Indonesia—and small Native populations all but ensure a colonial stranglehold.

Of course, the function of imperialism is exploitation of the colony: its lands and oceans, labor, women, and, in the Pacific, its mythic meaning as a "South Sea paradise." Moreover, any material aid to the colonies is an extension of exploitation, given to strengthen the economic dependency that binds colony to colonizer, just as teaching Natives to speak English, watch television, and consume alcohol creates a clever web of psychological dependency from which the colonized find it nearly impossible to disentangle. Generations become addicted to the worst cultural habits of the colonial society, which increases both ignorance of, and alienation from, the Native culture.[1] Indeed, cultural hegemony is the cutting edge of the imperial enterprise, which explains why cultural nationalism becomes such a crucial Native strategy in the battle for decolonization.[2]

In Hawai'i and Aotearoa (New Zealand), for example, teaching the Native languages in immersion schools has been at the forefront of a cultural resurgence that also includes reclaiming ancestral lands and moves toward various forms of self-government. In situations such as these, language instruction is understood to be both a cultural and a political assertion: *cultural* because it seeks to preserve the core of a way of thinking and being that is uniquely Native, and *political* because this attempt at preservation takes place in a system where the dominant group has employed legal and social means to deny the use and inheritance of the Native language by Natives themselves.[3]

An ideology of racism justifies the denial of Native culture with blanket claims such as that "Natives have no culture" comparable to the hegemonic one or even a valuable culture beyond mere ornamentation. This is especially true in Hawai'i, where mass tourism thrives on the commercialization of every aspect of Hawaiian culture. Indeed, one result of commercialization is a widely held belief that Hawaiian culture—including the *hula,* Hawaiian values of generosity and love such as *aloha,* and the Hawaiian extended family—is particularly suited to the "visitor" industry, which, in turn, encourages and preserves Hawaiian culture. The truth, of course, is the opposite: the myth of happy Hawaiians waiting to share their culture with tourists was invented to lure visitors and to disparage Native resistance to the tourist industry.

Behind this crude type of racism are other, subtler kinds of responses to Native cultural assertion premised on racist beliefs that Natives do not understand or even know their culture well enough to assert it. Therefore, the reasoning is, they are arguing for something devised on the spot or, what is more malevolent, they are asserting something political, not cultural. Examples of this include accusations by anthropologists and other alleged "experts" that Native nationalists "invent" cultural traditions for purely political ends or that the culture they practice is not "authentic."[4]

Because of colonization, the question of *who* defines *what* is Native, and even *who* is defined as Native has been taken away from Native peoples by Western-trained scholars, government officials, and other technicians. This theft in itself testifies to the pervasive power of colonialism and explains why self-identity by Natives of *who* and *what* they are elicits such strenuous and sometimes vicious denials by the dominant culture.[5]

These kinds of racist claims are thrown up into the public arena precisely when Native cultural assertion is both vigorous and strong-willed. Representatives of the dominant culture, from anthropologists and historians to bureaucrats and politicians, are quick to feel and perceive danger because, in the colonial context, all Native cultural resistance is political; it challenges hegemony. On one level, this challenge often draws out a rabid insistence on the use of the dominant language, or the general privilege of the dominant culture, in every aspect of life. On another level, mainstream scholars and officials seek to undermine the legitimacy of Native representatives by attacking their motives, or sanity, in asserting Native culture.

But motivation is usually laid bare through the struggle for cultural expression. Nationalists offer explanations at every turn: in writing, in public forums, and in acts of resistance, including passive resistance. To Natives, the burst of creative outpouring that accompanies cultural nationalism is self-explanatory: a choice has been made for things Native over things non-Native. Politically, the choice is one of decolonization.

Language, in particular, can aid in decolonizing the mind. Thinking in one's own cultural referents leads to conceptualizing in one's own world view, which, in turn, leads to disagreement with and eventual opposition to the dominant ideology. Native groups that insist on exclusive membership, that redefine authority as that which is Native, and that begin to create cultural artifacts that reflect Native history, values, and hopes are the products of decolonizing minds. These groups develop under conditions of heightened consciousness that often result in nationalist political movements. The direct links between mental and political decolonization are clearly observable to representatives of the dominant culture, not only to those oppressed and struggling to strengthen such links. This is why thinking and acting as a Native under colonial conditions is a highly politicized reality, one filled with intimate oppositions and powerful psychological tensions.

Despite its obvious presence, cultural nationalism is not the only arena of resistance or even the most visible one in the Pacific. First World militarization of the region is more contested since the Pacific evolved from a strange place with a few watering ports and frontier outposts in the eighteenth and nineteenth centuries into a strategic area for superpower nuclear politics, ocean and land mining, and First World dumping in the twentieth century. In the last ten years, another threat has evolved from the "South Sea paradise" myth: mass-based corporate tourism and its demand for lush islands and prurient exotica.

The seeming contradiction in this First World policy of poisoning Pacific Islands while using them as vacation destinations is explained by the utter arrogance of the imperialist nations. Without doubt, Euro-Americans and the (non-nuclear) Japanese see Islanders as racially and culturally inferior. To the predators, the Pacific is vast and far away from the centers of "civilization," rendering it most suitable for dangerous projects (such as nuclear testing and storage of weapons) and romantic holidays. The sheer stupidity of nuclearization in the Pacific (or anywhere else) is lost on colonial nations, such as the United States and France, because their belief in their own superiority translates into a sense of smug invincibility. To the *haole* world, Euro-American civilization will triumph over every difficulty, even nuclear holocaust. The absurd political position called "nuclear survivability" is the result.[6] Here, for example, is a typical enunciation of its appalling posture toward mass death:

> The worst-case scenarios of hundreds of millions dead and widespread destruction would be an unprecedented global calamity, but not necessarily the end of history. . . . (One) of the most important continuities of the nuclear era is that wars can still be fought, terminated, and survived. Some countries will win a nuclear conflict and others will lose, and it is even possible that some nuclear wars may ultimately have positive results (as World War II did). Reconstruction will begin, life will continue, and most survivors will not envy the dead.[7]

Opposition to this madness across national and cultural boundaries has been strong and articulate among Pacific Islanders. Thus, there has been organized diplomatic and popular resistance to nuclearization, especially testing and transport of weapons; regional support of independence movements in Kanaky (New Caledonia), West Papua, East Timor, Belau, and Tahiti; scrutiny of foreign exploitation of resources in the region, significantly through driftnetting, fisheries, mines, and resort development; and increasing fear of foreign cultural dominance that threatens commercialization and eventual loss of Native cultures. When viewed through island rather than continental eyes, Pacific peoples live in the largest danger zone in the world.

Because of their familial attachment to both land and sea, Pacific Islanders know a solidarity of geography and culture. Despite their diversity, they are all Island peoples in struggle with larger predatory powers. Pacific Island solidarity, then, has been formed in the teeth of First World aggression or aggression by regional powers, such as Indonesia, that are supported by First World institutions such as the World Bank and the American government.

From genocide in West Papua and East Timor to the murder of Kanak revolutionaries and leaders in New Caledonia, to the deaths of Native people from nuclear radiation in Micronesia and Tahiti, to Belau and its plunge into violence and, after years of resistance to the Americans, its signing of an undemocratic Compact of Free Association, to the Rongelap and Enewetok Islanders dispossessed and homeless, to Guam and the Northern Mariana Islands suffering from tourism and military exploitation, to Hawai'i and Aotearoa, where the Native people are an oppressed minority in their own land, Pacific Islanders are engaged in resistance struggles that are but the latest stage in the revolutionary era that advanced the freedom of African, Latin American, and Asian peoples.[8]

French colonialism illustrates this reality in French-occupied Polynesia and New Caledonia. Independence movements exist in both colonies, represented by the Polynesian Liberation Front in Tahiti and the Kanak Socialist National Liberation Front (FLNKS) in New Caledonia. Kanak resistance has gained support from the South Pacific Forum (SPF) countries, comprised of independent nations in the South Pacific. With the aid of the SPF, the Kanaks were able to relist New Caledonia on the agenda of the United Nations' Committee on Decolonization. This successful drive stunned the French, partly because it came as a result of regional cooperation between the Kanaks, Australia, New Zealand, Fiji, and the Melanesian spearhead group of Vanuatu, the Solomon Islands, and Papua New Guinea.

But the Pacific desire for a peaceful transition to independence for New Caledonia has been blunted. The French massacre of Independentists in a hostage crisis on Ouvea in the Loyalty Islands in May of 1988 and the subsequent signing of the Matignon Accord pose a grave threat to Kanak self-determination. As a result of the accord, two FLNKS leaders were assassinated by a rival faction on the 1989 anniversary of the French massacre. This latest violence has split the FLNKS, leaving it weakened in the face of French imperialism.[9] For the present, the drive toward independence has been derailed. In French-occupied Polynesia, meanwhile, the French have finally acceded to international demands to end their nuclear testing policy. Native resistance, meanwhile, in the form of Oscar Temaru's Ia Mana Te Nunaa has taken the lead in Tavini Huratira, the Polynesian Liberation Front. Temaru is the mayor of the second largest city in Tahiti, Faaa.

But in true colonial fashion, French policies have continued to benefit non-Polynesians, leaving the majority of Natives in poor economic and social circumstances. This planned inequality, in turn, has increased support of the nationalist movement. When coupled with French military action against strikers and other dissidents in recent years, French policy has served to unite and expand the resistance front in the form of a Pan-Pacific Nuclear-Free and Independent Movement as well as in established government organizations such as the South Pacific Forum.

Regionally, France continues to proffer large aid packages—for example, to Fiji and the Cook Islands—in the hopes of tilting the anti-French stand. But denial of adverse environmental and health effects from testing remains the steadfast—and absurd—French posture. The French may have ceased testing nuclear weapons, but the effects of radiation on the people of the area will continue for millenia.[10]

A more vicious battle rages over the independence of West Papua (Irian Jaya) from Indonesia. There, a severe refugee problem has been created for Papua New Guinea as thousands of border crossers have fled Indonesian troops seeking to crush the Free West Papua Movement. The Australian and Papua New Guinea governments have thus far been reluctant to condemn Indonesian atrocities, despite clear evidence of their existence. Meanwhile, the Indonesian "transmigration" policy of settling large numbers of their people in West Papua (officially to "civilize" the "backward" Melanesians) amounts to genocide for West Papuans.

Simultaneously the Indonesian occupation of East Timor (since 1975) and genocide against its Melanesian people continues. Despite

United Nations General Assembly condemnations, and appeals from many organizations in the Asia-Pacific region, Indonesia has refused to negotiate with the East Timor resistance front, called Fretilin. Described as a "hidden holocaust in the Pacific," the situation in East Timor has taken the lives of over 200,000 people through famine, torture, killings, bombings, and disappearances. The Indonesian military and business elites control the economy and political life of East Timor and have put in place a policy of systematic exclusion and marginalization of the Melanesian Natives.[11]

In the so-called United Nations Trust possessions, meanwhile, there is clear American opposition to Native sovereignty. Belau's nuclear-free Constitution (which bans passage of nuclear ships and weapons through its waters) has been forcefully resisted by the United States. The Americans have continued to insist that their naval operations be excluded from this ban. Belauans, meanwhile, had refused to change their Constitution. In the balance is the sovereign integrity of the Belauan people. After several referenda decidedly against changing the Constitution to suit American demands, the political crisis escalated into violence. One Belauan president has been murdered, one has committed suicide, activists for the anti-nuclear Constitution have been killed, and a heroic effort has been mounted by the women in Belau to urge the U.S. Congress to agree to a compact that accepts Belau's antinuclear Constitution. But the Bealuans have not been successful.

All this political violence has led to economic violence in the small nation of 15,000 people. As an example, a U.S. General Accounting Office report on the situation in Belau from August 1985 to August 1988 found Reagan Administration complicity in Belau's economic woes. Ranging from refusals to monitor expenditure of federal funds in Belau to overlooking serious charges of intimidation and reprisals against Belauans opposed to the compact, the Reagan Administration actually encouraged the economic deterioration and political chaos in Belau. With recent passage of the compact, Belau has finally come under near total American control. Economic and political sabotage by the Americans has consigned the tiny nation to the agony of dependency.

Beyond Belau, the long-negotiated covenants with the Commonwealth of the Northern Mariana Islands (CNMI), the Marshall Islands, and the Federated States of Micronesia (FSM) reveal that full decolonization has not occurred since the United States maintains permanent military rights to these areas, including "Star Wars" testing sites in the Marshall Islands.

On a larger scale, the question of how and when a United Nations trusteeship is terminated has been raised by confusing and unilateral actions on the part of the United States regarding FSM, the Marshall Islands and the CNMI. In 1986, for example, President Reagan declared that for these three territories, the trusteeship was no longer in effect but did in fact continue for the Republic of Belau. A year later, however, the United States stated to the United Nations Trusteeship Council that the Micronesian Trusteeship remained in force.

The failure of the United States to return sovereignty to the Trust Territories (as required by United Nations mandate) is proof—if any more is needed—of American colonialism (just as radiation poisoning in Enewetok, Bikini, Rongelap, and elsewhere is evidence of American colonialism). Of course, dispossession of Native peoples was the origin, and continues to be the core, of U.S. foreign policy. From the Indians of the Americas to Pacific Island Natives, to the indigenous peoples of Asia, the United States has an unbroken record of invasion, land theft, and genocide.[12]

Indeed, as the preeminent military power in the world, the United States has dealt with the Pacific, since World War II, as if it were an American ocean. From an indigenous perspective, this makes the United States the most powerful imperialist nation in the Pacific. The continuing ravages of colonialism are what the United States has bequeathed to Hawaiians, Micronesians, and Samoans.

Hawai'i was territorially incorporated into the United States after an American military occupation in support of a takeover of the Hawaiian government by missionary descended businessmen in 1893. Forced annexation occurred in 1898. Hawaiian citizenship was unilaterally changed by the United States to American citizenship in 1900.

Tiny Guam became part of the Pacific spoils of World War II and went from Japanese occupation to American occupation without so much as a vote yea or nay by its indigenous people. Belau, and the rest of Micronesia, were transferred by the United Nations to American control, forever altering their ability to be sovereign. So-called "American" Sāmoa, meanwhile, is divided from so-called "Western" Sāmoa, never to be united or independent. All of these cases demonstrate America's hegemony in the Pacific. United States control has meant land dispossession, economic dependency, cultural exploitation, and, in many cases, death and disease for America's captive Native peoples. Such disregard for Native self-determination explains the presence of so many nationalist movements in *all* the U.S. possessions.

The belligerent American presence has been magnified by their policy of "nuclear superiority." Nuclearization of the seas, including open ports and sea lanes for nuclear ships, is the basis of this policy. Access to strategic mineral resources is also included, as is the "right of strategic denial." Here, access to the Pacific Islands to any present or potential enemy is denied by the United States. Additionally, whatever political changes take place, the governments of these islands must remain friendly to the interests of the United States.[13] Islanders accurately perceive this American posture as the primary threat to their physical and cultural existence in the Pacific. First, the very size and breadth of the American presence is a danger in itself. Second, expanded nuclear arsenals on land and in the oceans and skies multiply the danger of errors and their catastrophic consequences. Third, the effects of American military testing have already meant the dispossession of many Island peoples in the Marshalls and elsewhere, despite continued resistance to American military aggression. Given this track record, increased militarization of the region holds the potential for increased dispossession of Pacific Islanders as bases, ports, storage and testing sites, and residential areas are taken for "defense" purposes. This is how the "interests" of the United States continue to mean degradation, suffering, and often death to Native peoples whose friendship and trust are always betrayed in the end.

Hawai'i, of course, is a supreme example of American aggression. Despite promises to support Hawaiian independence in the nineteenth century, the American invasion of Hawai'i in 1893 was a prelude to the extinguishment of Hawaiian sovereignty in 1898 when, against the expressed wishes of the Hawaiian people, Hawai'i became a territorial possession of the United States. Today, Hawai'i serves as the center for the American commander-in-chief of the Pacific and the forward-basing point for American forces in the region, including nuclear submarines. Tragically for the Native people, Hawai'i is the most militarized of America's colonial possessions in the Pacific, rendering it a likely target in time of war.

At present, our Native people of Hawai'i are crowded into urban areas or rural slums. And our socioeconomic, health, and educational profiles are depressingly poor. The military, in the meantime, controls huge land areas for bases and settlements, while its personnel receive subsidies and other economic privileges. Despite political rhetoric praising the alleged benefits of the military, Hawaiians have suffered enormously from its presence.

South Pacific Islanders can learn from Hawai'i in other ways. The overpowering impact of mass tourism on island cultures is best studied in Hawai'i, where the multibillion dollar industry has resulted in grotesque commercialization of Hawaiian culture, creation of a racially-stratified, poorly paid servant class of industry workers, transformation of whole sections of the major islands into high-rise cities, contamination and depletion of water sources, intense crowding with densities in the worst areas beyond that of Hong Kong, increases in crimes against property and violent crime against tourists, and increasing dependency on multinational investments, particularly from Japan. Today, Hawai'i suffers six and a half million tourists annually, over thirty visitors for every Native Hawaiian.

Indeed, Japan is moving into the Pacific with aggressive economic penetration as investors and as tourists in Vanuatu, Tahiti, Micronesia, Fiji, Sāmoa, and elsewhere. In Hawai'i, meanwhile, Japanese firms have purchased over nine billion dollars worth of real estate since the 1970s. Despite a recent downturn in Japanese investment in the nineties, Japan remains a dominant presence, in terms of tourists and investors, in our Native homeland.

For Pacific peoples, such proliferating investment means further loss of economic control and cultural survival. If the Hawaiian experience with tourism has taught anything, it is that inundation of small land bases and populations by hordes of visitors depletes the Native culture to a point of irreparable damage. Moreover, the people live in a hostage economy where tourist industry employment means active participation in their own degradation.

But if mass-based, corporate tourism is dangerous, so is dependency on foreign exploitation of the region's resources, from sea lanes and harbors to land areas and deep sea fish. Add to this, the First World's interest in seabed minerals, communication and information control, and extended maritime jurisdictions, and Pacific Islanders appear to be swamped by a global economy in which they are both small and vulnerable. Weak, dependent economies are the "norm" among South Pacific states. On a per capita basis, they are the most aid-dependent economies in the world.[14]

In fact, it is precisely the minute size and isolation of most Pacific Islands (in comparison to the big Euro-American and Asian powers) that makes them so attractive to the depredations of larger, less isolated, more urbanized nations whose economies and politics depend on constant profit, constant military readiness, and constant mobility.

The myth of an unspoiled paradise somewhere in the Pacific is belied, of course, by the realities of nuclear poisoning, impoverishment, racism, and exploitation. But it is the myth that drives foreign investment and lures foreign tourists.

At the risk of overgeneralizing, I would suggest the following needs as crucial to the survival of Pacific Islanders.

Self-Determination

New Caledonia, West Papua, East Timor, New Zealand, Tahiti, Belau and the other Trust Territories, Sāmoa, Guam, and Hawai'i all have Native movements for various forms of political and economic autonomy. For example, the Organization of People for Indigenous Rights in Guam, like groups elsewhere under the American imperium, is seeking some form of Native autonomy, including a land base for economic self-sufficiency. In Hawai'i, meanwhile, the Native people have been struggling for self-determination for the last decade. The major actors in this drama are a government-created Native council called the Office of Hawaiian Affairs; a Native initiative for self-government called Ka Lāhui Hawai'i; and the state and federal governments. Nearly two million acres of Native trust lands and billions of dollars of revenues are at stake. Predictably, all politicians, including the governor, the U.S. senators, and the trustees of the Office of Hawaiian Affairs, are in opposition to the Native initiative. As in the rest of the Pacific, so in Hawai'i: the forces arrayed against sovereignty support non-Native control of Native lands and assets.

Nuclear-Free Pacific

This issue is tied closely to the independence issue. Since it has been the United States, France, and the former Soviet Union who threaten the region through nuclearization, it is they who must abide by the South Pacific Forum's Nuclear-Free Zone protocols. Only the Russians and Chinese have said they will honor that treaty. Moreover, the treaty is not as strong as it might be, allowing Australia to continue to export uranium and leaving the question of allowing nuclear weapons transport to each South Pacific nation. As Vanuatu's Walter Lini has argued, a nuclear-free South Pacific means no nuclear material of any kind. Finally, the treaty does not include Hawai'i or the Trust Territories, all of which must negotiate separately with the United States. The case of Hawai'i may be the worst because it is heavily saturated with American military, including the Seventh Fleet, and thus could serve as a flash point for nuclear exchanges and accidents.

Protection of Natural and Cultural Resources

Apart from landbased resources, this area of concern includes protection of (and fair rates for) fish, seabed minerals, and other ocean/land privileges negotiated with foreign countries. Of paramount importance here is protection of the ocean environment.

An example of regional cooperation on a major issue is the statement adopted at the twentieth meeting of the South Pacific Forum in Tarawa that declared the South Pacific a "driftnet-free" region. Japan, which attended the forum, continues to refuse to stop driftnetting. Korea and Taiwan have also refused. Undoubtedly, forum members will raise the driftnet issue at the United Nations. Meanwhile, Japan is sure to continue its "checkbook diplomacy" in the Pacific, hoping to secure allies in their driftnet war. At present, the estimated Pacific Island aid package from Japan is over $70 million U.S. dollars.

Hand in hand with protection of the ocean and land environments goes protection of the many Native cultures, which are dependent on the island/sea ecosystem. At issue is the rapid and severe impact of foreign cultures and economies on peoples who are dependent on subsistence lifeways with little or no advanced technology. When coupled with the effects of tourism, rapid introduction of mass communication (for example, television and radio) and transport can destroy cultures in less than a generation. Familiar social problems (crime, family breakdown, suicide, and violence) follow, and the Native people are consigned to an oppressive destiny they have few means of controlling.

Foreign Policies and Regional Security

Pacific Island nations need to venture out from under the Euro-American umbrella, as Kiribati and Vanuatu did in their respective agreements with the former Soviet Union. This means increased involvement with other nations (in the Third World, for example), with international organizations (such as the United Nations), and with other Pacific Islanders (for example, the subregional Melanesian spear-head group of Vanuatu, the Solomon Islands, and Papua New Guinea).

Within the Pacific Basin, cultural experiences and geographic similarity can be used as a foundation for regional cooperation to resolve disputes and to present unified positions on crucial issues, such as nuclearization of the Pacific. Here, economic and political efforts have led to the creation of regional organizations like the Forum Fisheries Agency, the Committee for the Coordination of Off-Shore Prospecting in the South Pacific, and the (South Pacific) Forum Secretariat, formerly the South Pacific Bureau for Economic Cooperation. The recently formed Committee on Regional Institutional Arrangements (CRIA) of the South Pacific Forum will work on the integration of the forum's intergovernmental agencies. This kind of joint effort must continue.

Native Hawaiians, like other Pacific Islanders, view the ancestral Pacific as the repository of their history, including great genealogies of fearless navigators who made their journeys from island to island and hemisphere to hemisphere with nothing but the stars to guide them. More the children of the sea than the land, Pacific Islanders know their survival as distinct peoples depends on the survival of the Pacific itself. The First World nations must still learn what Pacific Islanders have known for millennia: upon the survival of the Pacific depends the survival of the world.

Notes

1. As for capitalizing "Native" in this essay and elsewhere, the issue is complex. The word is colonial in origin, like "black" as a description of Africans transplanted to America. But just as "black" was politicized, used for self-identification, and capitalized, so "Native" has undergone similar transformations.

I capitalize it to emphasize the political distance between that which is Western and that which is Native. But I also do it to highlight the word and therefore its referent. In Hawai'i, we generally call ourselves Hawaiians. But since the sovereignty movement, the consciousness that we are Natives and not immigrants to Hawai'i has meant a greater identification with the term Native, especially as immigrant history here has been glorified and falsified at the expense of Natives. It is typically American to reiterate the claim that "we are all immigrants." My use of Native is in opposition to that: the capital letter reminds the reader that some of us are not immigrants.

Thus, my usage is political on a geographic level (we are Native to Hawai'i and therefore not American), on an ideological level (we are neither Western nor Eastern but Native Pacific Islanders), and on a cultural level (we are not transplants who are "new" to Hawai'i but an ancient people who have learned to live in and with our Native place and whose culture is the least destructive and the most beneficial to the land).

2. For examples of "cultural nationalism" among indigenous peoples, see the following: Donna Awatere, *Maori Sovereignty* (Auckland, New Zealand: Broadsheet, 1984); Amilcar Cabral, *Return to the Source: Selected Speeches of Amilcar Cabral* (New York: Monthly Review Press, 1973); Vine Deloria, Jr., *God is Red* (New York: Dell, 1973); Russell Means, "Fighting Words on the Future of the Earth," *Mother Jones* (December 1980); Ngũgĩ wa Thiong'o, *Decolonizing the Mind* (London: Heinemann, 1986).

3. For examples of the importance of language revival in Hawai'i and Aotearoa (New Zealand), see Larry Kimura, "Native Hawaiian Culture," in *Native Hawaiians Study Commission Report* (Washington D.C.: Department of the Interior, 1983), vol. 1, pp. 173–197; and Donna Awatere, *Maori Sovereignty*, pp. 92–108. For a careful exploration of the link between the use of Native languages and decolonization, see Ngũgĩ wa Thiong'o, *Decolonizing the Mind.*

4. See Jocelyn Linnekin, "Defining Tradition: Variations on the Hawaiian Identity," *American Ethnologist* 10 (1983): 241–252. Also by the same author, *Children of the Land: Exchange and Status in a Hawaiian Community* (New Brunswick: Rutgers University Press, 1985). For my review of Linnekin's *Children of the Land*, see *The Hawaiian Journal of History* 20 (1986): 232–235. For a sweeping condemnation of nearly every cultural revival in the Pacific, see a particularly racist and dismissive article by Roger M. Keesing, "Creating the Past: Custom and Identity in the Contemporary Pacific," *Contemporary Pacific* 1(1 & 2) (1989): 19–24. Also, see my response, "Natives and Anthropologists: The Colonial Struggle," in *Contemporary Pacific* 3(1) (1991): 111–117. For examples of tourist industry apologists and their assertions that tourism encourages Hawaiian culture, see A. A. Smyser, "Hawaiian Problems," *Honolulu Star-Bulletin* (June 30, 1982), and my reply, "A Hawaiian View of Hawaiian Problems," *Honolulu Star-Bulletin* (July 15, 1982).

5. Native Hawaiians are defined by the federal government as those Hawaiians with 50 percent or more blood quantum. Hawaiians with less than 50 percent blood are not considered to be "Native" by the federal government and are thus not entitled to lands and monies set aside for those with 50 percent blood quantum See the *Federal-State Task Force Report on the Hawaiian Homes Commission Act* (Honolulu: Federal-State Task Force, 1983).

6. See Peter Hayes, Lyuba Zarsky, and Walden Bello, *American Lake: Nuclear Peril in the Pacific* (Ringwood, Australia: Penguin Books, 1986), pp. 337–357.

7. *American Lake*, p. 337.

8. See *Pacific News Bulletin* (Pacific Concerns Resource Center, Australia) 3 (1988): 2, 4, 8.

9. See Stephen Henningham, "Keeping the Tricolor Flying: The French Pacific into the 1990s," *Contemporary Pacific* 1(1 & 2) (1989): 97–132. See also, *Pacific Islands Monthly* (June 1988 and 1989; July and October 1989) and *Pacific News Bulletin* 3 (1988): 3.

10. Henningham, "Keeping the Tricolor Flying." Also, *Pacific News Bulletin* 4 (1989): 11. See also, David Robie, *Blood on Their Banner: Nationalist Struggles in the South Pacific* (London: Zed Books, 1989).

11. See *Pacific Islands Monthly* (March 1998). Also *Pacific News Bulletin* 2 (1987): 2 and 3 (1988): 4, 6, 8.

12. See a most detailed, rigorous, and insightful argument that U.S. foreign policy has been and continues to be one of expansionism based on uninterrupted American dispossession of indigenous peoples from the Indians of the Americas to Pacific Islanders to Asian peoples, in Richard Drinnon, *Facing West: The Metaphysics of Empire-Building and Indian Hating* (Minneapolis: University of Minnesota Press, 1980).

13. For an elaboration of the "right of strategic denial," see John Dorrance, *Oceania and the United States: An Analysis of U.S. Interests and Policy in the South Pacific,* The National Defense University, Monograph Series No. 80–86 (Washington, D.C.: U.S. Government Printing Office, 1980). For a critique of this, see James Anthony, "Great Power Involvement in Oceania: Implications for, and Appropriate Responses from, Pacific Island Microstates." Paper prepared for the United Nations University's Project on Militarization in the Pacific, Honolulu, Hawai'i, 1985.

14. "Sovereignty and Independence in the Contemporary Pacific," in *Contemporary Pacific* 1(1 & 2) (1989): 79–83.

Americans find it hard to believe that Native Hawaiians want to be self-governing. Here, Kalani 'Ohelo, long-time activist, states his preference very clearly. If some 6.5 million tourists who visit Hawai'i each year would take his advice, Hawaiians would be one step closer to sovereignty. (Photo by Ed Greevy.)

As unrestrained tourism development took over land and water in the 1970s, beach villages sprang up along the shorelines of each island. At Sand Island, near the industrial sections of Honolulu, one such village took a stand against eviction. Here, one of the leaders, Puhipau Ahmad, is arrested by state police for trespassing in 1980. (Photo by Ed Greevy.)

Sand Island Beach village in the 1970s, where some 138 families constructed housing out of used lumber and cardboard. Most of the families were Hawaiian, all of them were unable to rent housing because of astronomical costs. The entire village was evicted and several arrests made in 1980. By 1990, the area had become a park with a very large homeless population living in constant fear of eviction. (Photo by Ed Greevy.)

The New World Order

We in the Pacific have been pawns in the power games of the "master" races since colonialism first brought Euro-Americans into our vast ocean home. After Western contact destroyed millions of us through introduced diseases, conversion to Christianity occurred in the chaos of physical and spiritual dismemberment. Economic and political incorporation into foreign countries (Britain, France, the Netherlands, the United States) followed upon mass death. Since the Second World War, we Pacific Islander survivors have been witnesses to nuclear nightmare.

Now, our ancestral homelands—Hawai'i and the Pacific—are planned convergence points of the realigned New World Order. In our geographic area, a coalition of wealthy political entities has resulted in extreme American militarization of our islands and increasing nuclearization of the Pacific Basin; exploitation of ocean resources (including toxic dumping) by Japan, Taiwan, Korea, the United States and others; commodification of island cultures by mass-based corporate tourism; economic penetration and land takeovers by Japan and other Asian countries; and forced outmigration of indigenous islanders from their nuclearized homelands that can only be termed *diaspora*.

Unregulated transnational corporate activity has resulted in tremendous environmental and cultural destruction as well as the steady death of our people due to inundation by a mad industrial nationalism.

But here, *industrial* is the key adjective. As indigenous peoples, *our* nationalism is born not of predatory consumption nor of murderous intolerance but of a genealogical connection to our place, Hawai'i and—by Polynesian geographical reckoning—to the Pacific.

In our genealogy, Papahānaumoku, "earth mother," mated with Wākea, "sky father," from whence came our islands, or *moku*. Out of our beloved islands came the *taro*, our immediate progenitor, and from the *taro*, our chiefs and people.

Our relationship to the cosmos is thus familial. As in all of Polynesia, so in Hawai'i: elder sibling must feed and care for younger sibling, who returns honor and love. The wisdom of our creation is reciprocal obligation. If we husband our lands and waters, they will feed and care for us. In our language, the name for this relationship is *mālama 'āina*, "care for the land," who will care for all family members in turn.

This indigenous knowledge is not unique to Hawaiians but is shared by most indigenous peoples throughout the world. The voices of Native peoples, much popularized in these frightening times, speak a different language than Old World nationalism. Our claims to uniqueness, to cultural integrity, should not be misidentified as "tribalism." We are stewards of the earth, our mother, and we offer an ancient, umbilical wisdom about how to protect and ensure her life.

This lesson of our cultures has never been more crucial to global survival. To put the case in Western terms: biodiversity is guaranteed through human diversity. No one knows how better to care for Hawai'i, our island home, than those of us who have lived here for thousands of years. On the other side of the world from us, no people understand the desert better than those who inhabit her. And so on and so on, throughout the magnificently varied places of the earth. Forest people know the forest; mountain people know the mountains; plains people know the plains. This is an elemental wisdom that has nearly disappeared because of industrialization, greed, and hatred of that which is wild and sensuous.

If this is our heritage, then the counter to the New World Order is not more uniformity, more conformity but more autonomy, more localized control of resources and the cultures they can maintain. *Human diversity ensures biodiversity*.

Unremittingly, the history of the modern period is the history of increasing conformity, paid for in genocide and ecocide. The more we are made to be the same, the more the environment we inhabit becomes the same: "backward" people forced into a "modern" (read "industrial") context can no longer care for their environment. As the people are transformed, or more likely, exterminated, their environment is progressively degraded, parts of it destroyed forever. Physical despoliation is reflected in cultural degradation. A dead land is preceded by a dying people. As an example, indigenous languages replaced by "universal" (read "colonial") languages result in the creation of "dead languages." But what is "dead" or "lost" is not the language but the people who once spoke it and transmitted their mother tongue to succeeding generations. Lost, too, is the relationship between words and their physical referents. In Hawai'i, English is the dominant language, but it cannot begin to encompass the physical beauty of our islands in the unparalleled detail of the Hawaiian language. Nor can English reveal how we knew animals to be our family; how we harnessed the ocean's rhythms, creating massive fishponds; how we came to know the migrations of deep-ocean fish and golden plovers from the Arctic; how we sailed from hemisphere to hemisphere with nothing but the stars to guide us. English is foreign to Hawai'i; it reveals nothing of our place where we were born, where our ancestors created knowledge now "lost" to the past.

The secrets of the land die with the people of the land. This is the bitter lesson of the modern age. Forcing human groups to be alike results in the destruction of languages, of environments, of nations.

The land cannot live without the people of the land who, in turn, care for their heritage, their mother. This is an essential wisdom of indigenous cultures and explains why, when Native peoples are destroyed, destruction of the earth proceeds immediately. In Hawai'i, the uprooting and great dying of my people was quickly followed by massive and irreparable changes on the land. Under American control, Hawai'i has been transformed into a tinsel version of the fragile beauty it once was. As a nineteenth-century plantation economy gave way to a modern tourist/military economy, our lands and waters have been increasingly poisoned, developed, or destroyed altogether. Militarism and tourism—twin engines of *haole* (white) American culture in Hawai'i—have increased their rapacious consumption of our physical and cultural heritage as we enter the twenty-first century.

Now, we Hawaiians have no control over the massive tourist industry, which imports more than six million foreigners into our tiny islands every year. Multinational corporations sell our beauty; the world's rich buy it in two- and four-week packages. These foreigners, mostly *haole* and Japanese, think of our homeland as theirs, that is, as a place they have a claim to visit, pollute, and destroy by virtue of their wealth. Our role, as indigenous people, is to serve and wait upon these visitors, to illuminate and fulfill their dreams. Throughout the Pacific Basin, First World tourists play out this racist fantasy of an "island vacation," ruining our waters and lands, degrading our living cultures. When they leave, tourists have learned nothing of our people or our place. They have not listened to the land nor have they heard her singing.

And still Western stupidity knows no bounds: our islands are also nuclear hot spots. While tourists flock to our homelands, the U.S. military continues to maintain bases and airfields and storage sites and dumping grounds and tracking stations. The *haole* war machine, including nuclear submarines and missiles, is well oiled and ready for deployment on a moment's notice. Hawai'i, like most of the Pacific, is a nuclearized paradise.

Of course, the rush to sameness is resisted by indigenous peoples everywhere. Indeed, indigenous peoples are among the most resilient in the face of the existing World Order.

And yet, Native peoples' resilience depends on certain physical conditions: our homelands must be protected from destructive developments, such as deforestation, industrial projects, and mass-based tourism; immigration and in-migration into Native areas must be regulated or restricted *by indigenous peoples for our benefit*; and indigenous human rights, like those enunciated in the current Draft United Nations Declaration on the Rights of Indigenous Peoples now being considered, must be guaranteed. These rights include rights to self-determination on an aboriginal land base; rights to our languages, to our religions, to our economies, to integrity as distinct peoples, to the security of our families, especially our children, and perhaps most urgently, the right to be protected from physical and cultural genocide. Above all, modern nation-states, especially the super industrial powers of Japan, the United States, and European countries, must honor and protect these rights because they are the nations most responsible for chronic violations.

But can we, as Native peoples, resist the planned New World Order by ourselves? Probably not. The state of the world gives us little hope. Native resistance can be and has been crushed. As indigenous nations die out, our peoples reach a point of irreparable harm. We cannot sustain our numbers, our cultures, our stewardship of the earth. Even while they plan our demise, First World countries and those aspiring to that status memorialize our passing. We are not heroes, or models, to an unsung world.

The choice is clear. As indigenous peoples, we must fight for Papahānaumoku, even as she—and we—are dying.

But where do people in the industrial countries draw *their* battle lines? On the side of mother earth? On the side of consumption? On the side of First World nationalism?

If human beings, Native and non-Native alike, are to create an alternative to the planned New World Order, then those who live in the First World must change their *culture*, not only their leaders.

Who, then, bears primary responsibility? Who carries the burden of obligation? Who will protect mother earth?

Part II

Sovereignty: The Hawai‘i Context

Kūpa'a 'Āina: Native Hawaiian Nationalism in Hawai'i

The overthrow of our Native government in 1893 and forced annexation to the United States in 1898 meant the beginning of a long period of political and cultural suppression as the *haole* sugar barons dominated Hawai'i. Organized as the Republican Party, the *haole* plantation aristocracy enjoyed unrestrained power: Asian settlers poured into Hawai'i to work *haole*-owned plantations, Native Hawaiians continued to decline in number, and the Republicans enjoyed total control of the government, transport, educational, and economic systems.

After an initial period of political activity focused on various home rule parties, and faced with the total dominance of the *haole* Republican Party, politically astute and educated Hawaiians created an oppositional Democratic Party. Accepting that Native control of the islands was lost with the overthrow and annexation, these Hawaiians fashioned a political unit within the construct of the American two-party system. They reasoned that political power was closed to them as long as Hawai'i was a territory. Under this status, the president of the United States would always control the appointment of the all-powerful governor, resulting in continued dominance of the plantation-owning Republican party. If Hawaiians and Asians were to have any participation in governing Hawai'i, they had to be able to capture the governor's office, from which all patronage flowed. To this end, politically

---

Kūpa'a 'Āina means "hold fast to the land."

active Hawaiians argued and organized for over fifty years to have Hawai'i become a state. Finally, two generations after annexation, Hawai'i became part of the Union in 1959. (Most Hawaiians did not vote on statehood, choosing instead to stay away from the polls.) Since 1959, every elected governor of Hawai'i has been a Democrat.[1]

Statehood began a fundamental transformation in Hawai'i's economy. From dependence on military expenditures and cash crops of sugar and pineapple in the first half of the twentieth century, the economy shifted to an increasing dependence on tourism and land speculation with rising investment by multinational corporations in the second half of the century.

Concentrated land ownership, a problem since the onslaught of plantation agriculture in the 1800s, had actually increased during the twentieth century. Small landowners controlled less than 10 percent of the land. The military, the state, large private estates, and foreign and American developers owned the remainder. As a result, large landlords drove up the price of land, capitalizing on the post-statehood rush toward commercial, especially hotel, development.

Already economically exploited and culturally suppressed, rural Hawaiian communities, which had been relatively untouched during the plantation period, were besieged by rapid development of their agricultural areas beginning in the late 1960s. These communities—among them Hāna, East Moloka'i, Keaukaha, Nānākuli, Wai'anae, Waimānalo, Kahalu'u—had managed to retain many traditional practices, such as taro farming, fishing, and the spoken Hawaiian language. Given the genocidal effects of colonialism, especially population collapse, these Hawaiian enclaves, although remnants of a once dynamic civilization, were nevertheless crucial to the perpetuation of Hawaiian culture. Their threatened extinction by urbanization and other forms of development was correctly perceived by many Hawaiians as a final attempt to rid their ancestral homeland of all things Native. It was predictable that the Hawaiian Movement would begin and flourish in rural areas, where the call for a land base would be the loudest.

Out of anti-eviction and other land struggles in rural areas threatened with urbanization was born a Native rights movement, similar to movements of other colonized Native peoples, such as the Tahitians and the Maori, in the Pacific. Beginning in 1970, the Hawaiian Movement evolved from a series of protests against land abuses, through various demonstrations and occupations to dramatize the exploitative conditions of Hawaiians, to assertions of Native forms of sovereignty based on indigenous birthrights to land and sea.

At the beginning of the seventies, communities identified their struggles in terms of the claims of "local" people. The term *local* included both Hawaiian and non-Hawaiian long-time residents of Hawai'i. The residency rights of local people were thus framed in opposition to the development rights of property owners like the state, corporations, and private estates.

But as the decade wore on, the assertion of indigenous Hawaiian claims as historically and culturally unique in Hawai'i began to characterize more community struggles. Independent of their "local," non-Native supporters, Hawaiians protested spreading urbanization by occupying lands or by resisting eviction from land scheduled for residential and commercial development. Mass demonstrations, legal actions, and cultural assertions, such as the construction of fishing villages, became commonplace. As a group, Hawaiians pushed their demands to the front of the movement. The rights of "locals" were not thereby opposed. But Hawaiians' historic and cultural claims to the land as the *first* and *original* claimants were increasingly seen, at least by Hawaiians, as primary.

A typical eviction struggle (and one that began the movement) occurred in 1970 in Kalama Valley on the island of O'ahu where the single largest private landowner in the State of Hawai'i—Bishop Estate—evicted farmers for an upper-income residential development by Kaiser-Aetna. The resistance called forth an outpouring of support from around the state. While the organizing core, Kōkua Hawai'i, lost the battle for residents' rights, the issue of land use and land claims would characterize public debate for the next thirty years.

The merging of land-rich but capital-poor landowners with out-of-state corporations became a familiar pattern. This combination enabled large resorts, replete with golf courses, condominiums, and restaurants, to spring up near beaches and on conservation land around the islands. Mostly descended from American missionaries and other entrepreneurs, the landowners—such as Campbell Estate, Castle & Cook, Dillingham Corporation, American Factors, and Alexander & Baldwin—linked up with American and Japanese multinational corporations to develop the Kona Coast of the Big Island of Hawai'i, the east end of Moloka'i, the south and north shores of Kaua'i, and the west side of Maui. Such resort and residential development spurred antidevelopment battles wherever it occurred.

In the meantime, Native political organizations moved to reclaim a land base. Legal corporations (for example, the Hawaiian Coalition of Native Claims), political groups, and loose-knit community coalitions argued for reparations from the United States for its role in the overthrow of the Hawaiian government in 1893, for forced annexation in 1898, and for the consequent loss of Hawaiian nationhood and sovereignty. Beyond this, legal claims were made (by such groups as *Ho'āla Kānāwai*, meaning "awaken the law") to nearly two million acres of Native "trust" lands—lands given by the U.S. government for exclusive Hawaiian use but owned and mismanaged by both the state and federal governments. And finally, claims to a land base were brought as a right of residence by virtue of indigenous status, called aboriginal rights.[2]

Along with these claims had come concerns over military expropriation and abuse of lands. The American military controls nearly 30 percent of the most populated island of O'ahu. Military lands, including trust lands, were taken by Executive Order during periods when the United States was at war (for example, 600,000 acres taken during World War II, including the entire island of Kaho'olawe and hundreds of acres of Native trust lands taken during the Vietnam War).[3]

By 1976, this concern had "exploded" over Kaho'olawe Island, the smallest of the eight major islands, a military bombing target since 1941, and the site of revived Hawaiian religious worship. Occupation by Native activists rallied Hawaiians statewide around several issues: destructive military land use in an archipelago where land is scarce; the assertion of the Native land use ethic—*mālama 'āina*, or "protect the land"—in opposition to military use; and the failure of the state to protect the land for the public. In 1990, after the death of two activists and the designation of the island as a national historic site, the bombing was finally halted, but the controversy surrounding military misuse of land has expanded to include illegal military use of Native trust lands (for which the military pays, in some cases, less than a dollar a year) and the colonial presence of the military on all islands.

By 1980, abuse of Hawaiian Homes trust lands (nearly 200,000 acres) by the state and federal governments had been challenged by demonstrations, occupations, and law suits because of the extent of illegal use for airports (for example, the Hilo, Kamuela, and Moloka'i airports), military reservations (for example, Lualualei Valley), public schools (such as, Nānākuli and Moloka'i high schools), public parks (such as, Anahola and Waimānalo beach parks), even private homes (for example, Kawaihae residential lots) and county refuse sites (such as Moloka'i dump). By 1998, all applications for pastoral and residential lots on the islands of O'ahu, Maui, Hawai'i, Kaua'i, and Moloka'i totalled over 29,000. Meanwhile, illegal and other non-Native uses existed on more than 130,000 acres of trust lands. Particularly galling to beneficiaries was their status as wards of the state, without litigation rights to challenge illegal uses in both state and federal courts.[4]

The other land trust—on ceded lands—had *never* been used by the state for Hawaiians, despite their beneficiary status. Thus, as Hawaiians came to link abuse of the trust lands with land dispossession at the time of the overthrow and annexation, they coalesced around a unified push for a land base. Land and money restitution from the American government for its historic role in the loss of Hawaiian domain and dominion could be coupled with Native control of the trust lands to form a land base as the anchor of Native sovereignty. In the eighties, various arguments for Hawaiian sovereignty were put forward by defendants in eviction arrests (for example, at Sand Island and Mākua Valley), by Hawaiian activists at the United Nations and other international forums, and by lawyers and political groups seeking redress for all manner of Native rights violations. International networking included exchanges of nationalists to Nuclear-Free and Independent Pacific conferences and Third World gatherings throughout the Pacific, the Americas, and Asia. What started as a call for restitution in the seventies had broadened into a clear demand for Native sovereignty in the eighties.

The strength of this push was not lost on politicians at both the state and federal levels. Long discounted as a minor voice because of their poor voting participation in the American-imposed electoral system, Hawaiians had come more and more to represent a potential pivotal swing group in elections. If organized, they could turn narrow defeats into narrow victories. Toward this end, Hawaiian claims were professed by candidates for the 1978 State Constitutional Convention (Con-Con), in various campaigns for the legislature and eventually the state house, and even in congressional races. The results were seen in an increase in the number of Hawaiian elected officials beginning in the late seventies; in the appointment of two presidential commissions in 1981 to review both the Hawaiian Homes trust and the general status of Hawaiians; and in the creation of an Office of Hawaiian Affairs (OHA) in 1978.[5]

The Office of Hawaiian Affairs, though ostensibly for representation of Hawaiian rights by Hawaiians (the only group allowed to vote for its all-Native trustees), was actually devised as an extension of the state. It was powerless as a mechanism of self-government, having no control over the trust lands (that is, no legal status to stop their takings or misuse) and no statutory strength to prevent abuses of

Hawaiian culture (for example, grotesque and servile representations of Hawaiians by the tourist industry).

Initially, OHA trustees were unpaid, resulting in a high turnover as board members moved on to gainful employment. Indeed, three members from the first board quit after one term to run for the legislature, using their visibility as trustees to aid in voter identification. Two chairpersons of the board misused OHA monies while in office, although only one was dismissed for the offense. Over its first ten years of existence, OHA had been plagued by scandals, some sex-related, others concerning mismanagement of funds, falsification of trustee credentials, and misrepresentation of programs to the state legislature.

Beyond its trustee problems, OHA has been accused by many Hawaiians of being a "do nothing" organization because most of its funding goes into personnel, office space, and administration, instead of programs for Native beneficiaries. And when OHA does take a position on a controversial issue, it is often on the side of destructive projects like freeways and commercial development.

But the worst aspect of OHA is its continued collaboration with the state Democractic party. Although overflowing with pro-Hawaiian rhetoric, OHA supports destructive developments, such as state geothermal energy projects on Hawai'i island that endanger pristine Native forests and threaten pollution of nearby communities and destabilization of the volcanic area where geothermal wells have been sunk. A megaresort called West Beach (one-fifth the size of Waikīkī), has also been supported by several OHA trustees, despite overwhelming evidence that its hotels, marinas, restaurants, and golf courses will damage fisheries, obliterate historic sites, drain scarce water resources, and forever pave over fertile lands.[6]

While OHA has closed ranks with the Democratic party, there has been a proliferation of sovereignty groups seeking some form of Native political control of a land base. One of these groups, Ka Lāhui Hawai'i, was born out of a core watchdog association that had lobbied for the Federal-State Task Force on the Hawaiian Homes Commission Act. After the task force report documenting both abuses of trust lands and recommendations, the community group called a constitutional convention of its own in 1987, with 250 delegates from around the archipelago meeting to create a constitution and to elect interim officials.

As a Native initiative for self-government, Ka Lāhui is a repudiation of OHA as the sole representative of the Hawaiian people. Within three years of its first convention in 1987, Ka Lāhui membership had grown thirty times, to 7,500, suggesting more than that Hawaiians did not support OHA. In fact, Ka Lāhui's large membership indicated support for sovereignty on the model of American Indian nations. Ka Lāhui served as a focus for discontent over continued state abuse of the trust lands and revenues, and it raised an issue that OHA had ignored: inclusion of Hawaiians in federal Indian policy that recognized over 300 Native nations in the United States while not extending this recognition to Hawaiians.[7]

By the end of 1988, the issue of "sovereignty" was identified with the issue of "nationhood." While OHA worked on a reparations package to be presented to Congress, a sovereignty conference was hosted at the state capitol. Six major groups presented positions on the structure of the Native land base, a mechanism for Hawaiian governance, and political strategies for the achievement of nationhood. The groups included Nā 'Ōiwi o Hawai'i (supporting more community education before any mechanism for government was established), the Protect Kaho'olawe 'Ohana (supporting decentralized, island-based, autonomous entities), E Ola Mau (a health professionals group supporting Ka Lāhui), the Council of Hawaiian Organizations (supporting a constitutionally established mechanism on a separate land base), the Institute for the Advancement of Hawaiian Affairs (supporting secession), and Ka Lāhui Hawai'i (supporting federal recognition of Hawaiians as a Native nation with all the rights of nationhood extended to Indian nations). Although OHA board members had been invited to participate, they declined.

All these groups developed their arguments from the prior existence of the Hawaiian nation, the culpability of the United States in the loss of Hawaiian domain and dominion in 1893, the unilateral change in Native citizenship that came with forcible annexation in 1898, and the internationally recognized right of all peoples to self-determination. The specifics of the Native Hawaiian-United States relationship had been linked with the universals of the human rights position to form a powerful defense of Hawaiian sovereignty.

In the simplest terms, sovereignty was defined, in the words of Ka Lāhui Hawai'i, as

> the ability of a people who share a common culture, religion, language, value system and land base, to exercise control over their lands and lives, independent of other nations.[8]

Given that the Hawaiian form of government had been overthrown in 1893, the first order of business for Hawaiians emerged as the creation of a mechanism for self-government.

What that mechanism will look like is still hotly debated by sovereignty groups today. But the level of commitment is so high that when Senator Inouye's Indian Affairs Committee came to Honolulu to hear testimony on reparations in the summer of 1988, Native groups argued for self-government, not merely reparations. In 1989 a series of repeat forums yielded the same response from the communities.

The most compelling defense of Hawaiian sovereignty was put to Senator Inouye as an extension of current federal policy regarding Native people controlled by America. In the 1970s President Nixon had officially changed U.S. Native policy from wardship to self-determination. The policies of termination (through which Indian tribes would cease to have federal recognition and therefore tribal land rights as well as other treaty rights) were to be replaced by a commitment to aid and encourage tribal self-government. This aid was to come not only in the form of monies for economic development projects on reservations but also as specific recognition of tribes by the federal government. Today, the U.S. government recognizes over 300 Indian nations. Under existing U.S. policy, relations between the federal government and these Indian tribes are described as "Nation-to-Nation."

In the Hawaiian case, there has not been any federal recognition of a Native claim to self-government. It is as if, in terms of federal policy, Hawaiians are still in the stage of "termination" rather than self-government. In practice, federal policy had straddled two poles, acknowledging Hawaiians as Natives for some purposes (such as for educational and health programs) but refusing to grant them the privileges of Native recognition in terms of self-government.

Inouye was shaken by this argument. He could not fail to see the injustice of federal recognition for one Native people and not another. Pressured by Hawaiians calling for self-government, and cornered by the press at the hearing, Inouye finally acknowledged that, "If native American Indians have claims to sovereignty, it's difficult to argue Hawaiians do not." As a self-proclaimed champion of Indian rights, Inouye had been forced to recognize the equal claims of another Native people (who were also from his home state) to self-determination.[9]

The 1988 public statement by Inouye that Hawaiians had a claim to as much self-government as Indians was an indication of how far the Hawaiian Movement had progressed. For years, the debate had been over whether Hawaiians deserved reparations. Governor Waihe'e had stated openly that he would be satisfied with an apology for the overthrow from the American government. OHA, meanwhile, had supported a large reparations package, to be dispersed through its offices.

But the reparations game had been surpassed by a historic evolution in Hawaiian consciousness. Faced with this reality, and sensing that they had been under-prepared and out-organized at the summer hearing (where they had argued for reparations), OHA came out for sovereignty. Acknowledging themselves as a state agency, they nevertheless asserted that OHA should be the governing structure of the Hawaiian nation.

This position was problematic for several reasons. First, OHA was not representative of all Hawaiian communities and never had been, since voting procedures overweighted the most populous island of O'ahu, resulting in a skewed representation for trustees from the Neighbor Islands. Second, any lands or monies transferred by the federal government to OHA would go to the state, *not* to the Hawaiian people, since OHA was a state agency; this would mean *less*, not *more*, control by Hawaiians over their future. Finally, giving OHA nation status would be akin to calling the Bureau of Indian Affairs (BIA) an Indian nation.

Nevertheless, OHA issued a detailed "Blueprint" for reparations in 1989, arguing their prior status as the representative organization of the Hawaiian people. Ignoring the argument for inclusion under federal Indian policy, OHA's Blueprint made no claims against the state of Hawai'i, despite documented abuse of its trust relationship to Hawaiians. Instead, all claims were made against the federal government for the overthrow and annexation, with the recommendation that OHA be allowed to control all Native assets.[10]

In February 1990, after thirty months of closed-door negotiations, OHA and the governor's office concluded an agreement to settle ceded lands claims against the state. In the settlement, Hawaiians lost their right to 1.5 million acres of ceded lands and OHA received $100 million in 1991 and $8.5 million every year thereafter. Thus, *money*, rather than *land* is at the heart of the settlement. As predicted by sovereignty groups for years, two state agencies conspired against the Hawaiian people to settle Native claims.

Under the guise of "cooperation," the Office of Hawaiian Affairs, the alleged Hawaiian governor, and the senior senator from Hawai'i reaffirmed state and federal control of all Hawaiian trusts;

continued wardship of Native Hawaiians; and denial of the human right of self-determination as well as the civil rights of Hawaiians as citizens of the state of Hawai'i.

In 1992, OHA held public hearings on their sovereignty plan. As expected, only OHA was mentioned in the plan as the agency responsible for Hawaiian self-governance. In conflicts involving land, resources, language, and other cultural issues, OHA continues to maintain they are the sole political representative of the Hawaiian people.

Of course, OHA has not gone unchallenged. Several groups, including the most mild-mannered and thoughtful, have publicly repudiated OHA, while creating their own sovereignty organizations.

The largest of these sovereignty groups, Ka Lāhui Hawai'i, has steadily increased its representation, numbering over 20,000 in 1998. Their response to OHA's ceded lands settlement has been clearly enunciated since 1994 in the Ka Lāhui Master Plan.

Ka Lāhui Master Plan: *Ho'okupu a Ka Lāhui Hawai'i*

As a Native initiative for self-government, Ka Lāhui is the best example of how self-determination can work in practice. Founded in 1987, Ka Lāhui had expanded into a nationwide structure with representative bodies throughout the archipelago by 1993.

In 1994, Ka Lāhui created the most comprehensive plan for the attainment of Hawaiian sovereignty yet devised. The Ka Lāhui Master Plan[11] was the brainchild of its leader, Mililani Trask, who had been engaged throughout the eighties in international activity. Participating at the United Nations with the Working Group on Indigenous Populations and with world leaders like the Dalai Lama and Rigoberta Menchu, Ms. Trask understood the necessity for a larger agenda beyond the state of Hawai'i. The benefit of her international experience and leadership is visible in the scope as well as the framing of the Master Plan. As a Native attorney, Ms. Trask was uniquely suited to the translation of international principles into Hawaiian values. The inclusive vision of the Master Plan follows, at one and the same time the language of international law *and* the cultural precepts of Native Hawaiians.

The Master Plan begins, in Part I, with an endorsement of fundamental principles, including a commitment to peace, disarmament, and non-violence. There is, as well, a recognition of the inalienable rights of Native Hawaiians and their descendants as called for in the United Nations Charter, the Draft United Nations Declaration on the Rights of Indigenous Peoples, and the International Covenant on Civil and Political Rights, as well as the International Covenant on Social, Economic and Cultural Rights.

Rights to self-determination and self-development follow, including the right to engage freely in traditional activities. But the crucial declaration in this section is the rejection of the wardship imposed by the United States as a result of the policy of Manifest Destiny in general and the Tyler Doctrine in particular, which extended that policy to the Pacific.

Later in the Master Plan, the rejection of wardship leads to the assertion of self-determination and sovereignty as attributes of Hawaiian human rights. Historically, Hawaiians had tried to escape wardship by entering the Democratic party, that is, by embracing the reality of American citizenship as they left the dispossession of the overthrow behind them. Now, in 1994, the very existence of the Ka Lāhui Master Plan revealed the failure of the Democratic party to resolve the land claims and self-government issues of Hawaiians.

Part I concludes with multiple assertions of jurisdiction by Ka Lāhui Hawai'i. These include the powers to determine membership, to administer justice, to exclude persons from the "National Territory," to regulate trade, to tax, and to claim sovereign immunity. This section reveals how Ka Lāhui views itself as a government, albeit one in exile and without U.S. recognition.

Part II addresses how Ka Lāhui functions and lists, among its many accomplishments, the following: the formation of a democratic and elective nation whose indigenous citizens exercise the franchise by electing representatives and thereby practice self-determination; the drafting of a constitution that includes spiritual, cultural, and traditional values; and the establishment of a respected international reputation, which includes membership in the Unrepresented Nations and Peoples Organizations (U.N.P.O.) at The Hague.

In Part III, the Master Plan details the historical relationship with the United States which evolved from a policy of peace and friendship between 1826 and 1842 into a policy of colonialism under the Tyler Doctrine, which imposed an American sphere of influence on Hawai'i to ward off the predations of Britain and France. All treaties and conventions negotiated between the United States and Hawai'i subsequent to 1842 favored the United States over Hawai'i.

At the 1893 overthrow of the Kingdom of Hawai'i by the forces of the United States and through the offices of the U.S. minister at the time, the policy of armed intervention (exercised in 1874 and again in 1889, with the landing of U.S. troops on Hawaiian soil) resulted in the overthrow of the Hawaiian government (1893) and annexation of the Hawaiian Islands to the United States in 1898. No Native vote in Hawai'i was ever taken on annexation nor was any vote ever envisioned. In 1900, Hawai'i became American property.

At the creation of the United Nations in 1946, Hawai'i was listed as a non-self-governing territory under U.S. administration. Such status was considered a "trust" relationship, whereby the United States had an obligation to promote the political aspirations of the Hawaiian people toward attaining self-government.

In 1959, Hawai'i became a state. The vote on statehood included only two options: continuation of territorial status or statehood. Neither commonwealth status nor independence appeared as choices on the ballot.

Of course, the imperial policy of the United States has continued to be one of nonrecognition, denial, and wardship under the state of Hawai'i. This condition of wardship has meant, for example, that the federal government negotiates only with the state of Hawai'i rather than with the Hawaiian people when Hawaiian issues are at stake. The state, meanwhile, has used the Hawaiian homelands trust, some 200,000 acres, and the ceded land trust, nearly 2 million acres, for their own purposes. Meanwhile, the civil rights of Hawaiians continue to be abused, as documented in reports by the Hawai'i Advisory Committee to the United States Commission on Civil Rights.[12]

Abandonment has been the policy of the Reagan, Bush, and Clinton administrations. All three presidents have asserted that no trust obligation on the part of the federal government exists. In practical terms, this has meant no oversight of state actions by the federal government. In 1993, the U.S. Congress passed the Apology Bill in which it is acknowledged that ". . . the indigenous Hawaiian people never directly relinquished their claims to their inherent sovereignty as a people or over their national lands to the United States, either through their monarchy or through a plebiscite or referendum."[13]

Despite the hopefulness that greeted the passage of the Apology Bill in Hawai'i, nothing substantive has changed regarding federal policy toward Hawaiians. While "reconciliation" between the Hawaiian people and the American government is cited, no process or mechanism for reconciliation is included in the bill.

In its Master Plan, Ka Lāhui accepted the U.S. apology and suggested its own process for reconciliation. The goals of reconciliation are listed as follows:

1. Final resolution of the historic claims relating to the overthrow; to state and federal misuse of Native trust lands and resources; to violations of human and civil rights; and to federally held lands and resources.
2. Termination of the U.S. policy of nonrecognition of Native Hawaiian self-determination, including repudiation of the policy of wardship.
3. Federal recognition of Ka Lāhui Hawai'i as the indigenous sovereign Hawaiian Nation, including recognition of the jurisdiction of Ka Lāhui Hawai'i over its national assets, lands, and natural resources.
4. A commitment to decolonize Hawai'i through the United Nations process for non-self-governing territories.
5. Restoration of traditional lands, natural resources, ocean and energy resources to the Ka Lāhui National Land Trust. These lands include Hawaiian home lands, the ceded lands, and federally held lands. These lands shall be segregated from other public lands.

The process of termination of wardship is detailed in the Master Plan and involves legislation by the state to segregate all Hawaiian trust lands and assets from the general public lands and assets and transfer them to the National Land Trust of the Hawaiian Nation.

The National Land Trust includes all state-held trust lands, surface water and groundwater, marine resources and fisheries to the 200-mile limit, energy resources, airspace, and the trust assets of the many private Hawaiian trusts, such as the Kamehameha Schools/Bishop Estate.

In the area of economic development, the master plan calls for the establishment of the National Land Trust and jurisdiction over its assets and revenues; the powers of taxation; community-based economic development; and international trade agreements.

On international issues, the Master Plan reiterates the call for decolonization, self-government, and reinscription on the United Nations list of non-self-governing territories.

No other Hawaiian entity—OHA, the private trusts, or voluntary associations such as the civic clubs—has even approached the level of analysis and practical self-government that Ka Lāhui Hawai'i has attained. Without doubt, the Master Plan, will remain the single greatest accomplishment of Ka Lāhui. As a *ho'okupu,* or gift, to the Hawaiian people, it will guide future discussions about sovereignty. The general attentive Hawaiian public has already absorbed so much of the language of the Plan that concepts such as reinscription at the United Nations, a National Land Trust, and termination of wardship have become central to larger sovereignty discussions in the Hawaiian community.

Worried by the resilience and creativity of Ka Lāhui Hawai'i and other sovereignty groups, the state of Hawai'i moved to blunt the nationalist front by calling for a false referendum, misnamed the Native Hawaiian Vote. Frontline organizing by Ka Lāhui and other sovereignty groups resulted in a resounding defeat of the alleged vote. Of the 82,000 ballots mailed, only 33,000 were returned. Of those, only 22,294 or 27 percent of eligible voters said "yes." Without a mandate, the state remained in a quandary about how to control the sovereignty front. The legislature had tried, through creation of the Hawaiian Sovereignty Elections Council (HSEC), to devise an oversight body with sufficient funding to hold the Native vote. But once again Ka Lāhui led a massive and successful effort to stop yet another state ploy to bring the issue of sovereignty under the control of the Democratic party.

Finally, as 1998 dawned and Hawaiians prepared to mark the centennial of annexation by well-organized protests, the legislature tried, as usual, to control the Hawaiian sovereignty front by submitting a Hawaiian Autonomy bill through the *haole* chair of the Hawaiian Affairs Committee, Ed Case.[14] Misjudging the level of consciousness among Hawaiians, Case did not anticipate the outpouring of resistance to the bill. For the first time, *hula hālau* joined with political groups in a unified march and demonstration at the capital, calling for defeat of the bill as well as for unity on the issue of Hawaiian sovereignty.

Correctly identifying the bill and its author as racist, Hawaiians finally said publicly and forcefully what some of their leaders had been saying for decades: Hawaiian sovereignty was to be decided by Hawaiians, not by the state or its agents. Moreover, the fact that Case was *haole* served to underscore the issue of racism. Once again, Hawaiian issues were being defined and directed by *haole*, that is, by foreigners. Case heard over and over in testimony that the bill was racist, that in fact he himself was racist for acting on behalf of the state against the claims of Hawaiians.

From the view at the end of the twentieth century, the role of the government appears exactly the same now as it did at the end of the nineteenth century. Then, in 1898, an all-*haole* Republic of Hawai'i gave the Hawaiian Islands and the birthright of the Hawaiian people to the white government of the United States of America. A century later, in 1998, a *haole* legislator is seeking to foreclose Hawaiian self-determination through the intervention of the state of Hawai'i.

Perhaps more than any other example, the Hawaiian autonomy bill illustrates how little has changed for Hawaiians. The settlers, white and Asian alike, continue to control the politics of Hawai'i. Native sovereignty continues to be the issue of the day, just as it was during the reign of our beloved Queen Lili'uokalani. And Hawaiians continue to understand their situation in the context of self-government and human rights, rather than in the more American frame of constitutional and civil rights.

As Hawaiians enter the new century, they are well-grounded in the lessons of their past: We are Hawaiians, not Americans.

Notes

1. For an analysis of the territorial period, see Noel Kent, *Hawai'i: Islands Under the Influence* (New York: Monthly Review Press, 1983).

2. For a more detailed account of the Hawaiian Movement in the context of colonialism, see my article, "Hawai'i: Colonization and De-Colonization," in Antony Hooper, editor, *Class and Culture in the South Pacific* (Suva, Fiji: University of the South Pacific, 1987). Also, Haunani-Kay Trask, "The Birth of the Modern Hawaiian Movement: Kalama Valley, O'ahu," in *Hawaiian Journal of History* 21 (1987): 126–153. For the relationship between missionary-descended landowners and development of resort and commercial property, see George Cooper and Gavan Daws, *Land and Power in Hawai'i* (Honolulu: Benchmark Books, 1986).

3. For a summary of military landholdings in the context of Hawai'i politics in the twentieth century, see Ian Lind, "Ring of Steel: Notes on the Militarization of Hawai'i," in *Social Process in Hawai'i* 31 (1984): 25–48.

4. For an early review of the problems with the Hawaiian Homes trust lands as well as some solutions, see the *Report of the Federal-State Task Force on the Hawaiian Homes Commission Act*. The report carefully documents illegal uses, wrongful takings, and below-market rentals. Recommendations are also

made, including a right to sue for aggrieved beneficiaries in both state and federal courts. For the latest report from the Hawai'i Advisory Committee to the United States Commission on Civil Rights regarding Hawaiian Homes, see *A Broken Trust, The Hawaiian Homelands Program: Seventy Years of Failure of the State and Federal Governments to Protect the Civil Rights of Native Hawaiians* (December 1991). Waiting list figures are available from the Department of Hawaiian Home Lands, State of Hawai'i.

5. The presidential commissions grew out of a decade of political activism around the issues of reparations and the abuse of the Hawaiian Homes trust lands. The Native Hawaiian Study Commission issued its report, including a minority report in vol. II, in 1983. By coincidence, the Federal-State Task Force on the Hawaiian Homes Commission Act issued its report in the same year. Both reports are excellent for background material on the two issues.

6. OHA's support for geothermal energy projects and for West Beach was, and remains, controversial both within Hawaiian communities and within the OHA Board of Trustees. Neither project was supported by the board unanimously.

7. *Faces of the Nation,* a video produced for Ka Lāhui Hawai'i by Nā Maka o Ka 'Āina Video, explains the origins and structure of Ka Lāhui, and contains valuable information about the governing body of Ka Lāhui. The constitution of the nation is contained in a booklet, *Ka Lāhui Hawai'i,* available from the Center for Hawaiian Studies, University of Hawai'i, Honolulu, Hawai'i, 96822.

8. This quotation is from the booklet *Ka Lāhui Hawai'i,* p. 2.

9. *Honolulu Star-Bulletin* (August 22, 1988).

10. "Blueprint for Native Hawaiian Entitlements" (September 1989) is available from the Office of Hawaiian Affairs, Honolulu, Hawai'i.

11. *Ho'okupu a Ka Lāhui Hawai'i–Ka Lāhui Master Plan* (see appendixes).

12. *A Broken Trust, The Hawaiian Homelands Program.*

13. Public Law 103–150, 103rd Cong., S.J. Res. 19 (23 November 1993).

14. Hawai'i State Legislature, House Bill 2340, *The Native Hawaiian Autonomy Act,* 1998.

At the federal trials of Hawaiian "trespassers" on Kaho'olawe Island, Hawaiians used symbols of our Native past to illustrate opposition to American colonization. The gourd helmet took on a new meaning in this context as a sign of resistance and pride. (Photo by Ed Greevy.)

Mililani Trask, governor of Ka Lāhui Hawai'i, and Haunani-Kay Trask, Director of the Center for Hawaiian Studies, lead a commemorative march to 'Iolani Palace, site of the overthrow of the Hawaiian government by U.S. Marines and white sugar planters in 1893. The biggest sovereignty organization, Ka Lāhui Hawai'i, organized the march, which turned out to be the single largest demonstration in the history of modern Hawai'i. Over 15,000 people participated, including international visitors from the American continent and the Pacific Islands. (*The Honolulu Advertiser* photo by Bruce Asato.)

Anti-eviction struggles characterized most protests during the 1970s. Workers, students, and other community people from all ethnic and racial groups coalesced to resist the rapid commercial and resort development of our shores and valleys. (Photo by Ed Greevy.)

Even our children protest the American military presence in Hawai'i. Here, the son of an activist holds a sign he painted himself. His target was the U.S. Navy and their use of Kaho'olawe as a bombing range since World War II. (Photo by Ed Greevy.)

During the 1970s, land struggles witnessed an amazing outpouring of leadership from young Hawaiians. One example is Hanale "Soli" Niheu, who led the Kalama struggle and went on through the 1980s to speak out for Native sovereignty both in Hawai'i and the South Pacific. A carpenter by trade, Soli continues to organize for Hawaiian self-determination in grassroots communities statewide. (Photo by Ed Greevy.)

The U.S. military has bombed many valleys and islands during its occupation of Hawai'i since the overthrow of our government in 1893. This bomb crater is but one among many in Mākua Valley, a large and once beautiful area on the leeward side of O'ahu where endangered species become extinct daily due to destructive military misuse. (Photo by Ed Greevy.)

George Helm and Kimo Mitchell were allegedly lost at sea (some think they were murdered) when they attempted to occupy Kaho'olawe Island in 1977 to stop military bombing. George, pictured here, came from the rural island of Moloka'i. He was best known for his beautiful falsetto voice, which entertained thousands of Hawaiians as well as tourists. Like many activists, George came to the movement through his musical talent, which he saw exploited by the tourist industry. Today, his legacy is political as well as cultural, since younger Hawaiians are inspired by both his resistance and his music. (Photo by Ed Greevy.)

Hawaiians protest the misnamed "Hawaiian Autonomy" bill, which actually sought to stop the drive to sovereignty. The protest signs correctly identified the bill's author, Ed Case, as a racist. (Photo by Ed Greevy.)

Women's *Mana* and Hawaiian Sovereignty

Like our Maori siblings who struggle for sovereignty in the far reaches of the vast South Pacific, we Hawaiians in the isolated North Pacific have been working for nearly thirty years to assert our genealogical claims as the indigenous people of Hawai'i. But unlike our Polynesian *'ohana* (family), we are not fighting within an independent island nation. Nor are we blessed with a large country where one island is sparsely populated. Nor are we fortunate enough to have but one major settler population, as Maori do, with which to battle.

As many of our South Pacific cousins argue, Hawaiians are among the most subordinated Natives in the Pacific Islands. Our land base is one-sixteenth the size of Aotearoa (New Zealand), and we are but one among five major ethnic groups in Hawai'i, two of which—the Japanese and the *haole*—are more populous and more economically powerful than Hawaiians. Our lands and waters have been inundated by foreigners, including American military personnel, and every kind of settler, particularly Asian immigrants and tourists.

The suffering and dispossession that Hawaiians have endured—and continue to endure—have been justified by a racist ideology that claims we are better off as American citizens than we ever were as citizens of our own independent nation of Hawai'i. Despite the historical fact that Hawaiians did not want to become American citizens, and protested to this effect at the time of the overthrow in 1893 and again at annexation in 1898, our citizenship status has, according to American patriots, placed us in a select class of human beings.

Allegedly, inclusion in the United States gave us "rights," the much-prized individual rewards that Americans wave in the faces of their conquered peoples like little American flags on the graves of fallen soldiers. Universal suffrage, private property, and public education are among these "rights," as are the trumpeted joys of mass consumption, mass communication, and mass popular culture. Americans truly believe that such "rights" are the measure of civilization worldwide. Indeed, according to American ideology, every human being—whether from Africa, India, and the former Soviet Union, or the Americas, the Pacific Islands and Asia—wants desperately to follow the American path by achieving such "rights." That these alleged "rights" were forced onto resisting peoples at the point of cannon and in the face of conquering armies is ignored in the case of Natives like my own people because the ideology of "rights" cannot abide the reality of imperialism.

By "rights" Americans do not mean Natives controlling their own affairs, holding their land and resources collectively as a people rather than as individuals, or learning and transmitting their own Native language, religion, and family structure.

Ideologically, "rights" talk is part of the larger, greatly obscured historical reality of American colonialism. The postwar American imperium is now global, as is the American denial that such an imperium exists. Part of this denial is the insistence that the United States has no colonies, only little island "democracies," such as Puerto Rico, Micronesia, and Hawai'i. In these far-flung colonies, the language of "civil rights" operates to legitimize American control.

For example, by entering legalistic discussions wholly internal to the American system, Natives participate in their own mental colonization. Once indigenous peoples begin to use terms like language "rights" and burial "rights," they are moving away from their cultural universe, from the understanding that language and burial places are born from our ancestral association with our lands of origin. These indigenous Native practices are not "rights" that are given as the largesse of colonial governments. These practices define, instead, who we are, where we live, and how we feel.

When Hawaiians begin to think otherwise, that is, to think in terms of "rights," the identification as "Americans" is not far off. Thus, soon after annexation some of our people argued and organized for statehood, including members of my own family, because they believed control over their destiny as Hawaiians would be gained with full American citizenship such as the right to vote for the governor of the state of Hawai'i. Decades of work went into the statehood effort, which was finally successful in 1959.

Now, some thirty years later, Hawai'i is less Hawaiian culturally, ecologically, and politically. Hawaiians themselves are fast outmigrating to California and other parts of the U.S. continent, and our islands have become the premier military fortress from which the United States patrols and nuclearizes the Pacific. Full American citizenship, that is, full American "rights," thus accelerated the de-Hawaiianization begun with the theft of our government, lands, and language in the 1890s.

For us nationalist Hawaiians, the lesson of statehood is a lesson of loss and despair: the loss of land, of self-government, of language; the despair of political powerlessness, of cultural prostitution, of economic exploitation.

The franchise has given Hawaiians no control over our home lands (nearly two million acres including water and subsurface minerals), since they are held in alleged "trust" by the state and federal governments, including the military. The right to a public education has not led to the creation of an educational system in the Hawaiian language, but rather to an education in a foreign language. And legal, that is, judicial access, has not been extended to Hawaiians as a people, despite ongoing political battles to wrest such access from the state. Still, in 1998, we have no standing in the courts to bring suit for breach of trust against our "trustees," the state and federal governments. Worse, the state continues to attempt a termination of their trust responsibilities by cash payoffs for all our lands. Now, post-statehood Hawai'i is a tinsel paradise for six and a half million tourists a year and a living nightmare for our impoverished, marginalized Native people.

While surviving as a Native person in any colonial situation is a strange mix of refusal, creation, and assertion, the Hawaiian situation is particularly galling, since the ideology of American democracy has both suppressed and co-opted Native resistance. When Hawaiians do begin to resist, we must start at the most elementary levels, such as challenging the preferability of Western dress or the superiority of the English language. Slowly, this kind of challenge can proceed to larger, more political resistance, such as antimilitary activity, efforts to preserve wetlands, forests, and other wild areas, and finally, a political struggle for self-determination.

The first stage of resistance involves a throwing off, or a peeling apart, of a forced way of behaving. Layers of engineered assimilation begin to come loose in the face of alternatives, *Native cultural alterna-*

tives. Usually, this process means tremendous psychological tension as a conscious rejection begins with cultural habits first ingrained by a colonial education, a foreign language, and a fearful daily relationship with the dominant, white class. Frantz Fanon identified this process as the birth of a new, revolutionary human being. Others, such as the African writer Ngũgĩ wa Thiong'o, call it "decolonizing the mind."

All across the Pacific Islands, and for at least the past forty years, Natives have been decolonizing their minds. Hawaiians, too, are participating in this same decolonizing process, often mistakenly referred to as "cultural revival." Anthropologists and politicians readily use this term because it has no political context: the primary emphasis is usually on trivializing quaint practices and beliefs rather than on supporting conscious Native resistance to cultural imperialism. But decolonization is political at the core because it functions to unscrew the power of the colonizing force by creating a new consciousness very critical of foreign terms, foreign definitions, and foreign solutions.

Predictably, dangers arise in the early stages of decolonization, just as they do in any radicalizing process. For example, participation in Native culture merely as recreational activity stunts the growth of a critical political posture. By definition, recreational culture is peripheral—on the fringes rather than at the center of daily life. As recreation, this kind of cultural participation does not pose a direct, political challenge to the dominant forces within society, that is, the very forces that control daily life. Worse, Hawaiian culture is constantly in danger of commercialization. The *hula* and Hawaiian language are easily incorporated into and transformed by tourist promotions, hotel festivities, and the ideological sea of commercialism that washes over our islands.

But paradoxically, recreational culture does create a rich medium for politicization. Even with the slick predations of tourism, things Hawaiian allow a reenactment of cultural ways tied to our land and our unique genealogical understanding of life. To counter the impulse toward commercialism, a politicizing agent must enter this medium, precipitating the growth of political consciousness. Sometimes, the agent is an elder whose cultural wisdom includes a sense of politics. At other times, the agent is an older friend or relative, what we call *kua'ana,* who consciously organizes and leads younger Hawaiians toward decolonization. These people operate in an already highly politicized world where the push for sovereignty has been in the air for over fifteen years now. Their function is thus greatly aided by a common public understanding that sovereignty is a familiar demand and, given global resistance by colonial powers, a much contested demand.

From my intimate participation in the Hawaiian movement for self-determination, it is obvious to me that these politicizing agents have most often been women—young, nationalist women. Occasionally, older women with cultural knowledge have evolved into nationalists, but they lead by virtue of their cultural *mana,* or power, rather than by political *mana.*

Mana

Now *mana,* in its Hawaiian sense, conveys an understanding that power is more than what the *haole* call "charisma," or personal attraction. Leaders possess *mana,* they embody and display it. But the source of *mana* is not reducible to personal ability or spiritual and genealogical ancestry. A high chiefly line may bequeath the potential for *mana,* but the actualization or achievement of *mana* in terms of political leadership requires more than genealogy, it requires specific identification by the leader with the people, just as the *ali'i,* or chiefs, in days of old were judged by how well they cared for their people.

The presence of a leader with *mana* presupposes that the people acknowledge *mana* as an attribute of political leadership. Part of the beauty of Hawaiian decolonization is the reassertion of *mana* in the sovereignty movement as a defining element of cultural and political leadership. Both the people and their leaders understand the link between *mana* and *pono,* the traditional Hawaiian value of balance between people, land, and the cosmos. Only a leader who understands this familial, genealogical link between Hawaiians and their land can hope to reestablish *pono,* the balance that has been lacking in the Hawaiian universe since the coming of the *haole.* The assertion of the value of *pono,* then, awaits a leader with *mana.*

In this decolonizing context, *mana* as an attribute of leadership is a tremendous challenge to the colonial system, which defines political leadership in terms of democratic liberalism, that is, in terms of electoral victory. But *mana* is also a tremendous challenge to aspiring Hawaiian leaders who want to achieve sovereignty. By definition and history, leaders embody sovereignty only if they are *pono,* that is, only if they believe in and work for the well-being of the land and the people. In this way, Hawaiian leaders exhibit *mana* and increase it *if* they speak and represent the needs of Hawaiians, *not* the needs of all citizens of Hawai'i, or of legislative districts, or of bureaucratic institutions. *Mana,* then, opposes the American system of electoral power while reclaiming a form of political leadership based on Hawaiian cultural beliefs.

Hawaiian politicians who have chosen to subsume Hawaiian well-being under the need for profit or see it as a peripheral issue to the larger concerns of all the people of Hawai'i *cannot* be *pono* leaders, nor can they be said to possess *mana.* Therefore, while the first elected Hawaiian governor, John Waihe'e, was Hawaiian in ancestry, he did not behave, during his gubernatorial terms, as a Hawaiian leader should; that is, he did not work for the well-being of his Native people. For example, Waihe'e submitted to the legislature a plan to extinguish all Hawaiian claims to our trust lands in exchange for money. On this point alone, Waihe'e demonstrated that he is not a Hawaiian leader in the traditional chiefly sense. Instead, Waihe'e was the leader of the Democratic party, a typically American political machine with the sole purpose of capturing and maintaining political office.

Women's *Mana*

Waihe'e is not alone as a Hawaiian politician. There are many others, including some female politicians, who have followed the male model of electoral politics. Indeed, a sizable number of Hawaiians have chosen to assimilate into the foreign American system, including the first Hawaiian senator in the U.S. Congress, Daniel Akaka. But while Hawaiian men have been transforming themselves into politicians, many Hawaiian women have chosen the path of decolonization, testing their leadership in the movement for sovereignty.

Because American culture, like Western civilization generally, is patriarchal, that is, structured and justified by values that emphasize male dominance over women and nature, American institutions reward men and male-dominant behavior with positions of power. This is how the patriarchy entrenches itself. Thus, the common reference to the public world, the world of politics and economics and bureaucracy as a "man's world" with the concomitant reference to the world of the family and of relationships as a "woman's world." Men are bred for power, women for powerlessness, except within their own sphere of the family.

Colonialism brought the replacement of the Hawaiian world by the *haole* world. Hawaiian women, including our chiefly women, lost their place just as Hawaiian men lost theirs. Like most indigenous peoples colonized the world over, our marginalization meant economic ghettoization. We were to become a semiskilled labor force for the *haole* capitalists. Above all, the loss of our land base denied us political and economic power.

During the long, sixty-year eclipse of the territorial period, when immigrant Asian labor continued to outnumber our Native people and the *haole* tried desperately to retain their dominant position, some of our Hawaiian men slowly entered the legislature, organizing with Asian immigrant descendants for statehood and what they saw as their eventual takeover of political power. At statehood, some of our Native men, including my father and uncles, continued the transition into electoral power. They had been schooled in the American system and believed that the only path to power lay through that system. Hawaiian ways, they reasoned, were gone forever; therefore, if Hawaiians were to improve their lot, they had to learn American ways. Of course, this is what Americanization seeks to do, namely, to convince conquered peoples they have no choice but to be Americanized. The ideology tells a tale of success: if one captures political power through the electoral process, one can do anything.

Anything, that is, except live as a Native person.

As our men sought power in the Americanized political system, they internalized the values of that system: politics is a man's world, family life is a woman's world. While some of our men, the most educated and articulate, rose up in the ranks of the political system, our women tended the home and worked at low-paying service jobs. Americanization had triumphed, at least on the surface.

But every generation surprises the one that preceded it. Poststatehood Hawai'i was not the dreamland of opportunity that my father's generation assumed. Corrupt electoral politics represented a collaborationist elite who, like the previous missionary party, looked to economic exploitation of Hawai'i and our Native culture to advance their power. Tourism came to replace sugar plantations, opening the floodgates to nearly seven million tourists a year from America, Japan, and Europe. Now, little more than a hundred years since the overthrow of our Native government, the spirit and bounty of my ancestral home have been plundered beyond imagining. Our Hawaiian people have been further marginalized, our living conditions and general health diminished, our lands developed and poisoned.

But in 1970, as if announced by oracle, voices of resistance and protest began to be heard from one end of our archipelago to the other. Beginning with antidevelopment struggles, the poorest and the least articulate began to stand firm against evictions, gathering up their courage to occupy trust lands abused by the military and the state, asserting the primacy of Native language as a form of sovereignty. Now, after twenty years, land rights have been encompassed by a push for self-determination.

And on the front lines, in the glare of public disapproval, are our women, articulate, fierce, and culturally grounded. A great coming together of women's *mana* has given birth to a new form of power based on a traditional Hawaiian belief: women asserting their leadership for the sake of the nation. At this very moment, nationalist women leaders are organizing and leading our people, even if that entails opposition to our Hawaiian men's leadership in the electoral system and in the movement.

While Hawaiian men have come to achieve their own place in the legislature and in the governor's office, Hawaiian female leadership has come to the fore in the sovereignty movement. Of course, this is not to say there are no male leaders in our movement. But they are not the most visible, the most articulate, nor the most creative. Nor are they the most recognized leaders by our own people. By any standard—public, personal, political—our sovereignty movement is led by women.

Part of the reason for this is simply colonialism: men are rewarded, including Native men, for collaboration. Women's role, if they are to be collaborators, is not to wield political power but to serve as an adjunct to men who do.

But I believe the main reason women lead the nationalist front today is simply that women have not lost sight of the *lāhui,* that is, of the nation. Caring for the nation is, in Hawaiian belief, an extension of caring for the family, the large family that includes both our lands and our people. Our mother is our land, *Papahānaumoku,* she who births the islands. Hawaiian women leaders, then, are genealogically empowered to lead the nation.

Predictably, however, genealogy is not a sufficient condition for leadership. A cursory glance at some of our highest ranking Native women and what they have chosen to do with their lives is a simple way of dispelling the notion that genealogy *determines* leadership or even *mana*. While our cultural genealogy is as protectors of the earth, our specific genealogies may carry *ali'i* rank. *Ali'i* rank does play some part in reinforcing leadership, but it is insufficient by itself to establish leadership.

No, the defining characteristic of leadership is *mana,* the ability to speak for the people and the land, to command respect by virtue of this ability, and to set the issues of public debate as those that benefit the *lāhui*. In formulating the sovereignty position, Hawaiian women have demonstrated most forcefully what *pono* leadership might be.

Predictably, none of our nationalist women leaders holds an elected political office, a reality that underscores their collective rather than individual focus and their mistrust of the American system. All our women leaders are attached to Hawaiian groups, whether political or cultural, and they are consciously aware of their conflict with Western ways. Consequently, when these women speak, they represent not only their groups but the Hawaiian people as *lāhui Hawai'i*. They all speak from their life experience as Hawaiians in defense of Hawaiian culture, the national culture of our people. This stance is often in opposition to elected leaders, including Hawaiian politicians, who are bound to a constituency and to the American government and who enter politics primarily for personal career advancement and economic gain.

But despite their shared commonalities, these women do not fit easily into a model of women's leadership in our movement. There is not a single mold, or even two molds, from which these women have been cast. In fact, our women leaders are better characterized by their amazing and delightful uniqueness. Their personal and familial biographies as well as their training and talents are as different from each other as that of any randomly chosen individuals.

What they do share is *mana,* exercised on behalf of the people. Where they exercise it—in government, in the protection of burial places, in the dance—is specific to each woman.

Three such women, whose public recognition has been substantial and whose dedication is unquestioned, include Dana Naone, poet, community organizer, political strategist, and protector of our ancestors' remains at our largest national cemetery at Honokahua, Maui; Pua Kanaka'ole Kanahele, *kumu hula* and protector of our deity, Pele, and her family of the volcano and the forest; and my sister, Mililani Trask, attorney, political organizer, and elected governor of our nation, Ka Lāhui Hawai'i, a native initiative for self-government.

Educated in Western schools whose purpose is forced assimilation into foreign ways, these women have nevertheless resisted physical and psychological and spiritual colonization in a system that is dominated by foreign investment, by local corruption, and by anti-Hawaiian institutions. Disappointing the hopes of anthropologists and politicians who predict our political demise, these women remain magnificently steadfast against the enormous forces of corporate tourism and the organized greed of our local Democratic party. And they have proven their commitment to protecting our Native heritage on the land, among our families, and in our hearts.

Lest anyone think the personal lives of these women will hold the key to their leadership, let me say that such a perspective is wholly Western, individually based, and plain wrong. Even knowing the economic class of these women will not explain why or how they have evolved into leadership positions or why and how they have been able to sustain their opposition.

The answer to such questions lies in their collective experience and identity as Hawaiians with the Hawaiian nation, that is, with our *lāhui.* In other words, no matter how effective colonialism has been in dismembering our culture and our people, it has not managed—yet—to kill all of us, to push all of us out of Hawai'i, to strangle our love for our people and our language and our land.

Our generation has witnessed a phenomenal energy by our women. On the Big Island of Hawai'i, Pua Kanahele has been the *kumu hula* (master teacher) of one of the most revered and traditional *hālau* (dance academy) in our islands. Keeper of the chants and the dance, *kumu hula* Kanahele has taken her cultural knowledge into the political arena to protect Pele, our deity of the volcano and her sister, Hi'iaka, who inhabits the forests of the volcano. Protesting geothermal energy development, Kanahele led the long struggle to stop both the drilling of wells into the breast of Pele, and the construction of energy plants. In addition, she has been a staunch supporter of the protection of ancient Native burials.

In the middle of our island chain, on the lovely island of Maui, Dana Naone has been working for years to protect wild areas, including burial sites, *heiau* (religious temples), beaches, and valleys. Her style has been quiet, dogged, and brilliantly political. Her leadership, unlike Pua Kanahele's, does not spring from a commitment to the traditional dance but rather from a sense of obligation to protect the land: *mālama 'āina.* Both women work in their own arenas, and both have dedicated their lives to the land and the indigenous people born from her.

Finally, my sister, Mililani Trask, has contributed in a political way to the preservation of our nation by creating a model for self-government, called Ka Lāhui Hawai'i. Trained as a lawyer and enormously gifted as a political theorist and strategist, Mililani convened a group of Hawaiians in 1987 to create Ka Lāhui Hawai'i, a Native initiative for self-government. Since then, Ka Lāhui has been the lead sovereignty organization in the Hawaiian nationalist front, with a membership in the thousands. Beyond this, Mililani has worked in the international arena with Nobel Peace Prize winner Rigoberta Menchu, with the Dalai Lama and his group, The Unrepresented Nations and Peoples Organization (U.N.P.O.), and with various Native groups, from the Indians of the Americas to the Aborigines of Australia.

What links these women leaders together, apart from their extraordinary talents, is an identification with our ancestral value of caring for the people and the land. This political/cultural assertion serves the nation not only as an opposing force to colonialism but as a Native reenactment of the reality that Hawai'i is *our* mother and we are her children. Our family responsibility, then, requires us to behave according to tradition. We must protect and preserve our family, that we may survive as inheritors of the lands of Hawai'i.

Kupuna (elder) Emma DeFries was one of the first of the older generation to support younger Hawaiians who occupied Kaho'olawe Island in protest of military bombing since 1941. She went to the island to conduct spiritual ceremonies and frightened the military with her magnetic personal *mana*. When she died, the vacuum created by her loss was enormous. (Photo by Ed Greevy.)

Lawyer, activist, and spiritual and political leader, Mililani Trask was the first Hawaiian leader to organize a nation on the model of American Indian nations. Today, she is recognized throughout the Pacific and the American continent for her tireless work on behalf of Hawaiians. (Photo by Ann Landgraf.)

Kia'āina Mililani Trask leading the January 17, 1993, sovereignty march to 'Iolani Palace. (Photo by Ed Greevy.)

Long-time activist in Hawaiian communities on Maui Island, Dana Naone Hall is a poet, mother, and Hawaiian nationalist whose major work has been to preserve the sanctity of Hawaiian burials and to stop golf courses, hotels, and other destructive development. Here, she stands on the shoreline at Waiheʻe where Japanese developers threaten destruction of ancient sites, including burials. She is a continuing source of inspiration for young Hawaiian women just entering our movement. (Photo by Margo Berdeshevsky.)

Mililani and Haunani-Kay Trask demonstrate at the State Capitol for water for Hawaiian homesteaders. (Photo by Ed Greevy.)

Neocolonialism and Indigenous Structures

In August 1990, my sister, Mililani, and I traveled to Karasjokka, Norway, to attend a world conference of Native women sponsored by the Sami people of the Arctic.

Despite profound geographic, cultural, and physical differences among the delegates attending, our similarities as colonized indigenous women—from the Americas, the Pacific, the Middle East, Africa, Europe and Asia—were obvious. This speech was intended to underscore our shared conditions and commonalities.

In this mysterious northern land of ice and eternal light, we, the indigenous women of the world, are embarking on a timely path. This week, history is being made by the very fact of this conference and its focus on indigenous women. We are here to speak for ourselves, to decide our own strategies, and to plan our own futures. We are not here as members of minority groups or as adjuncts to male organizations but as Native women determined to link our peoples in a common cause for self-determination.

We come from diverse communities at varied levels of forced assimilation, economic exploitation, religious missionizing, political and cultural oppression, and physical extermination as peoples. Many of us are survivors of earlier genocidal campaigns, while some of us are no doubt fighting current genocidal campaigns. Clearly, we are vastly different from each other, not only geographically, but culturally, linguistically, and historically as well.

And yet, I believe, we share many more similarities than differences. We have a common heritage as aboriginal peoples, that is, as First Nations of the world. We are all land-based people, and some of us also sea-based people, who are attuned to the rhythms of our homelands in a way that assumes both protection of and an intimate belonging to our ancestral places. We have all been colonized by imperialist powers more or less resistant to our human needs for self-determination and self-government. And, at this moment, we face grave problems that range from environmental poisoning, nuclear radiation, and high infant mortality to land dispossession, economic marginalization, and militarization of our areas.

These large commonalities have brought us together as indigenous women fighting for our peoples, our lands, and our very survival.

In this context of shared experiences, I have been asked to address neocolonialism and the co-optation of indigenous sociopolitical structures. Obviously, these categories are both large and extremely varied. Our cultures, our geographies, and our responses to colonialism shape how and what we experience as Native nations. But given this, and acknowledging that I am working at a broad level of generalization, I will attempt an outline of concerns that others here should feel free to enlarge, modify, or otherwise change.

For the purposes of discussion, I have defined neocolonialism as the experience of oppression at a stage that is nominally identified as independent or autonomous. I use *nominally* to underscore the reality that independence from the colonial power is legal but not economic. Some examples of neocolonialism include the control by multinational corporations of former territorial colonies. Latin American, African, and Asian countries come to mind. Other examples include the persistence of social and cultural practices imposed by colonial powers during the first stages of imperialism even after independence, for example, Anglo-American legal and land tenure systems in places as diverse as the Philippines, Fiji, and parts of Africa. Finally, neocolonialism refers not only to dominant colonial retentions but also to psychological injuries suffered by the colonized that continue to wound our internal and external lives.

Part of neocolonialism, of course, is the ideological position that all is well; in other words, that decolonization has occurred. Therefore, problems and conflicts are post-colonial and the fault of the allegedly independent peoples. Nothing could be more inaccurate.

To begin with, indigenous peoples *by definition* lack autonomy and independence. In the modern, post-war world, we are surrounded by other, more powerful nations that desperately want our lands and resources and for whom we pose an irritating problem. This is just as true for the Indians of the Americas as it is for the tribals of India and the aborigines of the Pacific. This economic reality is also a political reality for most if not all indigenous peoples. The relationship between ourselves and those who want control of us *and* our resources is not a *formerly* colonial relationship but an *ongoing* colonial relationship. That is to say, we are not now autonomous yet dependent. Rather, we are dependent *and* subjugated. Part of our subjugation is the unequal relationship to our numerous colonizers.

In the world system today, natural and human resources, markets, and technology determine the value of indigenous peoples to the colonial powers. Tragically, this is a truism for every woman in this room. Thus, land is no longer our mother, source of physical and spiritual sustenance. She is now a resource for consumption and profit. Our children are no longer the flower of our nations but the labor units of industry and the military. Our cultures are no longer the expressions of harmony and beauty between our people and our gods but the source of entertainment and recreation for the world's rich. Our spiritual values and philosophical systems are no longer the guides to daily and generational life but the playthings of First World adventurers. Even our ancestors, long dead, have not escaped these degradations. Their bones and artifacts are now displayed in museums and antique shops as "primitive" curiosities.

These transformations continue to occur not only as a result of brute physical and economic violence but also as a by-product of skillful co-optation of our own cultural forms. At the risk of over-generalizing, I want to suggest five areas in which co-optation occurs and then use a vivid example from my own culture to illustrate how successfully "colonial" such co-optation can be.

I begin with our own self-definitions, that is, with how and what we call ourselves. Unless I am mistaken, most indigenous nations simply say they are the "people" or the "people of the land," or "human beings." The sense of this identity is an attachment to place and a differentiation from other living things in the natural world.

Under colonialism, this identification is transformed into pejorative categories that take on legal force. For example, the U.S. government has defined a Native Hawaiian as someone with 50 percent or more blood quantum. Those who meet this blood requirement are eligible for lands and revenues. Those who do not meet this test are completely dispossessed. As a result, our people are divided by race, something foreign to us and to our identity as a nation.

Beyond the question of who is and is not indigenous looms the power to define and thus to determine who we, as Native peoples, will be in the future. Imposed systems of identification are instituted to separate our people from our lands and from each other in perpetuity. Again using my own people as an example, the white people who created our classification hoped that Hawaiians of 50 percent or more blood quantum would eventually die out, thus leaving our lands and revenues not to Hawaiians of less than 50 percent blood but to the state and federal governments.

The experience of a legal identity is, as all identities, both psychological and political. Who we believe ourselves to be is often *not* what the colonial legal system defines us to be. This disjunction causes a kind of suffering nearly impossible to end without ending the colonial definitions of who we are. Barring this, we are constantly in struggle with government agencies and, sometimes, with our own people. We are besieged by state powers attempting to decrease our numbers and therefore our claims by merely defining us out of existence. Or, we are categorized in a manner alien to our cultures in the hopes of strangling our ancestral attachments to our own people.

If we are tribal, the colonial power defines us so as to minimize the powers of the tribe. If we are not tribal, the colonial power uses our self-definition against us by claiming that we are not indigenous because we are not tribal. If we are of mixed bloodlines, we are often not indigenous enough and therefore not able to claim lands. But if we are not of mixed blood, we are required to substantiate our ancestry.

Definition, then, has served to co-opt our identity. Naming has been, for many of us, a theft of matrilineal descent by Western patriarchal descent. In the case of Hawaiians, legal imposition of Christian, English, and patrilineal names meant the loss of our ancestral names. This imposed system greatly weakened and, in some areas, destroyed our indigenous practice of genealogical naming.

Definitions of who we are closely parallel where we live and with whom we live. Thus, our extended families have suffered incessant pressures to fragment into nuclear units of only parents and children. In nuclear families, women's power, as the power of the mother generally, is reduced from life-giver to domestic servant. When industrial capitalism penetrates our societies, our people are driven into the labor market, where production takes place outside the family, which declines to a mere consumer unit. This sundering of our functions also severs our people from their traditional work. The devaluing of traditional, cultural kinds of work accompanies the forcing of our people into the labor market. Depending on where we live, women's "work" then ranges from domestic labor and prostitution to sales clerkship and *hula* dancing. Such work has no meaning and no status in our cultures; therefore, we lose both our traditional work and the high valuation that attached to our roles.

In the Pacific, "big nation" dominance has meant that labor markets develop to serve the needs of American, French, Japanese, New Zealand, and Australian interests. Two well-known cases will suffice to illustrate my point.

American military dominance in the Pacific has meant that enormous amounts of land, water, and other resources are diverted to satisify American military needs. The Marshall Islands and Hawai'i are clear examples of how a dominant power's so-called "national interests" result in the loss of lands and the skewing of employment opportunity because of the burdensome presence of military personnel, bases, training areas, and ports. Such a large military presence both directs the kinds of employment that will develop and limits the opportunity for work in traditional fields such as agriculture and fishing. A substantial military presence also creates a second economy, with special privileges for its personnel, including housing, elite consumer goods, and exclusive recreational areas. This misuse of land is coupled with the ill-effects of the military on Islanders' physical and mental health. Finally, there is the ultimate injury: the frightening risk of becoming "strategically important" in the game of superpower politics.

If the American military exemplifies one way in which foreign impingement structures labor demand, Japanese corporate invasion of the Pacific, meanwhile, spells dangerous foreign control of fragile island economies and, in the case of tourist investments, the inundation of small land bases and populations by hordes of visitors. The indigenous people are then presented with the alleged opportunity of waiting on tourists, cleaning their rooms, selling them artifacts, and smiling for a living.

In the case of Hawaiian women, the definition of us as alluring, highly eroticized Natives is anchored by a tourist economy that depends on the grossest commercialization of our culture. Because of mass-based corporate tourism, our women have become purveyors of our dances, our language, our islands, in other words, all that is beautiful about us. This is cultural prostitution, often with our own people's willing, if unexamined, participation.

We, in the Pacific, do not take this kind of cultural degradation lightly. The Japanese in particular are investing heavily all over the Pacific, including Fiji, Vanuatu, Tahiti, Sāmoa, and of course, most spectacularly in my own Native land, Hawai'i. The disastrous effects of mass tourism on island cultures is best observed in Hawai'i, where the multibillion dollar industry has resulted in grotesque commercialization of our Native culture, creation of a racially stratified, poorly paid servant class of industry workers, transformation of whole sections of our major islands into high-rise cities, contamination and depletion of water sources, intense crowding—with densities in the worst areas exceeding that of Hong Kong—increases in crimes against property and violent crime against tourists, and increasing dependency on corporate investments.

The co-optation of indigenous ways does not work without complicitous Natives. Some of our people are bought, some are crushed between impossible demands, others are squeezed until they become but images of their former selves. Those who resist often find the price too high. In Hawai'i—the world's most isolated archipelago—Native resistance no longer results in death or imprisonment, as it once did, but now brings chronic unemployment or threats of law suits or constant hounding and public ridicule that threatens our sanity. For the sake of our loved ones, our families, our elders, and our relatives, we participate in the wage system because we feel there is no other way.

And yet, throughout our Native nations, there are attempts to rebuild self-sufficiency projects that begin with our traditional subsistence activities—such as farming, fishing, and gathering—and proceed outward to Native crafts, and further still to the performing arts, such as dance and theater. These are healthy signs of resistance to co-optation, but not all of us have this opportunity.

While our naming and our family structures have been subjugated to Western systems, so too have our land tenure and inheritance customs been co-opted. Land, once held in common for use by all has nearly everywhere come under the threat of private property tenure, and all the bureaucratic papers that trail along with it, like deeds, mortgages, and bank notes. The constant fighting over land and water that we see throughout Indian country, in Hawai'i, New Zealand, Australia, and other parts of the world is played out in the language of property law. The inevitable conflict between land that is collectively held and land that is individually owned will never cease because it is a conflict between cultures whose values are directly opposed.

For our peoples, this means only ill-health, poor living conditions, urbanization, and continued theft. As the industrial countries increase their stockpiles of waste and weapons, they will need to bury them somewhere. Of course, that unspecified "somewhere" is our Native lands and waters. Thus, Japanese plans to bury their nuclear waste in the Mariana trench; the Euro-American plan to incinerate chemicals on Johnston Island in the Pacific; French testing of nuclear weapons in Tahiti and their pretense that radiated water does not circulate throughout the Pacific. I understand that here, in Samiland, there are plans to bury nuclear waste in the Arctic. As with our labor, so with our lands: we are reserved for First World needs.

And this leads me to political co-optation. Our leaders are tremendously vulnerable to the pressures of colonial governments, insidious anthropologists, greedy financiers, and a host of other predators. The politics of co-optation, in other words, are treacherous and not immediately obvious.

For example, it seems that some of our people, once educated in colonial systems and yearning for colonial things, have a very difficult time returning to help their nations. This is not to say that we do not need lawyers, scientists, and other technical people who are familiar with the colonizer and colonial ways.

But as peoples, we need to convey to our younger siblings that learning about and understanding the outside world has a goal other than individual success or money. *Our* goal is to help our people. Co-optation occurs so frequently once our people leave us, which is why the colonizer tries to take our children, to force our families into urban areas, and to separate our generations. Indeed, the entire policy of the United States regarding its Native people can be seen as various confusions over how to destroy or co-opt us. The failure of the first policy leads to the inevitability of the second.

The United States now seeks to avoid confrontation with us by creating false Native governments, like tribal councils, or in Hawai'i the Office of Hawaiian Affairs. The Brazilian, New Zealand, Canadian, and other governments seek to do the same. Once these false fronts are in place, agreements for natural resources, militarization, waste burial, and a host of other things are immediately drawn up and signed. Co-optation triumphs in the guise of Native self-determination.

In Hawai'i, the effectiveness of co-optation is very visible. We have had a Hawaiian governor who behaves like a white man. We have Hawaiian representatives in the electoral system, including the Congress of the United States, who think, talk, and act like capitalist entrepreneurs bargaining off our natural and human resources. And I have Hawaiian students at the university who yearn to sell our culture in the tourist spots in our islands.

All these Hawaiians think, to greater or lesser degrees, that they are helping their people. Personal advancement has become the proof of self-determination, a ridiculous belief but one that is nevertheless strongly held. The breakdown of collective identification, which I referred to earlier, has set in motion an increasing individualist identification fed by popular culture, the structure of the market, and the bureaucracy of everyday life. As a result, personal achievement becomes the mirage of our movement, beckoning our people down a path of falsity and emptiness.

For my people, and perhaps for many others, neocolonialism *is* co-optation. Apart from the loss of our lands, the fracturing of our identities and collectivities, and the psychological impairment of our understanding, co-optation is the ever-ready reply from Native sell-outs to those of us who continue to organize among our people. Our young people, especially, are vulnerable to co-optation.

The problem, then, for all of us, is to strengthen our resolve; to learn from each other about strategies and linkages; and to create alternatives. This last possibility is the most difficult to fulfill.

But that is why we are here. Not merely to meet, exchange, and console, but to fashion new ways of resisting, of continuing as Native people. Specifically, we are here to build women's organizations focused on the needs of other women and their families and to work these organizations into political forces that will continue to be the backbone of our people.

And for this, we are remarkably gifted. At home, our movement is led by women, like the Kia'āina of our nation, my sister, Mililani. The few men present are overshadowed by our strong women leaders who constantly confront establishment Hawaiians who have become politically assimilated. Indeed, everywhere in the Pacific strong indigenous female leadership is the norm: in Belau, where women traveled to the

U.S. Congress to lobby against the Reagan-inspired economic and political chaos that has drowned that tiny nation in violence; in Aotearoa and Te Wai Pounamu, also called New Zealand, where articulate women leaders are fighting for language, land, and cultural rights; in Guam, where indigenous Chamorro women are organized to gain some form of autonomy from the U.S. government; in West Papua and East Timor, where genocide by Indonesia has driven out thousands of refugees and given rise to new, young leadership; in Kanaky, also known as New Caledonia, where the Kanak liberation front is locked in a battle with the French; in Tahiti, where the Polynesian Liberation Front is pushing for independence and, of course, in the Pan-Pacific Nuclear-Free and Independent Pacific Movement, where indigenous women from throughout the Pacific, such as Hilda Lini of Vanuatu and Hilda Harawira of Aotearoa, have been guiding lights.

Let me suggest, in closing, a few things to keep in mind. We need to be inclusive in our categories of analysis. We need to work toward resolutions regarding land and resources, family issues, militarization and nuclearization and, of course, self-government.

Let me offer now a favorite saying of Hawaiians. It was uttered by one of our great chiefs before the worst battle of his life:

Imua e na poki'i
Forward my younger siblings

A inu i ka wai 'awa'awa
And drink the bitter water

A loa'a ka lei
Of opposition until we wear the lei

O Ka Lanakila
of Victory.

Part III

The Colonial Front: Historians, Anthropologists, and the Tourist Industry

From a Native Daughter

E noiʻi wale mai nō ka haole, a,
ʻaʻole e pau nā hana a Hawaiʻi ʻimi loa

Let the *haole* freely research us in detail
But the doings of deep delving Hawaiʻi
will not be exhausted.

Kepelino
Nineteenth-century Hawaiian historian

When I was young the story of my people was told twice: once by my parents, then again by my school teachers. From my *ʻohana* (family), I learned about the life of the old ones: how they fished and planted by the moon; shared all the fruits of their labors, especially their children; danced in great numbers for long hours; and honored the unity of their world in intricate genealogical chants. My mother said Hawaiians had sailed over thousands of miles to make their home in these sacred islands. And they had flourished, until the coming of the *haole* (whites).

At school, I learned that the "pagan Hawaiians" did not read or write, were lustful cannibals, traded in slaves, and could not sing. Captain Cook had "discovered" Hawaiʻi, and the ungrateful Hawaiians had killed him. In revenge, the Christian god had cursed the Hawaiians with disease and death.

I learned the first of these stories from speaking with my mother and father. I learned the second from books. By the time I left for college, the books had won out over my parents, especially since I spent four long years in a missionary boarding school, called the Kamehameha Schools, for Hawaiian children.

When I went away, I understood the world as a place and a feeling divided in two: one *haole* (white) and the other *kānaka* (native). When I returned ten years later with a Ph.D., the division was sharper, the lack of connection more painful. There was the world that we lived in—my ancestors, my family, and my people—and then there was the world historians described. This world, they had written, was the truth. A primitive group, Hawaiians had been ruled by bloodthirsty priests and despotic kings who owned all the land and kept our people in feudal subjugation. The chiefs were cruel, the people poor.

But this was not the story my mother told me. No one had owned the land before the *haole* came; everyone could fish and plant, except during sacred periods. And the chiefs were good and loved their people.

Was my mother confused? What did our *kūpuna* (elders) say? They replied: Did these historians (all *haole)* know the language? Did they understand the chants? How long had they lived among our people? Whose stories had they heard?

None of the historians had ever learned our mother tongue. They had all been content to read what Europeans and Americans had written. But why did scholars, presumably well-trained and thoughtful, neglect our language? Not merely a passageway to knowledge, language is a form of knowing by itself; a people's way of thinking and feeling is revealed through its music.

I sensed the answer without needing to answer. From years of living in a divided world, I knew the historian's judgment: *There is no value in things Hawaiian; all value comes from things* haole.

Historians, I realized, were very like missionaries. They were a part of the colonizing horde. One group colonized the spirit; the other, the mind. Frantz Fanon had been right, but not just about Africans. He had been right about the bondage of my own people: "By a kind of perverted logic, [colonialism] turns to the past of the oppressed people, and distorts, disfigures, and destroys it."[1] The first step in the colonizing process, Fanon had written, was the deculturation of a people. What better way to take our culture than to remake our image? A rich historical past became small and ignorant in the hands of Westerners.

And we suffered a damaged sense of people and culture because of this distortion.

Burdened by a linear, progressive conception of history and by an assumption that Euro-American culture flourishes at the upper end of that progression, Westerners have told the history of Hawai'i as an inevitable if occasionally bittersweet triumph of Western ways over "primitive" Hawaiian ways. A few authors—the most sympathetic—have recorded with deep-felt sorrow the passing of our people. But in the end, we are repeatedly told, such an eclipse was for the best.

Obviously it was best for Westerners, not for our dying multitudes. This is why the historian's mission has been to justify our passing by celebrating Western dominance. Fanon would have called this missionizing, intellectual colonization. And it is clearest in the historian's insistence that pre-*haole* Hawaiian land tenure was "feudal," a term that is now applied, without question, in every monograph, in every schoolbook, and in every tour guide description of my people's history.

From the earliest days of Western contact, my people told their guests that *no one* owned the land. The land—like the air and the sea—was for all to use and share as their birthright. Our chiefs were *stewards* of the land; they could not own or privately possess the land any more than they could sell it.

But the *haole* insisted on characterizing our chiefs as feudal landlords and our people as serfs. Thus, a European term that described a European practice founded on a European concept of private land tenure—*feudalism*—was imposed upon a people halfway around the world from Europe and vastly different from her in every conceivable way. More than betraying an ignorance of Hawaiian culture and history, however, this misrepresentation was malevolent in design.

By inventing feudalism in ancient Hawai'i, Western scholars quickly transformed a spiritually based, self-sufficient economic system of land use and occupancy into an oppressive, medieval European practice of divine right ownership, with the common people tied like serfs to the land. By claiming that a Pacific people lived under a European system—that the Hawaiians lived under feudalism—Westerners could then degrade a successful system of shared land use with a pejorative and inaccurate Western term. Land tenure changes instituted by Americans and in line with current Western notions of private property were then made to appear beneficial to our people.

But in practice, such changes benefited the haole, who alienated Hawaiians from the land, taking it for themselves.

The prelude to this land alienation was the great dying of the people. Barely half a century after contact with the West, our people had declined in number by eighty percent. Disease and death were rampant. The sandalwood forests had been stripped bare for international commerce between England and China. The missionaries had insinuated themselves everywhere. And a debt-ridden Hawaiian king (there had been no king before Western contact) succumbed to enormous pressure from the Americans and followed their schemes for dividing up the land.

This is how private property land tenure entered Hawai'i. The common people, driven from their birthright, received less than one percent of the land. They starved, while huge *haole*-owned sugar plantations thrived.

And what had the historians said? They had said that the Americans "liberated" the Hawaiians from an oppressive "feudal" system. By inventing a false feudal past, the historians justify—and become complicitous in—massive American theft.

Is there "evidence"—as historians call it—for traditional Hawaiian concepts of land use? The evidence is in the sayings of my people and in the words they wrote more than a century ago, much of which has been translated. Historians however, have chosen to ignore any references here to shared land use. But there is incontrovertible evidence in the very structure of the Hawaiian language. If the historians had bothered to learn our language (as any American historian of France would learn French), they would have discovered that we show possession in two ways: through the use of an "a" possessive, which reveals acquired status, and through the use of an "o" possessive, which denotes inherent status. My body *(ko'u kino)* and my parents *(ko'u mākua),* for example, take the "o" form; most material objects, such as food *(ka'u mea'ai),* take the "a" form. But land, like one's body and one's parents, takes the "o" possessive *(ko'u 'āina).* Thus, in our way of speaking, land is inherent to the people; it is like our bodies and our parents. The people cannot exist without the land, and the land cannot exist without the people.

Every major historian of Hawai'i has been mistaken about Hawaiian land tenure. The chiefs did not own the land, they *could not* own the land. My mother was right, and the *haole* historians were wrong. If they had studied our language, they would have known that no one owned the land. But was their failing merely ignorance, or simple ethnocentric bias?

No, I did not believe them to be so benign. As I read on, a pattern emerged in their writing. Our ways were inferior to those of the West, to those of the historians' own culture. We were "less developed," or "immature," or "authoritarian." In some tellings we were much worse. Thus, Gavan Daws, the most famed modern historian of Hawai'i, had continued a tradition established earlier by missionaries Hiram Bingham and Sheldon Dibble, by referring to the old ones as "thieves" and "savages" who regularly practiced infanticide and who, in contrast to "civilized" whites, preferred "lewd dancing" to work. Ralph Kuykendall, long considered the most thorough if also the most boring of historians of Hawai'i, sustained another fiction, that my ancestors owned slaves, the outcast *kauwā*. This opinion, as well as the description of Hawaiian land tenure as feudal, had been supported by respected sociologist Andrew Lind. Finally, nearly all historians had refused to accept our genealogical dating of A.D. 400 or earlier for our arrival from the South Pacific. They had, instead, claimed that our earliest appearance in Hawai'i could only be traced to A.D. 1100. Thus, at least seven hundred years of our history were repudiated by "superior" Western scholarship. Only recently have archaeological data confirmed what Hawaiians had said these many centuries.[2]

Suddenly the entire sweep of our written history was clear to me. I was reading the West's view of itself through the degradation of my own past. When historians wrote that the king owned the land and the common people were bound to it, they were saying that ownership was the only way human beings in their world could relate to the land, and in that relationship, some one person had to control both the land and the interaction between humans.

And when they said that our chiefs were despotic, they were telling of their own society, where hierarchy always resulted in domination. Thus, any authority or elder was automatically suspected of tyranny.

And when they wrote that Hawaiians were lazy, they meant that work must be continuous and ever a burden.

And when they wrote that we were promiscuous, they meant that lovemaking in the Christian West was a sin.

And when they wrote that we were racist because we preferred our own ways to theirs, they meant that their culture needed to dominate other cultures.

And when they wrote that we were superstitious, believing in the *mana* of nature and people, they meant that the West has long since lost a deep spiritual and cultural relationship to the earth.

And when they wrote that Hawaiians were "primitive" in their grief over the passing of loved ones, they meant that the West grieves for the living who do not walk among their ancestors.

For so long, more than half my life, I had misunderstood this written record, thinking it described my own people. But my history was nowhere present. For we had not written. We had chanted and sailed and fished and built and prayed. And we had told stories through the great bloodlines of memory: genealogy.

To know my history, I had to put away my books and return to the land. I had to plant *taro* in the earth before I could understand the inseparable bond between people and *'āina.* I had to feel again the spirits of nature and take gifts of plants and fish to the ancient altars. I had to begin to speak my language with our elders and leave long silences for wisdom to grow. But before anything else, I had to learn the language like a lover so that I could rock within her and lay at night in her dreaming arms.

There was nothing in my schooling that had told me of this or hinted that somewhere there was a longer, older story of origins, of the flowing of songs out to a great but distant sea. Only my parents' voices, over and over, spoke to me of a Hawaiian world. While the books spoke from a different world, a Western world.

And yet, Hawaiians are not of the West. We are of *Hawai'i Nei,* this world where I live, this place, this culture, this *'āina.*

What can I say, then, to Western historians of my place and people? Let me answer with a story.

A while ago I was asked to share a panel on the American overthrow of our government in 1893. The other panelists were all *haole.* But one was a *haole* historian from the mainland who had just published a book on what he called the American anti-imperialists. He and I met briefly in preparation for the panel. I asked him if he knew the language. He said no. I asked him if he knew the record of opposition to our annexation to America. He said there was no real evidence for it, just comments here and there. I told him that he did not understand and that at the panel I would share the evidence. When we met in public and spoke, I said this:

There is a song much loved by our people. It was written after Hawai'i had been invaded and occupied by American marines.

Addressed to our dethroned Queen, it was written in 1893 and tells of Hawaiian love of our homeland as well as our feelings against annexation to the United States.

Kaulana nā pua a'o
Hawai'i
Kūpa'a mahope o
ka 'āina
Hiki mai ka 'elele o ka loko 'ino
Palapala 'ānunu me ka pākaha.

Famous are the children of
Hawai'i
Who cling steadfastly to
the land.
Comes the evil-hearted with
A document greedy for plunder.

Pane mai Hawai'i moku o
Keawe.
Kōkua nā Hono a'o
Pi'ilani.
Kāko'o mai Kaua'i o Mano
Pa'apū me ke one o
Kakuhihewa.

Hawai'i, island of Keawe,
answers.
The bays of Pi'ilani [of Maui,
Moloka'i, and Lana'i] help.
Kaua'i of Mano assists
Firmly together with the sands of
Kakuhihewa.

'A'ole 'a'e kau i ka pūlima
Maluna o ka pepa o ka 'enemi
Ho'ohui 'āina kū'ai hewa
I ka pono sivila a'o
ke kanaka

Do not put the signature
On the paper of the enemy.
Annexation is wicked sale
Of the civil rights of the
Hawaiian people.

'A 'ole mākou a'e minamina
I ka pu'ukālā a ke aupuni.
Ua lawa mākou i ka pōhaku,
I ka 'ai kamaha'o o ka 'āina.

We do not value
The government's sums of money
We are satisfied with the stones,
Astonishing food of the land.

Mahope mākou o Lili'ulani
A loa'a 'ē ka pono o
ka 'āina.
(A kau hou 'ia e ke kalaunu)
Ha'ina 'ia mai ana ka puana
Ka po'e i aloha i ka 'āina.

We support Lili'uokalani
Who has earned the right to
the land.
(She will be crowned again)
The story is told
Of the people who love the land.[3]

This song, I said, continues to be sung with great dignity at Hawaiian political gatherings, for our people still share the feelings of anger and protest that it conveys.

But our guest, the *haole* historian, answered that this song, although beautiful, was not evidence of either opposition or of imperialism from the Hawaiian perspective.

Many Hawaiians in the audience were shocked at his remarks, but, in hindsight, I think they were predictable. They are the standard response of the *haole* historian who has no respect for Native memory.

Finally, I proceeded to relate a personal story, thinking that surely such a tale could not want for authenticity, since I myself was relating it. My *tūtū* (grandmother) had told my mother, who had told me, that at the time of the overthrow a great wailing went up throughout the islands, a wailing of weeks, a wailing of impenetrable grief, a wailing of death. But he remarked again, this, too, is not evidence.

And so, history goes on, written in long volumes by foreign people. Whole libraries begin to form, book upon book, shelf upon shelf. At the same time, the stories go on, generation to generation, family to family.

Which history do Western historians desire to know? Is it to be a tale of writings by their own countrymen, individuals convinced of their "unique" capacity for analysis, looking at us with Western eyes, thinking about us within Western philosophical contexts, categorizing us by Western indices, judging us by Judeo-Christian morals, exhorting us to capitalist achievements, and finally, leaving us an authoritative-because-Western record of their complete misunderstanding?

All this has been done already. Not merely a few times, but many times. And still, every year, there appear new and eager faces to take up the same telling, as if the West must continue, implacably, with the din of its own disbelief. But there is, as there has been always, another possibility. If it is truly our history Western historians desire to know, they must put down their books, and take up our practices: first, of course, the language, but later, the people, the *'āina,* the stories. Above all, in the end, the stories. Historians must listen; they must hear the generational connections, the reservoir of sounds and meanings.

They must come, as American Indians suggested long ago, to understand the land. Not in the Western way, but in the indigenous way, the way of living within and protecting the bond between people and *'āina*. This bond is cultural, and it can be understood only culturally. But because the West has lost any cultural understanding of the bond between people and land, it is not possible to know this connection through Western culture. This means that the history of indigenous people cannot be written from within Western culture. Such a story is merely the West's story of itself.

Our story remains unwritten. It rests within the culture, which is inseparable from the land. To know this is to know our history. To write this is to write of the land and the people who are born from her.

Notes

1. Frantz Fanon, *The Wretched of the Earth* (New York: Grove Press, 1968), p. 210.

2. Gavan Daws, *Shoal of Time: A History of the Hawaiian Islands* (Honolulu: University of Hawai'i Press, 1968). Hiram Bingham, *A Residence of Twenty-one Years in the Sandwich Isles* (Hartford, CT: H. Huntington, 1848); reprinted in 1981 (Tokyo: Charles E. Tuttle). Sheldon Dibble, *A History of the Sandwich Isles* (Honolulu: Thrum Publishing, 1909). Ralph Kuykendall, *The Hawaiian Kingdom, 1778–1854: Foundation and Transformation* (Honolulu: University of Hawai'i Press, 1978); originally published in 1938. Andrew Lind, *An Island Community: Ecological Succession in Hawai'i* (Chicago: University of Chicago Press, 1938). H. David Tuggle, "Hawai'i," in *The Prehistory of Polynesia*, Jessie D. Jennings, ed. (Cambridge, Harvard University Press, 1979). See also Abraham Fornander, *An Account of the Polynesian Race, Its Origins, and Migrations and the Ancient History of the Hawaiian People to the Times of Kamehameha I* (Rutland and Tokyo: Charles E. Tuttle, 1969); originally published in 1878–1889. Lest one think these sources antiquated, it should be noted that there exist only a handful of modern scholarly works on the history of Hawai'i. The most respected are those by Kuykendall (1938) and Daws (1968) and a social history of the twentieth century by Lawrence Fuchs, *Hawai'i Pono: A Social History* (New York: Harcourt Brace & World, 1961). Of these, only Kuykendall and Daws claim any knowledge of pre-*haole* history, while concentrating on the nineteenth century. However, countless popular works have relied on these two studies, which, in turn, are themselves based on primary sources written in English by extremely biased, anti-Hawaiian Westerners, such as explorers, traders, missionaries (e.g., Bingham [1848] and Dibble [1909]), and sugar planters. Indeed, a favorite technique of Daws'—whose *Shoal of Time* is the most acclaimed and recent general history—is the lengthy quotation, without comment, of the most racist remarks by missionaries and planters. Thus, at one point, half of a page is consumed with a "white man's burden" quotation from an 1886 *Planters Monthly* article ("It is better here that the white man should rule.") Daws's only comment is, "The conclusion was inescapable" (p. 213). To get a sense of such characteristic contempt for Hawaiians, one has to read only the first few pages, where Daws refers several times to the Hawaiians as "savages" and "thieves" and where he approvingly has Captain Cook thinking, "It was a sensible primitive who bowed before a superior civilization" (p. 2). See also—among examples too numerous

to cite—his glib description of sacred *hula* as a "frivolous diversion," which, instead of work, the Hawaiians "would practice energetically in the hot sun for days on end . . . their bare brown flesh glistening with sweat" (pp. 65–66). Daws, who repeatedly displays an affection for descriptions of Hawaiian skin color, taught Hawaiian history for some years at the University of Hawai'i. He once held the Chair of Pacific History at the Australian National University's Institute of Advanced Studies.

3. Samuel H. Elbert and Noelani Mahoe, *Nā Mele o Hawai'i Nei: 101 Hawaiian Songs* (Honolulu: University of Hawai'i Press, 1970), pp. 62–64.

What Do You Mean "We," White Man?

On a recent Saturday night, I watched a 1932 film, *The Mummy,* starring Boris Karloff. The movie opens in Egypt, where two British archaeologists and a non-Native believer in what is described as the "Egyptian occult" are debating whether to open an unearthed treasure, some 3,700 years old. Engraved with a death curse, the artifact troubles the occult believer, who argues against its opening to the senior archaeologist. The two discuss the issue outside the tomb, leaving a junior archaeologist within. The believer of the "Egyptian occult" states the Native case, once removed, that any disturbance will anger the gods, who must surely take their just revenge. The senior archaeologist replies that "in the interests of science," the discovery must be investigated. Even if he subscribed to Egyptian beliefs, he says, he would not allow them to deter the progress of his work. His friend issues a final warning, then departs in fear.

During their discussion, the eager junior archaeologist has opened the box, withdrawn a mysterious scroll, and begun to translate it, thus awakening our friend, Boris Karloff, long asleep in his mummy case standing uncovered against the tomb wall. As Karloff makes off with the scroll, the junior archaeologist succumbs to the ancient curse, laughing idiotically, forever lost to insanity.

I, of course, cheered this turn of events.

But alas, Native Hawaiians do not, as far as I know, possess anything so powerful and immediate as the curse of the Egyptian gods to threaten those who disinter our cultural remains. In other respects, however, we are remarkably similar to the Egyptians.

Like Egypt, Hawai'i is part of a white colonial empire. Hawaiian culture and people are dominated by a long-distance power, the United States of America, whose settlers flood our land. We are fair game for tourists, adventurers, politicians, and, of course, purveyors of intellectual colonialism, including historians, anthropologists, and archaeologists. Our culture is seen—as is Egyptian culture in the film—to be foreign, prescientific, and representative of the threatening-because-potentially-uncontrollable unknown. Most important, Hawaiians, like Egyptians, are those being disinterred, studied, and removed to museums. The entire subject of the film assumes the power of the British colonizers to control the Egyptian colonized, just as the practice of archaeology in Hawai'i assumes the power of foreigners to dig up and study our remains. Hawaiians, like Egyptians, are but the backdrop for history: we do not make our own history; we merely watch as others concoct a history for us. The film's racist assumptions, like the assumptions of archaeology and anthropology in Hawai'i, are clear: these Natives are not *real* people (meaning white people) who have a *real* culture (meaning European culture) deserving of the kind of respect that operates between equals. Therefore, Native customs and beliefs are of little consequence; they cannot be seriously compared to "scientific" concerns, nor can they limit or direct, not to mention stop altogether, the work of "scientists." The attraction of the film for Euro-American audiences is that Native resistance, in the form of the mummy, will pit the feared, colonized world of the "occult" Egyptians against the safe, rational world of the "scientific" British. The fantasy life of the colonizers will be satisfied while their worst fears are laid to rest: the mummy will fight, but he will lose. Cultural dominance is reified in film artifact.

In Hawai'i, the politics of colonial anthropology and archaeology are not publicly debated or even acknowledged by its practitioners in the university or the museum or the field, and certainly not in the contract firm. Because most archaeology in Hawai'i is "contract" archaeology, that is, archaeology done for hire to satisfy state or federal requirements, professional ethics often take a back seat to the demands of speedy development. Simply said, contract firms find that monetary self-interest requires that they discover no significant sites, especially religious sites, that might trigger statutory oversight and eventual protection. That these realities are an outgrowth of colonial domination is also ignored, or flat-out denied, as are the political and ethical implications arising out of such origins. While thoughtful scholars and organizations in other places try to address their roles in dispossessing and further colonizing the people they study, anthropologists and archaeologists in Hawai'i (most of whom are white American) refuse to see Hawaiians as a colonized people whose Native land is a colonial possession of the United States.[1] Worse, they avoid the simple observation that most, if not all, anthropology and archaeology in Hawai'i is done by non-Natives for non-Natives. Indeed, I do not know of any published piece written by an anthropologist on Hawai'i which questions the presence of anthropologists or archeologists here or challenges their assumed intention of "scholarship" or analyzes the racist assumptions of foreigners who believe a few years training in an American university (or any other university) qualifies them to study, describe, and pass judgment upon Hawaiian culture and Hawaiian people. There is a singular lack of controversy here while a phalanx of academic colonizers prepares our burial grounds for development, characterizes our cultural beliefs as ideological inventions for political ends, and determines what is and who is Hawaiian.[2]

Despite raging battles in the Hawaiian community over disinterment of our ancestral bones (for example, Honokahua on Maui and the Pele Cave in Puna), the bombing of our sacred places (Kaho'olawe Island, Mākua, Pōhakuloa), industrial development of our forests and oceans (such as geothermal energy production and manganese nodule mining), resort development of our shorelines and valleys, which forecloses Hawaiian fishing and agricultural projects (for example, the West Beach project on O'ahu), and highway development of our valleys (H-3 freeway), anthropologists and archaeologists have vigorously resisted examining their work and its political impact as they aid state and private developers in transforming our lands and waters. They have run away from the accurate Native accusation that their arguments are used by our colonizers—for example, the U.S. military, the resort industry, the state government, and other anthropologists—in furthering our degradation, our suffering, and our powerlessness. When criticized by Hawaiians in struggle, their defense is a retreat into "science" or "scholarly endeavor," as if these projects have no historical contexts and are not themselves subject to error, racist intent, and political usage. Anthropologists and archaeologists have gone on the offensive, attacking Natives who oppose them as "ignorant about their culture" or "romantic and mixed up."[3]

Here, the hidden racism of anthropology and archeology is made manifest through Native challenge. When push comes to shove, anthropologists and archaeologists say what they really think: *they* are the experts on Native culture; *they* have superior knowledge of it. Natives, by comparison, are uninformed and untrained, and should not, therefore, have control over their sites and culture. In this political context, foreign "experts" with the support of local and state government, including planning and other legal processes, are pitted against "emotional" Natives who have nothing to rely upon but their personal and cultural integrity in asserting that their sacred places and beloved lands must not be damaged. This situation is obviously colonial. The indigenous people, once rulers of their own destiny, are totally subjugated to the technocrats of another culture dedicated to endless profit on the ancestral birthsands of the Native people.

It is not merely that Hawaiians are institutionally powerless to decide how and whether their people and their cultural remains should be studied *at all*. It is that a whole way of life, of being in and with the world, has been obliterated. The destiny that is left to Native people then becomes an imposed life of never ending struggle in a losing war.

The daily experience of resistance for Hawaiians is bitter, indeed. When we challenge what experts say and write, we are attacked for not knowing what and who we are, for being grossly political or for "*haole* bashing." Because we are presumed to be inferior in terms of Western training and concepts, the public debate never approaches the issues but always falls back on disparagement of our psychological state or our emotional and rational equilibrium. In other words, we are characterized in terms reserved for the infirm or the mentally incompetent. Many Hawaiians, myself included, have been branded as "crazies," simply because we assert the priority of our cultural values—for example, that land is our ancestor and that burial grounds are sacred—over the American insistence that all value proceeds from moneymaking. (In the Hawaiian way of thinking, a value that holds money and "science" as the promise of human fulfillment is itself crazy.) If this public disparagement does not stifle our resistance, then the counterattack becomes an economic one. Thus, there have been various attempts to have us fired from our jobs, or to prevent us from getting jobs, especially if they have some professional status that would challenge archaeologists and anthropologists.

While Hawaiians suffer this colonial yoke, anthropologists deny the very methodology of their work as exploitative. To Native peoples, anthropology is based on a peculiarly Western belief that studying books and learning to do fieldwork bequeaths a right to go halfway around the world to live with, observe, and write about another people. Moreover, this exploitation of a people's hospitality and generosity does not carry with it any responsibility of repayment in kind, or of privilege and privacy. At some time in their professional lives, anthropologists live with Natives who are in struggle, dispossessed, and, in some cases, endangered. But in the interests of knowledge or science or some other abstraction, the anthropologist has no obligation to aid the people he or she studies, to withhold information that threatens the people or is considered sacred or privileged to them, or to be a part of their struggles, whatever they may be. In other words, the anthropologist is a taker and a user. And if the people who are taken suffer from the anthropologist's work, too bad. No moral or ethical responsibility attaches to the anthropologist or the archeologist.

Familiar examples come from places where Native peoples are being removed or killed at an incredible rate, such as the Amazon or the Philippines or tribal areas in India. But this colonial exploitation is also occurring right here and right now in Hawai'i.

Jocelyn Linnekin, former student of Marshall Sahlins and a tenured professor in the Department of Anthropology at the University of Hawai'i-Mānoa, has written a book—*Children of the Land*—and an article, "Defining Tradition: Variations on the Hawaiian Identity," in which she asserts that modern-day Hawaiians have "invented" what they claim is a traditional value of love and caring for the land. She refers to this value, called *'aloha 'āina* or *mālama 'āina,* as a "slogan" (rather than a real cultural value) that is used by the Protect Kaho'olawe 'Ohana and other Hawaiian groups in their efforts to stop military bombing of Kaho'olawe. She goes on to say that the sacred meaning of Kaho'olawe was invented because Hawaiian nationalists needed a "political and cultural symbol of protest" in the modern period. Despite nineteenth-century evidence of Kaho'olawe's importance, Linnekin argues that the island's meaning has been created for the purposes of Hawaiian political maneuvering today.[4]

In her article, Linnekin writes, "For Hawai'i, 'traditional' properly refers to the precontact era, before Cook's arrival in 1778" (p. 242). But later, on the same page, she admits that "tradition is fluid. . . ." Still, despite this confusion, she criticizes Hawaiians for a "reconstruction of traditional Hawaiian society" in the present. Linnekin's difficulty stems from the kind of wrong-headedness that insists on hard-edged bifurcations of reality: pre-Western culture versus post-Western culture.

But what constitutes "tradition" to a people is ever changing. Culture is not static, nor is it frozen in objectified moments in time. Without doubt, Hawaiians were transformed drastically and irreparably after contact, but remnants of earlier lifeways, including values and symbols have persisted. One of these values is the Hawaiian responsibility to care for the land, to make it flourish, called *mālama 'āina* or *aloha 'āina.* To Linnekin, this value has been invented by modern Hawaiians to protest degradation of the land by developers, the military, and others. What Linnekin has missed here—partly because she has an incomplete grasp of "traditional" values but also because she does not understsand and thus misapprehends Hawaiian cultural nationalism—is simply this: The Hawaiian relationship to land has persisted into the present. What has changed is ownership and use of the land (from collective use by Hawaiians for subsistence to private use by whites and other non-Natives for profit). Asserting the Hawaiian relationship in this changed context results in politicization. Thus, Hawaiians assert a "traditional" relationship to the land not for political ends, as Linnekin argues, but because they continue to believe in the cultural value of caring for the land. That land use is now contested makes such a belief political. This distinction is crucial because the Hawaiian cultural motivation reveals the persistence of traditional values, the very thing Linnekin claims modern Hawaiians have "invented."

In her book, Linnekin severely criticizes Hawaiian nationalists, arguing that their nationalism is so much ideological fodder in the fight for land claims while disparaging their cultural origins as something less than "Hawaiian." She mistakenly says the Hawaiian movement is urban in origin and even misunderstands the lack of nationalism in other ethnic groups.[5]

Apart from the factual errors Linnekin has made—the movement is *rural* in origin; *aloha 'āina* is a traditional value; Hawaiians are nationalist and other ethnic groups are not because we are the only group in Hawai'i to have been made, literally, nationless in the land of our birth—her position that we have "invented" our traditions has now been repeated by other anthropologists, such as the anti-Native professor, Roger Keesing; by newspapers, such as the *New York Times* and the *San Francisco Chronicle/Examiner,* and worst of all for

Hawaiians, by the U.S. Navy as justification for ongoing destruction of Hawaiian lands.[6]

In short, because Linnekin wanted to publish an allegedly scholarly article applying the "inventing tradition, inventing culture" school of thought to Hawaiians, we, the Native people, are now faced with a proliferating ideology that is hurting our *real* culture everyday, hurting *real* Hawaiians everyday, and that is being used over and over to undermine *our* claim to say who and what we are.

Of course, Hawaiian nationalists' claim to knowledge is our life experiences as Natives within a culture that is 2,000 years old. Linnekin's claim to knowledge is her brief training (in Michigan) as an anthropologist. But the problem is more serious than epistemology. In a colonial world, the work of anthropologists and other Western-trained "experts" is used to disparage and exploit Natives. Thus, what Linnekin writes about Hawaiians has more potential power than what Hawaiians write. Proof of this rests in the use of Linnekin's argument by the U.S. Navy that Hawaiian nationalists have invented the sacred meaning of Kaho'olawe Island. Here, the connection between anthropology and the colonial enterprise is explicit. When Natives accuse Western scholars of exploiting them, they have in mind the exact kind of situation I am describing.

Beneath this academic reaction to Native assertions of our own culture is the entire question of evidence. How could an obviously wrong-headed statement about Hawaiians inventing their love for the land become such an oft-repeated "fact"? The answer is simple: a different standard of proof operates when Natives are involved. Every reiteration of the "fact" of our cultural invention reinforces it as a truism. Because of deep-rooted racism at the core of Western history, negative descriptions are believed without the slightest shred of evidence because the people in question are Natives. Were the same statements to be made about white people, careful examination of evidence and demands for more of it would be assumed. Not so with Natives.

I teach a course in Hawaiian studies called "Myths of Hawaiian History." I devised the course after concluding that so much of what passed for Hawaiian history was nothing more than a series of political myths created by foreigners and designed to disparage our people. Many of the myths—such as infanticide as a common practice in pre-*haole* Hawaiian culture—were invented by missionaries. But what is perhaps more telling is that these same myths are repeated today by anthropologists and archaeologists. Thus the "great" Marshall Sahlins (like the less great Eleanor Nordyke and Gavan Daws) asserts that

Hawaiians practiced infanticide but offers as evidence only doubtful missionary hearsay. The fashionable Valerio Valeri argues that Hawaiian land tenure was feudal, but his only evidence is alleged linguistic similarities between Hawaiian and European terms, hardly a sound evidentiary base. Patrick Kirch, a leading figure in Hawaiian archaeology, has written that tuberculosis was a "common pathology" in pre-*haole* Hawai'i, which, in turn, is exaggerated by archaeologist Paul Cleghorn, who claims that "many" Hawaiians suffered from it. At this writing, no evidence exists that there was *any* tuberculosis in pre-*haole* Hawai'i.[7]

And the list of lies told by credible, professional academics about us Native Hawaiians goes on and on. Indeed, it could be said that anthropologists and archaeologists are inventing our culture at an unbelievable rate.

To bewildered non-Natives, it may not be clear why we Natives are so upset about all this or even what infanticide, feudalism, and tuberculosis have in common as descriptions of pre-*haole* Hawaiian society. Suffice it to say that these fabrications, when taken together, form a tidy racist profile of a people who, in Western thinking, are primitive (because they practice baby killing), backward (because they have feudal land tenure), and diseased. The value of this description, although false, is simply that Western impact is then seen to be beneficial for Hawaiians, since it meant an end to infanticide, the liberation of private property, and the excusing of diseased Westerners, such as the celebrated Captain Cook, and the resulting massive depopulation of Hawaiians. I could go on with this list, which also includes other myths and other inventors from fields such as history, demography, and politics. But the point has been made: when it comes to Natives, negative statements are eagerly believed with but the thinnest evidence or none at all because of the general racist belief in Native cultural and physical inferiority.

As a Native Hawaiian who has participated for nearly fifteen years in the current efforts of my people to sustain their peoplehood, and nationhood, I have fought with anthropologists and archaeologists many times: to stop disinterment, to insist on accurate representation of the Hawaiian movement, to end osteological and DNA analysis. At each juncture, I feel that we Hawaiians have no likelihood of convincing either the anthropologists or the archaeologists of our position. They seem, almost to a person, to reject our arguments against "scientific" study, so-called cultural analysis, and all the rest. Worse, some of them have tried to injure our employment opportunities, to question our motives and our sanity, even to assert that they are themselves Native to Hawai'i.

All this has brought me to the following position. First, all anthropology and archaeology on Hawaiians should stop. There should be a moratorium on studying, unearthing, slicing, crushing, and analyzing us.

Second, while this moratorium is in place, there needs to be serious discussion among anthropologists and archaeologists about their political roles, their place in Hawai'i, and their responsibility to the Hawaiian people. Some departure points here could be the kind of ethical discussions that take place among atomic scientists and geneticists regarding the potential damage of their work to other people. This is especially true of work on the contemporary Hawaiian Movement that is used daily by our enemies to disparage and attack us. In other words, there needs to be some internal discussion among anthropologists and archaeologists about the impact of their work on living Hawaiians and the ethical conflicts that spring from their research. There needs to be an equal discussion between these two groups and leaders in the Hawaiian community.

Third, Hawaiians must lead an independent, professional investigation into the Bishop Museum, the largest and oldest research museum focusing on the Pacific Islands, with particular interest in traditional Hawaiian culture. Serious questions remain concerning the quality and professional integrity of their contract archaeology, including questions of falsification of reporting on sites and mismanagement of state funds. In the last ten years, Bishop Museum has come under increasing fire from the Hawaiian community, practicing archaeologists, and other state agencies for shoddy work and an arrogant disregard of Hawaiian cultural expertise in identifying religious sites.

Fourth, anthropologists and archaeologists working in Hawai'i need to acknowledge and address the racist inheritance of their fields as well as their own individual prejudices against a Native culture and people classifed by Euro-American "civilization" as inferior and savage. For many Hawaiians, including myself, archaeologists who dig up our ancestors for money or glory are *maha'oi haole*, that is, rude and intrusive white people who go where they do not belong. It is simply wrong, culturally, for non-Natives to dig up our ancestors, to break their bones, to remove them for highways and hotels, and to publish about them. Unlike white people, our culture is not obsessed with "scientific" study of human skeletons. We have much *aloha* for our ancestors and think of their burials as worthy of both ceremony and respect. This is why many of us Hawaiians do not support disinterment and analysis of our ancestral remains. I cannot reconcile grave robbing of my own people to increase "scientific" knowledge. Some things are sacred, even though, to the West, nothing is. To me and to most Natives, bones, graves, and rituals are sacrosanct. No exceptions.

For those who know little about such things outside Hawai'i, let me just say that in the Maori and aboriginal situations, in my understanding, the Native peoples exert much more control over what and how work is done regarding their culture and their artifacts. And in entirely independent countries, the Native people decide everything. Period. In this, as in so much else, Hawai'i is far behind other Pacific nations.

Finally, I reiterate something all colonialists despise: Native land belongs to Native people. They are the only residents with a genealogical claim to their place. That Euro-Americans violently disagree with this does not make it less true. Indeed, violent disagreement is violent precisely to the degree that the presence of Euro-Americans is dominant. In the Americas, white people insist on the fiction of "discovery" of two continents where more than 150 million people lived at the time of conquest. The genocide that followed contact continues today, but that, too, is a story of denial.

In Hawai'i, Hawaiians are categorized as just another group of immigrants who happened along some 2,000 years before whites and Asians. Words like "indigenous" are never used by scholars or lay people to describe Hawaiians. Nor is the word "settler" used to describe immigrants. As racist as this obviously is, the denial of Native history, culture, and humanity is central to the colonial endeavor. Archaeology and anthropology, in Hawai'i as elsewhere, are integral parts of the mammoth Euro-American project to dominate the human and natural world.

For those who disagree, there is really no middle ground. Non-Natives, no matter how long their residence in Hawai'i, should acknowledge their status as settlers, that is, uninvited guests in our Native country. Hawaiians are the only Native people. No other people—Asian, white, etc.—can or should claim Native status. Put differently, we are *not* all immigrants. Therefore, those who are Native Hawaiians have the only honest claim to decide what is researched and published about us and what is *kapu* (sacred).

This is my challenge and my hope.

Notes

1. Cultural Survival, Inc. (out of Harvard University), and the International Work Group on Indigenous Affairs (out of Denmark) are two non-Native groups that have been working for some time to aid indigenous peoples the world over. Initiated by anthropologists, these groups have sought to present the plight of Native peoples in such a way as to support them in their struggle for survival. The formation of both groups was a response to the complicity of anthropologists in the destruction of indigenous cultures and peoples.

For a critique of anthropologists and other scholars in terms of their exploitation of Native peoples, see Edward W. Said, "Representing the Colonized: Anthropology's Interlocutors," *Critical Inquiry* 15 (Winter 1989): 205–225. Said concludes his survey with these words: "Perhaps anthropology as we have known it can only continue on one side of the imperial divide, there to remain as a partner in domination and hegemony" (p. 225). For an article that seeks to create a typology of archaeologies, see Bruce G. Trigger, "Alternative Archaeologies: Nationalist, Colonialist, Imperialist," *Man* (N.S.) 19, 355–370. In this fine piece, the present form of archaeology done by Americans—and, therefore, done in Hawai'i—is situated historically as part of the so-called American "New Archaeology," which Trigger argues is an outcome of postwar American imperialism. In Trigger's words, ". . . the New Archaeology asserts the unimportance of national traditions themselves and of anything that stands in the way of American economic activity and political influence." This arrogant stand is surely what has been operating in Hawai'i with contract archaeology, in which any Native opposition to unearthing burial grounds and preparing sites for construction projects is seen as an impediment to "science." Moreover, the view that Hawaiians should have control over what happens to the record of their past, especially in terms of their own cultural values, is dismissed as "romanticism" when, in truth, it is a challenge to the imperialist notion that national traditions should be subordinated to the harsh realities of life in capitalist society. Hawaiian resistance can be seen as an assertion of an alternative tradition, one that is decidedly non-American, and for which the past is a direct link with the present, a present that is living rather than scholarly and artifactual.

2. The Society for Hawaiian Archaeology is not Hawaiian in any of its parts but is, rather, a professional organization whose ideology reflects the needs of predominantly *haole* archaeologists in Hawai'i for continued private and state support in archaeological work. The questions of who is an "expert" on things Hawaiian, of who has a claim to speak for the Hawaiian past, of the involvement of archaeologists in the destruction of things Hawaiian, and more

have been systematically ignored by the Society. So, too, has any interaction with Hawaiians who protest their work. Generally, the relationship between activist Hawaiians and archaeologists is filled with conflict and distrust. From the Hawaiian point of view, this is healthy, since without such opposition the voice of our ancestors would be stilled and the heritage of our children would be lost.

3. The controversy over the huge cemetery at Honokahua on Maui (which involved the potential removal of nearly 2,000 ancient Native skeletons for the building of a Japanese-financed hotel on missionary-owned land) revealed what many archaeologists actually think about Hawaiians. For example, disparaging comments were heard from the head of the archaeology firm—Rosendahl—that had the contract to remove the burials. These comments questioned the motivation, intelligence, and emotional stability of protesting Hawaiians. Moreover, this controversy spilled into the Honolulu dailies, which repeated charges that Hawaiians who resisted the unearthing were emotional as opposed to the archaeologists who were merely doing their job. To my knowledge, not a single archaeologist sided with the resistance efforts. Indeed, the president of the Society for Hawaiian Archaeology, Professor Terry Hunt, wrote to the governor asking that remains at Honokahua be made available for osteological analysis. This position came long after the issue had exploded into a statewide concern involving thousands of protesting Hawaiians throughout the archipelago. Thus, no matter how serious our resistance, archaeologists continue to believe and assert that "science" should determine the fate of Native remains.

4. See Jocelyn Linnekin, "Defining Tradition: Variations on the Hawaiian Identity," *American Ethnologist* 10 (1983): 241–252.

5. Jocelyn Linnekin, *Children of the Land: Exchange and Status in a Hawaiian Community* (New Brunswick: Rutgers University Press, 1985). For a reading of Linnekin's work and a critique of her posture as a Western-trained anthropologist misrendering Hawaiian culture, see my review of her book in *The Hawaiian Journal of History* XX (1986): 232–235. For a careful analysis of both Linnekin's argument and my own as a Native nationalist, see Jeffrey Tobin, "Cultural Construction and Native Nationalism: Report from the Hawaiian Front," in *boundary* 2, vol. 21 (Spring 1994): 111–133.

6. See the racist article by Roger M. Keesing, "Creating the Past: Custom and Identity in the Contemporary Pacific," *Contemporary Pacific* 1 (1989): 19–42. Also, see my response in "Natives and Anthropologists: The Colonial Struggle," *Contemporary Pacific* 3 (1991): 111–117. Keesing repeats Linnekin's charges that modern-day Hawaiians have invented their love of the land. His only citations for this assertion come from *haole* sources. As for Kaho'olawe, Linnekin's falsehoods are repeated by a fellow anthropologist, one Tom Keane, who was contracted by the Navy to write their cultural analysis of Kaho'olawe. The study is entitled *Kaho'olawe Island, Hawai'i Cultural Significance Overview.* The Sunday *San Francisco Chronicle/Examiner* (March 4, 1990) reprinted a piece from the *New York Times* on Natives inventing their culture. Hawaiians were included as one example of this invention. No citation followed. Linnekin's

false claim has become such a common property that, apparently, no citations are needed.

7. See Sahlins, *Islands of History* (Chicago: University of Chicago Press, 1985), p. 23; Kirch, *Feathered Gods and Fishhooks* (Honolulu: University of Hawai'i Press, 1985), p. 243; and Cleghorn, review of *Feathered Gods and Fishhooks*, in *Journal of the Polynesian Society* 96 (1987): 133. For an analysis of all references, both missionary and scholarly, on the myth of infanticide in traditional Hawai'i, see David Stannard, "Recounting the Fables of Savagery: Native Infanticide and the Functions of Political Myths," *Journal of American Studies* 25 (1991): 3, 381–418. On the absence of tuberculosis in Hawai'i prior to the arrival of *haole*, see David Stannard, *Before the Horror: The Population of Hawai'i on the Eve of Western Contact* (Honolulu: Social Science Research Institute, University of Hawai'i, 1989), pp. 77–78.

"Lovely Hula Hands": Corporate Tourism and the Prostitution of Hawaiian Culture

I am certain that most, if not all, Americans have heard of Hawai'i and have wished, at some time in their lives, to visit my Native land. But I doubt that the history of how Hawai'i came to be territorially incorporated, and economically, politically, and culturally subordinated to the United States is known to most Americans. Nor is it common knowledge that Hawaiians have been struggling for over twenty years to achieve a land base and some form of political sovereignty on the same level as American Indians. Finally, I would imagine that most Americans could not place Hawai'i or any other Pacific island on a map of the Pacific. But despite all this appalling ignorance, five million Americans will vacation in my homeland this year *and* the next, and so on, into the foreseeable capitalist future. Such are the intended privileges of the so-called American standard of living: ignorance of and yet power over one's relations to Native peoples. Thanks to postwar American imperialism, the ideology that the United States has no overseas colonies and is, in fact, the champion of self-determination the world over holds no greater sway than in the United States itself. To most Americans, then, Hawai'i is *theirs:* to use, to take, and, above all, to fantasize about long after the experience.

Just five hours away by plane from California, Hawai'i is a thousand light years away in fantasy. Mostly a state of mind, Hawai'i is the image of escape from the rawness and violence of daily American life. Hawai'i—the word, the vision, the sound in the mind—is the fragrance and feel of soft kindness. Above all, Hawai'i is "she," the Western image of the Native "female" in her magical allure. And if luck prevails, some of "her" will rub off on you, the visitor.

This fictional Hawai'i comes out of the depths of Western sexual sickness that demands a dark, sin-free Native for instant gratification between imperialist wars. The attraction of Hawai'i is stimulated by slick Hollywood movies, saccharine Andy Williams music, and the constant psychological deprivations of maniacal American life. Tourists flock to my Native land for escape, but they are escaping into a state of mind while participating in the destruction of a host people in a Native place.

To Hawaiians, daily life is neither soft nor kind. In fact, the political, economic, and cultural reality for most Hawaiians is hard, ugly, and cruel.

In Hawai'i, the destruction of our land and the prostitution of our culture is planned and executed by multinational corporations (both foreign-based and Hawai'i-based), by huge landowners (such as the missionary-descended Castle & Cook of Dole Pineapple fame), and by collaborationist state and county governments. The ideological gloss that claims tourism to be our economic savior and the "natural" result of Hawaiian culture is manufactured by ad agencies (such as the state-supported Hawai'i Visitors Bureau) and tour companies (many of which are owned by the airlines) and spewed out to the public through complicitous cultural engines such as film, television and radio, and the daily newspaper. As for the local labor unions, both rank and file and management clamor for more tourists, while the construction industry lobbies incessantly for larger resorts.

The major public educational institution, the University of Hawai'i, funnels millions of taxpayer dollars into a School of Travel Industry Management and a business school replete with a Real Estate Center and a Chair of Free Enterprise (renamed the Walker Chair to hide the crude reality of capitalism). As the propaganda arm of the tourist industry in Hawai'i, both schools churn out studies that purport to show why Hawai'i needs more golf courses, hotels, and tourist infrastructure and how Hawaiian culture is "naturally" one of giving and entertaining.

Of course, state-encouraged commodification and prostitution of Native cultures through tourism is not unique to Hawai'i. It is suffered by peoples in places as disparate as Goa, Australia, Tahiti, and the southwestern United States. Indeed, the problem is so commonplace that international organizations—for example, the Ecumenical Coalition on Third World Tourism out of Bangkok, the Center for

Responsible Tourism in California, and the Third World European Network—have banded together to help give voice to Native peoples in daily resistance against corporate tourism. My focus on Hawai'i, although specific to my own culture, would likely transfer well when applied to most Native peoples.[1]

Despite our similarities with other major tourist destinations, the statistical picture of the effects of corporate tourism in Hawai'i is shocking:

> *Fact:* Nearly forty years ago, at statehood, Hawai'i residents outnumbered tourists by more than 2 to 1. Today, tourists outnumber residents by 6 to 1; they outnumber Native Hawaiians by 30 to 1.[2]
>
> *Fact:* According to independent economists and criminologists, "tourism has been the single most powerful factor in O'ahu's crime rate," including crimes against people and property.[3]
>
> *Fact:* Independent demographers have been pointing out for years that "tourism is the major source of population growth in Hawai'i" and that "rapid growth of the tourist industry ensures the trend toward a rapidly expanded population that receives lower per capita income."[4]
>
> *Fact:* The Bank of Hawai'i has reported that the average real incomes of Hawai'i residents grew only *one* percent during the period from the early seventies through the early eighties, when tourism was booming. The same held true throughout the nineties. The census bureau reports that personal income growth in Hawai'i during the same time was the lowest by far of any of the fifty American states.[5]
>
> *Fact:* Groundwater supplies on O'ahu will be insufficient to meet the needs of residents and tourists by the year 2000.[6]
>
> *Fact:* According to *The Honolulu Advertiser,* "Japanese investors have spent more than $7.1 billion on their acquisitions" since 1986 in Hawai'i. This kind of volume translates into huge alienations of land and properties. For example, nearly 2,000 acres of land on the Big Island of Hawai'i was purchased for $18.5 million and over 7,000 acres on Moloka'i went for $33 million. In 1989, over $1 billion was spent by the Japanese on land alone.[7]

Fact: More plants and animals from our Hawaiian Islands are now extinct or on the endangered species list than in the rest of the United States.[8]

Fact: More than 29,000 families are on the Hawaiian trust lands list, waiting for housing, pastoral, or agricultural lots.[9]

Fact: The median cost of a home on the most populated island of O'ahu is around $350,000.[10]

Fact: Hawai'i has by far the worst ratio of average family income to average housing costs in the country. This explains why families spend nearly 52 percent of their gross income for housing costs. [11]

Fact: Nearly one-fifth of Hawai'i's resident population is classified as *near-homeless,* that is, those for whom any mishap results in immediate on-the-street homelessness.[12]

These kinds of statistics render a very bleak picture, not at all what the posters and jingoistic tourist promoters would have you believe about Hawai'i.

My use of the word *tourism* in the Hawai'i context refers to a mass-based, corporately controlled industry that is both vertically and horizontally integrated such that one multinational corporation owns an airline and the tour buses that transport tourists to the corporation-owned hotel where they eat in a corporation-owned restaurant, play golf, and "experience" Hawai'i on corporation-owned recreation areas and eventually consider buying a second home built on corporation land. Profits, in this case, are mostly repatriated back to the home country. In Hawai'i, these "home" countries are Japan, Taiwan, Hong Kong, Canada, Australia, and the United States. In this sense, Hawai'i is very much like a Third World colony where the local elite—the Democratic Party in our state—collaborate in the rape of Native land and people.[13]

The mass nature of this kind of tourism results in megaresort complexes on thousands of acres with demands for water and services that far surpass the needs of Hawai'i residents. These complexes may boast several hotels, golf courses, restaurants, and other "necessaries" to complete the total tourist experience. Infrastructure is usually built by the developer in exchange for county approval of more hotel units. In Hawai'i, counties bid against each other to attract larger and larger complexes. "Rich" counties, then, are those with more resorts, since they will pay more of the tax base of the county. The richest of these is the City and County of Honolulu, which encompasses the entire island of O'ahu. This island is the site of four major tourist destinations, a major international airport, and 80 percent of the resident population of Hawai'i. The military also controls nearly 30 percent of the island, with bases and airports of their own. As you might imagine, the density of certain parts of Honolulu (e.g., Waikīkī) is among the highest in the world. At the present annual visitor count, more than five million tourists pour through O'ahu, an island of only 607 square miles.

With this as a background on tourism, I want to move now into the area of cultural prostitution. *Prostitution* in this context refers to the entire institution that defines a woman (and by extension the *female*) as an object of degraded and victimized sexual value for use and exchange through the medium of money. The *prostitute* is a woman who sells her sexual capacities and is seen, thereby, to possess and reproduce them at will, that is, by her very "nature." The prostitute and the institution that creates and maintains her are, of course, of patriarchal origin. The pimp is the conduit of exchange, managing the commodity that is the prostitute while acting as the guard at the entry and exit gates, making sure the prostitute behaves as a prostitute by fulfilling her sexual-economic functions. The victims participate in their victimization with enormous ranges of feeling, from resistance to complicity, but the force and continuity of the institution are shaped by men.

There is much more to prostitution than my sketch reveals but this must suffice, for I am interested in using the largest sense of this term as a metaphor in understanding what has happened to Hawaiian culture. My purpose is not to exact detail or fashion a model but to convey the utter degradation of our culture and our people under corporate tourism by employing *prostitution* as an analytic category.

Finally, I have chosen four areas of Hawaiian culture to examine: our homeland, our *one hānau* that is Hawai'i, our lands and fisheries, the outlying seas and the heavens; our language and dance; our familial relationships; and our women.

The *mo'olelo,* or history of Hawaiians, is to be found in our genealogies. From our great cosmogonic genealogy, the *kumulipo,* derives the Hawaiian identity. The "essential lesson" of this genealogy is "the interrelatedness of the Hawaiian world, and the inseparability of its constituents parts." Thus, "the genealogy of the land, the gods, chiefs, and people intertwine one with the other, and with all aspects of the universe."[14]

In the *mo'olelo* of Papa and Wākea, "earth mother" and "sky father," our islands were born: Hawai'i, Maui, O'ahu, Kaua'i, and Ni'ihau. From their human offspring came the *taro* plant and from the *taro* came the Hawaiian people. The lessons of our genealogy are that human beings have a familial relationship to land and to the *taro,* our elder siblings or *kua'ana.*

In Hawai'i, as in all of Polynesia, younger siblings must serve and honor elder siblings who, in turn, must feed and care for their younger siblings. Therefore, Hawaiians must cultivate and husband the land that will feed and provide for the Hawaiian people. This relationship of people to land is called *mālama 'āina* or *aloha 'āina,* "care and love of the land."

When people and land work together harmoniously, the balance that results is called *pono.* In Hawaiian society, the *ali'i,* or "chiefs," were required to maintain order, an abundance of food, and good government. The *maka'āinana* or "common people," worked the land and fed the chiefs; the *ali'i* organized production and appeased the gods.

Today, *mālama 'āina* is called *stewardship* by some, although that word does not convey spiritual and genealogical connections. Nevertheless, to love and make the land flourish is a Hawaiian value. *'Āina,* one of the words for "land," means "that which feeds." *Kama'āina,* a term for native-born people, means "child of the land." Thus is the Hawaiian relationship to land both familial and reciprocal.

Hawaiian deities also spring from the land: Pele is our volcano, Kāne and Lono our fertile valleys and plains, Kanaloa our ocean and all that lives within it, and so on with the numerous gods of Hawai'i. Our whole universe, physical and metaphysical, is divine.

Within this world, the older people, or *kūpuna,* are to cherish those who are younger, the *mo'opuna.* Unstinting generosity is a prized value. Social connections between our people are through *aloha,* simply translated as "love" but carrying with it a profoundly Hawaiian sense that is, again, familial and genealogical. Hawaiians feel *aloha* for Hawai'i from whence they come and for their Hawaiian kin upon whom they depend. It is nearly impossible to feel or practice *aloha* for something that is not familial. This is why we extend familial relations to those few non-Natives whom we feel understand and can reciprocate our *aloha.* But *aloha* is freely given and freely returned; it is not and cannot be demanded or commanded. Above all, *aloha* is a cultural feeling and practice that works among the people and between the people and their land.

The significance and meaning of *aloha* underscores the centrality of the Hawaiian language or *'ōlelo,* to the culture. *'Ōlelo* means both "language" and "tongue"; *mo'olelo,* or "history," is that which comes from the tongue, that is, "a story." *Haole,* or white people, say that we have oral history, but what we have are stories, such as our creation story, passed on through the generations. This sense of history is different from the *haole* sense of history. To Hawaiians in traditional society, language had tremendous power, thus the phrase, *i ka 'ōlelo ke ola; i ka 'ōlelo ka make*—"in language is life, in language is death."

After nearly two thousand years of speaking Hawaiian, our people suffered the near extinction of our language through its banning by the American-imposed government in 1900, the year Hawai'i became a territory of the United States. All schools, government operations and official transactions were thereafter conducted in English, despite the fact that most people, including non-Natives, still spoke Hawaiian at the turn of the century.

Since 1970, *'ōlelo Hawai'i,* or the Hawaiian language, has undergone a tremendous revival, including the rise of language immersion schools. The state of Hawai'i now has two official languages, Hawaiian and English, and the call for Hawaiian language speakers and teachers is increasing every day.[15]

Along with the flowering of Hawaiian language has come a flowering of Hawaiian dance, especially in its ancient form, called *hula kahiko.* Dance academies, known as *hālau,* have proliferated throughout Hawai'i, as have *kumu hula,* or dance masters, and formal competitions where all-night presentations continue for three or four days to throngs of appreciative listeners. Indeed, among Pacific Islanders, Hawaiian dance is considered one of the finest Polynesian art forms today.

Of course, the cultural revitalization that Hawaiians are now experiencing and transmitting to their children is as much a *repudiation* of colonization by so-called Western civilization in its American form as it is a *reclamation* of our own past and our own ways of life. This is why cultural revitalization is often resisted and disparaged by anthropologists and others: they see very clearly that its political effect is decolonization of the mind. Thus our rejection of the nuclear family as the basic unit of society and of individualism as the best form of human expression infuriates social workers, the churches, the legal system, and educators to this day. Hawaiians continue to have allegedly "illegitimate" children, to *hānai,* or "adopt," both children and adults outside of sanctioned Western legal concepts, to hold and use land and water in a collective form rather than a private property form, and to proscribe the notion and the value that one person should strive to surpass and therefore outshine all others.

All these Hawaiian values can be grouped under the idea of *'ohana,* loosely translated as "family," but more accurately imagined as a group of both closely and distantly related people who share nearly everything, from land and food to children and status. Sharing is central to this value, since it prevents individual decline. Of course, poverty is not thereby avoided; it is only shared with everyone in the unit. The *'ohana* works effectively when the *kua'ana* relationship (elder sibling/younger sibling reciprocity) is practiced.

Finally, within the *'ohana,* our women are considered the lifegivers of the nation and are accorded the respect and honor this status conveys. Our young women, like our young people in general, are the *pua,* or "flower" of our *lāhui,* or our "nation." The renowned beauty of our women, especially their sexual beauty, is not considered a commodity to be hoarded by fathers and brothers but an attribute of our people. Culturally, Hawaiians are very open and free about sexual relationships, although Christianity and organized religion have done much to damage these traditional sexual values.

With this understanding of what it means to be Hawaiian, I want to move now to the prostitution of our culture by tourism.

Hawai'i itself is the female object of degraded and victimized sexual value. Our *'āina,* or lands, are not any longer the source of food and shelter, but the source of money. Land is now called "real estate," rather than "our mother," Papa. The American relationship of people to land is that of exploiter to exploited. Beautiful areas, once sacred to my people, are now expensive resorts; shorelines where net fishing, seaweed gathering, and crabbing occurred are more and more the exclusive domain of recreational activities such as sunbathing, windsurfing, and jet skiing. Now, even access to beaches near hotels is strictly regulated or denied to the local public altogether.

The phrase, *mālama 'āina*—"to care for the land"—is used by government officials to sell new projects and to convince the locals that hotels can be built with a concern for "ecology." Hotel historians, like hotel doctors, are stationed in-house to soothe the visitors' stay with the pablum of invented myths and tales of the "primitive."

High schools and hotels adopt each other and funnel teenagers through major resorts for guided tours from kitchens to gardens to honeymoon suites in preparation for post-secondary school jobs in the lowest paid industry in the state. In the meantime, tourist appreciation kits and movies are distributed through the state Department of Education to all elementary schools. One film, unashamedly titled *What's in It for Me?*, was devised to convince locals that tourism is, as the newspapers never tire of saying, "the only game in town."

Of course, all this hype is necessary to hide the truth about tourism, the awful exploitative truth that the industry is the major cause of environmental degradation, low wages, land dispossession, and the highest cost of living in the United States.

While this propaganda is churned out to local residents, the commercialization of Hawaiian culture proceeds with calls for more sensitive marketing of our Native values and practices. After all, a prostitute is only as good as her income-producing talents. These talents, in Hawaiian terms, are the *hula;* the generosity, or *aloha,* of our people; the *u'i,* or youthful beauty of our women and men; and the continuing allure of our lands and waters, that is, of our place, Hawai'i.

The selling of these talents must produce income. And the function of tourism and the State of Hawai'i is to convert these attributes into profit.

The first requirement is the transformation of the product, or the cultural attribute, much as a woman must be transformed to look like a prostitute—that is, someone who is complicitous in her own commodification. Thus *hula* dancers wear clownlike makeup, don costumes from a mix of Polynesian cultures, and behave in a manner that is smutty and salacious rather than powerfully erotic. The distance between the smutty and the erotic is precisely the distance between Western culture and Hawaiian culture. In the hotel version of the *hula,* the sacredness of the dance has completely evaporated, while the athleticism and sexual expression have been packaged like ornaments. The purpose is entertainment for profit rather than a joyful and truly Hawaiian celebration of human and divine nature.

The point, of course, is that everything in Hawai'i can be yours, that is, you the tourists', the non-Natives', the visitors'. The place, the people, the culture, even our identity as a "Native" people is for sale. Thus the word "Aloha" is employed as an aid in the constant hawking of things Hawaiian. In truth, this use of *aloha* is so far removed from any Hawaiian cultural context that it is, literally, meaningless.

Thus, Hawai'i, like a lovely woman, is there for the taking. Those with only a little money get a brief encounter, those with a lot of money, like the Japanese, get more. The state and counties will give tax breaks, build infrastructure, and have the governor personally welcome tourists to ensure that they keep coming. Just as the pimp regulates prices and guards the commodity of the prostitute, so the state bargains with developers for access to Hawaiian land and culture. Who builds the biggest resorts to attract the most affluent tourists gets the best deal: more hotel rooms, golf courses, and restaurants approved. Permits are fast-tracked, height and density limits are suspended, new groundwater sources are miraculously found.

Hawaiians, meanwhile, have little choice in all this. We can fill up the unemployment lines, enter the military, work in the tourist industry, or leave Hawai'i. Increasingly, Hawaiians are leaving, not by choice but out of economic necessity.

Our people who work in the industry—dancers, waiters, singers, valets, gardeners, housekeepers, bartenders, and even a few managers—make between $10,000 and $25,000 a year, an impossible salary for a family in Hawai'i. Psychologically, our young people have begun to think of tourism as the only employment opportunity, trapped as they are by the lack of alternatives. For our young women, modeling is a "cleaner" job when compared to waiting on tables or dancing in a weekly revue, but modeling feeds on tourism and the commodification of Hawaiian women. In the end, the entire employment scene is shaped by tourism.

Despite their exploitation, Hawaiians' participation in tourism raises the problem of complicity. Because wages are so low and advancement so rare, whatever complicity exists is secondary to the economic hopelessness that drives Hawaiians into the industry. Refusing to contribute to the commercialization of one's culture becomes a peripheral concern when unemployment looms.

Of course, many Hawaiians do not see tourism as part of their colonization. Thus, tourism is viewed as providing jobs, not as a form of cultural prostitution. Even those who have some glimmer of critical consciousness do not generally agree that the tourist industry prostitutes Hawaiian culture. This is a measure of the depth of our mental oppression: we cannot understand our own cultural degradation because we are living it. As colonized people, we are colonized to the extent that we are unaware of our oppression. When awareness begins, then so, too, does decolonization. Judging by the growing resistance to new hotels, to geothermal energy and manganese nodule mining, which would supplement the tourist industry, and to increases in the sheer number of tourists, I would say that decolonization has begun, but we have many more stages to negotiate on our path to sovereignty.

My brief excursion into the prostitution of Hawaiian culture has done no more than give an overview. Now that you have read a Native view, let me just leave this thought with you. If you are thinking of visiting my homeland, please do not. We do not want or need any more tourists, and we certainly do not like them. If you want to help our cause, pass this message on to your friends.

Notes

1. The Center for Responsible Tourism and the Third World European Network were created out of the activism and organizing of the Ecumenical Coalition on Third World Tourism (ECTWT). This umbrella organization is composed of the following member bodies: All Africa Conference of Churches, Caribbean Conference of Churches, Christian Conference of Asia, Consejo Latinoamericano de Iglesias, Federation of Asian Bishops Conference/Office of Human Development, Middle East Council of Churches, Pacific Conference of Churches. In addition, sister organizations, like the Hawai'i Ecumenical Coalition on Tourism, extend the network worldwide. The ECTWT publishes a quarterly magazine with articles on Third World tourism and its destructive effects from child prostitution to dispossession of Native peoples. The address for ECTWT is P.O. Box 24, Chorakhebua, Bangkok 10230, Thailand.

2. Eleanor C. Nordyke, *The Peopling of Hawai'i*, 2nd ed. (Honolulu: University of Hawai'i Press, 1989), pp. 134–172.

3. Meda Chesney-Lind, "Salient Factors in Hawai'i's Crime Rate," University of Hawai'i School of Social Work. Available from author.

4. Nordyke, *The Peopling of Hawai'i*, pp. 134–172.

5. Bank of Hawai'i Annual Economic Report, 1984.

6. Estimate of independent hydrologist Kate Vandemoer to community organizing group *Kūpa'a He'eia*, February 1990. Water quality and groundwater depletion are two problems much discussed by state and county officials in Hawai'i but ignored when resort permits are considered.

7. *The Honolulu Advertiser*, April 8, 1990.

8. David Stannard, Testimony against West Beach Estates. Land Use Commission, State of Hawai'i, January 10, 1985.

9. Department of Hawaiian Home Lands, phone interview, March 1998.

10. *Honolulu Star-Bulletin*, May 8, 1990.

11. Bank of Hawai'i Annual Economic Report, 1984. In 1992, families probably spent closer to 60 percent of their gross income for housing costs. Billion-dollar Japanese investments and other speculation since 1984 have caused rental and purchase prices to skyrocket.

12. This is the estimate of a state-contracted firm that surveyed the islands for homeless and near-homeless families. Testimony was delivered to the state legislature, 1990 session.

13. For an analysis of post-statehood Hawai'i and its turn to mass-based corporate tourism, see Noel Kent, *Hawai'i: Islands Under the Influence.* For an analysis of foreign investment in Hawai'i, see *"A Study of Foreign Investment*

and Its Impact on the State," (Honolulu: Hawai'i Real Estate Center, University of Hawai'i, 1989).

14. Lilikalā Kame'eleihiwa, *Native Land and Foreign Desires* (Honolulu: Bishop Museum Press, 1992), p. 2.

15. See Larry Kimura, "Native Hawaiian Culture," *Native Hawaiians Study Commission Report,* vol. 1, pp. 173–197.

Part IV

Native Hawaiians in a White University

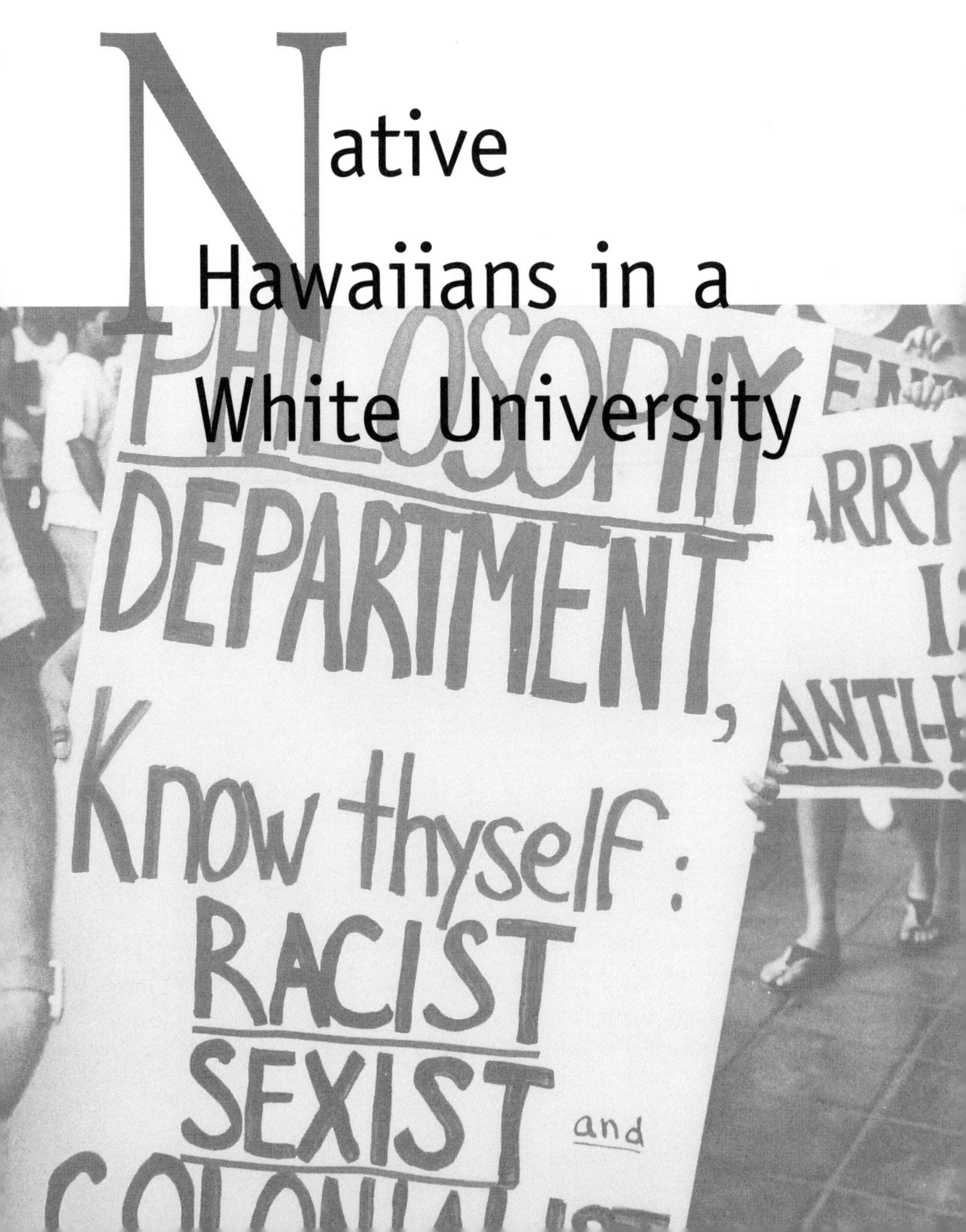

Racism against Native Hawaiians at the University of Hawai'i: A Personal and Political View

The Colonial Context

Since the eighteenth-century arrival of Westerners in my Native land, Hawai'i has been much vaunted as a "paradise" of sunny beaches, lush, unspoiled valleys, erupting volcanoes, and happy Natives. Thanks to Hollywood movies and tourist industry propaganda, this paradisal myth endures. To the West, and increasingly to Japan, Hawai'i represents a Pacific playground for escape or romance or recreation. It is a fantasy, a state of mind.

But for Hawaiians, this image is nothing but the usual colonial propaganda.

And it is only in a context of colonialism that formal education in Hawai'i can be understood. Indeed, public education in Hawai'i is similar in purpose to Francophone education in French-controlled Tahiti and English education in Commonwealth New Zealand.[1]

The University of Hawai'i stands atop the educational pyramid of public schools as the flagship campus for the state. With over 40,000 full- and part-time students, it is a living symbol of colonization. In many ways, the university is an educational equivalent to the American military command center in Hawai'i. Both serve as guardians of white dominance, both support the state economy, and both provide a training ground for future technocrats.

Just as universities in other colonies function to legitimate and entrench the power of the colonizing culture, so the University of

Hawai'i functions to maintain *haole* (white) American control.[2] The standard American university curriculum, bureaucratic structure, and white male-dominated faculty characterize the institution. In addition, there is a School of Travel Industry Management, a Chair of Free Enterprise (renamed the Walker Chair to avoid the crassness of the original title), and a Hawai'i Real Estate Center, which support the local tourist industry. An affiliated East-West Center, a creature of the federal government, was established as a counterinsurgency think tank during the Vietnam War and continues as a gathering place for military, government, and corporate interests focused on Asia and the Pacific Basin. All this exists on a tiny Polynesian island that is part of the most isolated archipelago in the world.

It also exists on the ancestral land base of the Hawaiian people. As a *haole* enclave in a local society where Asians are the largest numerical group and whites and Hawaiians are each about a fifth of the one million residents in Hawai'i, the University is a nineteenth-century throwback to the first stages of white colonialism. People of color comprise more than 75 percent of the student body, while the faculty is more than 75 percent white. Along with the sugar companies and the banks, the university is one of the few remaining institutions where no attempts have been made to add a little Native color to the visible white reality.

In 1981, I entered this bastion of white power as an assistant professor of American Studies. I was an active member and occasional spokesperson for various struggles in the Hawaiian Movement. And I had recently completed a doctoral dissertation on feminist theory at the University of Wisconsin. Like dozens of other Hawaiians who had been sent to the metropole to become assimilated professionals, I had returned to colony Hawai'i as a Native nationalist. My growing public persona was that of an indigenous critic of American imperialism in Hawai'i. And although I was identified by the *haole* press as one of the more militant activists in the movement, nothing I did or said was beyond the bounds of critical public dissent.

But in a colony, any dissent is threatening, especially by Natives. My application and hiring unleashed forces of racism and political suppression in the department that lasted until I was transferred to another academic unit (as part of a settlement of a racism/sexism grievance) in the fall of 1986. Between my hire and my transfer, I lived through a five-year battle (with student-community support) against all manner of oppressive and exploitative conditions: racism by individual faculty and by the institution as a whole; attempts to prevent my written and verbal expressions of critical political views; violation of the academic freedom to teach certain subjects and ideas; and petty daily harassment on the job. At times, even the recognition of my humanity as a Hawaiian was at issue.

But, with the help of supporters, including my faculty union, I prevailed. The struggle consumed over five years of my life and yet, like most victorious resistance efforts, it was, in the end, a victory for more than myself. The ultimate success of one Hawaiian woman who fought the *haole* world and won is a tale worth recounting.

Racism and Suppression of Political Views

The Scene

The strange origins of an American Studies department in colony Hawai'i deserve some background. Evolving out of the federal government's East-West Center in the early sixties, the department had been chaired by the same man for nearly twenty years when I applied for my job. By his own proud admission, he had worked for the Central Intelligence Agency prior to his appointment at the East-West Center and the university. He also was well known as an adversary of the small liberal community on campus and had been known to make disparaging remarks about oppositional people of color, including Hawaiians. As chair, he had hired the early members of the department, including two of his former students. Structurally, he had enormous power, with only weak advisory committees beneath him. As a result, his long tenure as chair had created a docile faculty too willing to be governed and too meek to demand a change in leadership.

By 1981, the department had nine full-time male faculty, one half-time female faculty, and two emeritus male faculty. Two of their number were Asian, the rest were white. None were Hawaiian.

Academically, only a third of the faculty had acceptable publishing records, including books. The remainder had published with vanity presses or, like the chair, had published only a few articles or nothing at all.

In ideological terms, the department represented a very "celebrate America," procapitalist, proempire perspective. The Black Civil Rights Movement, the antiwar movement, and the women's movement did not appear in the teaching of most faculty. Intellectually, the faculty were (and still are) in a presixties mode. Indeed, there was no Third World or Marxist analysis of America at all. And there was surely no attention paid to the Hawaiian Movement or to the military/tourist exploitation of Hawai'i because of its colonial status. The Hawaiian people, beyond our tourist manifestations, were completely unknown to the faculty, just as Maori communities in New Zealand would be unknown to English professors at the University of Auckland. Finally, the characteristic isolation of academics from the surrounding community was compounded by the racism of a faculty who felt superior to the general public, including students, because they were overwhelmingly Asians and Hawaiians or, as Americans are fond of repeating, "nonwhite."

Culturally, this superiority showed its hand in a number of ways. Disparaging remarks were often made by faculty about pidgin-speaking local students who could not (rather than would not) speak what the faculty called "standard English." The lack of knowledge about American cultural institutions—such as the *New York Times* or championship baseball teams—on the part of students irritated faculty who bemoaned the "provincialism" of life in Hawai'i. (Indeed, one adjunct faculty wrote an entire book about this "provincialism," which, predictably, was published by a vanity press and wound up as required reading in his courses.) Local cultural traits—for example, ethnic humor or habits of local dress—were ridiculed by many faculty as backcountry buffoonery. And Hawaiian culture, when noticed at all, was relegated to the entertainment/recreational category of an occasional *hula* (dance) festival or commercial *lū'au* (feast).

In reality, most of the American studies faculty behaved like colonial settlers on the outskirts of empire, enduring their postings until a better opportunity came along.

Act One: In the Land of the White Man

By February of 1981, I had applied for a position in American Studies that called for expertise in women's studies and in a cross-cultural field (in my case, Hawai'i and the Pacific). Some fifty-one other candidates had applied, and the department personnel committee had chosen six semifinalists, myself included.

On February 23, the department selected their top two choices: one white female candidate about to complete a Ph.D. in American Studies at an Ivy League university, and myself, about to complete a Ph.D. in political science from the University of Wisconsin. The meeting was very long (a total of six hours divided into afternoon and evening sessions) and contentious. My politics were openly discussed and one faculty member (who was Asian) asserted that my hire would be inappropriate because I was "radical." This was only the first salvo.

The field had been narrowed, but my hire was yet to come. Sometime in late February, the chair removed several pages listing community service from my vita, which had been placed on file for departmental perusal. When discovered by one of my faculty supporters, the chair said he meant only to "balance" the vitae, since the other candidate did not have a list of community activities. The other finalist, meanwhile, was flown in from the American continent for an interview and public lecture. She stayed at the chair's house, where he also arranged for a reception in her honor. As a Hawaiian candidate, and an activist one at that, no such amenities were extended to me.

By the middle of March, when both candidates were being interviewed, relations between some of my faculty supporters and the chair had deteriorated. To fulfill the requirements of due process (and steer clear of administrative oversight), some faculty insisted that I should also be hosted at a reception. A hastily arranged one was held at a faculty member's house, but by this time any "routine" interview process was beyond salvage. It was clear, at least to me, that I was treading on whites-only territory. Despite the presence of two Asians in the department (both of whom self-identified as assimilationist and spoke openly against my hire because I was an activist), my presence was perceived, at least by the chair, as a Hawaiian encroachment.

On March 20, the faculty voted. According to my supporters, the meeting was filled with such argument and accusation regarding my "radicalism" on behalf of Hawaiians that everyone felt exhausted in the end. After an initial tie vote, I was selected on the second ballot, which visibly upset the chair. Later, he would tell other faculty they betrayed him by voting for a "troublemaker." As in the past, the faculty assumed he would follow established procedures and offer the job to the chosen candidate, that is, to me. Instead, he called the other finalist, said the faculty was hopelessly "split" and the position "frozen." I, of course, never heard from him.

Two weeks of silence elapsed before I called the personnel committee chair to tell him I had heard nothing. He was flabbergasted. As a white, Yale-educated male faculty member, he had nothing in his personal experience to prepare him for the chair's overt and boastful racism. While we spoke, I noted that the department chair might withdraw the position rather than follow the faculty mandate to hire me, a suggestion that elicited laughter and a reply that I was "paranoid."

On April 10, at a faculty meeting called by the chair, he read a prepared statement. The following is a direct quotation from the chronology of events kept by the personnel committee.

> [The chair said] he believed the university and the department were not democracies, that they were rather "authoritarian and paternalistic" in fact. He went on to state that the Provost, the Chancellor, and the President of the University had all been approached by him and they had agreed to block Trask's appointment. Consequently, no one was to be hired for the slot which had been empty for several years.
>
> Not a single faculty member spoke in support of the chair's actions. The response, on the contrary, was at first shock over the violating of department collegiality, openness, and agreed-upon procedures, and then a unanimous request that the chair reconsider his stand.

Faculty supporters later told me the chair said I was "unqualified" for the job but gave no reasons why he thought so.

The day after this debacle, I gathered together a group of student and community supporters and resource people (attorneys, researchers, photographers) to strategize our position. Given the faculty's vote and thus their confidence in my credentials, and given the historic antagonism between whites and Hawaiians, it was clear to us that the chair's actions were racist. Of course, the American Studies faculty would continue to deny that racism was involved at all, choosing instead to dig up the familiar academic smokescreen of lack of "collegiality" by the chair. As Hawaiians, however, our experience told another story. All the obvious signs of racism were present in the chair's behavior: fear at my application; nervousness in my presence; procedural "irregularities" during the interview process; vociferous denial of racist behavior; and finally, outright rejection of my hire.

But the worst was yet to come. On April 16, the chair called another meeting with me and four faculty who supported me.

When the meeting began, there was a menacing strangeness in the air. As we took our seats, the chair turned off all lights, and in the unannounced and eerily threatening dark he began a slide show. His narrating voice, tight with anger, seeped out of the projection booth. One by one, horrifying slides of Nazi victims at Buchenwald hit the screen. After a few minutes, the chair began making references to his heritage as a Jew, which, he heatedly insisted, made it impossible for him to be a racist. No one, to my knowledge, had accused him of racism, nor did he say anyone had. I felt him to be on the jagged edge of insanity.

When the slides were finished, none of the faculty spoke. I began to wonder why I had ever wanted a job in such a crazy department. The chair came to the table in a trembling fury, saying, to our complete surprise, he would hire me. He had failed, he went on, to secure a part-time, nontenure-track position he called a "compromise." Thus, he was forced to offer the original position for which I had interviewed.

Various faculty tried, in a timid and roundabout way, to tell him that his behavior was "inappropriate" and that I was being unjustly treated. One professor, who was also Jewish, pleaded with him about his attitudes regarding Hawaiians, intimating that his reference to the Jewish holocaust was both strange and irrelevant. None of the faculty mentioned the slide show directly, pretending they had not seen it. Neither did anyone express anger at the chair's intimidation in the meeting. The sense of the faculty seemed to be that he was still the chair and deserved their deference no matter how obscenely he behaved.

I had been spoken about in the third person for twenty minutes with not a single verbal acknowledgement of my presence in the room. Although all faculty invited by the chair had voted for me, none felt any obligation to speak to me directly. The scene moved toward the bizarre.

Not knowing what else to do or say, and feeling both humiliated and very angry, I asked for an opportunity to speak, which was granted, almost gladly, by the faculty. Of course, the chair still refused to recognize me. I recited the recent events that brought us to the present, reminding everyone, especially the chair, that I had survived a national search. I noted that the other finalist (who was *haole*) would never have been mistreated if she had been selected. To me, this was evidence enough that I was suffering discrimination because of my race and my politics. The chair's earlier comment that I was "unqualified" only underscored my point. I concluded by saying a letter of intent to hire should be drawn up immediately.

The faculty eagerly agreed. They understood events were out of control but were reluctant, even nervous, about moving ahead. They appeared incredibly cowed; to me, they seemed terrified.

Naturally, the chair refused to give me a letter. A few days later, after he let it be known to several faculty that he was reconsidering his announced decision to offer me the position, the personnel committee met with him, said they would not support his continuing refusal, and communicated as much to the chancellor. Several meetings ensued between the faculty and the administration in which the faculty continued to argue violations of procedures and "collegiality" by the chair. Eventually, the chancellor was asked by the faculty for a change in chairmanship and for permission to hire me.

Nothing happened.

"Racism" was never uttered by any of the faculty. Privately, some faculty told me they found events inexplicable, and when I proffered racism as an explanation, they became silent. I felt their world locked in everlasting refusal.

Our committee proceeded to assemble representatives from a half-dozen Hawaiian communities, from departments across the campus, and from student organizations. A meeting was planned between department representatives and our group.

In many ways, the encounter was a good illustration of the tensions between whites and Hawaiians in the colony. Although the behavior of our committee members was respectful, the department's two representatives, both white men, were visibly frightened by the physical presence of so many Hawaiians. The chair of my support group (also a white man and a faculty member from another department) presented our demand that I be hired as soon as possible. The rest of the committee expressed the general concern that I was being treated badly because I was Hawaiian and that various Hawaiian communities, once the word was out, would look very unfavorably on the situation.

Our support committee had decided it was absolutely crucial for the department to understand their situation. Accustomed to secrecy, they were being told that public exposure was imminent if I was not hired. In the long run, this constant threat of exposure kept the faculty moving toward a resolution.

By the end of April, there was a new acting chair. (The previous one had finally been forced to resign.) I was in the last stages of completing the dissertation, and my support committee was still planning strategy in the event that a letter was not tendered to me.

May and June were hectic. Department instability continued because the acting chair was to leave soon for a foreign country and another chair would need to be appointed. I was offered the job and, of course, accepted. But I began to be seen, in the subtlest of ways, as the source of embarrassment, much in the way rape victims are seen because they have brought shame to families or communities.

In addition, my high visibility as a spokesperson for Hawaiian rights continued to be discussed in various faculty meetings as already disruptive to the department given my problematic hire. My critical stance on the United States as an imperialist power in Hawai'i and around the world was seen as potentially dangerous if students were affected by my ideas. Slowly, my faculty supporters began to feel uncomfortably in the minority.

In July, four months after the faculty had voted for me, I defended my dissertation at Wisconsin, and became an assistant professor of American Studies at the University of Hawai'i. The struggle to get me hired was over, but undercurrents of bitterness remained only to resurface later.

Act Two: In the Land of the White Woman

Between the fall of 1981 and the fall of 1984 the chair of the department was a white woman. At first, I felt relief at having a new chair, especially one who had voted for me. A month into her appointment, however, I began to sense that nothing had changed. Intellectual, political, even stylistic differences became the source of heated conflict between us. Her belief that there existed a correct way—a culturally correct way—of speaking and behaving made it clear to me how white hegemony in Hawai'i and on the campus would mean a tight constraint on *my* cultural behaviors. I was to start acting, as we say in Hawaiian, as a *ho'ohaole,* someone who behaves like a white person. I was shocked, bemused, furious, and depressed. Very depressed.

I was told, for example, what to teach and what not to teach. In my required reading of an introductory course on American society, I had included sections on racism and capitalism as basic American institutions and ideologies. The chair pressured me to remove those sections and supplant them with units on the family and Christianity. I refused, but the disagreement left a bitter feeling between us.

Regarding faculty meetings, the chair tried to tell me what to say and what not to say, even how I should speak. After one faculty meeting, she took me aside to say that I should "treat the faculty appropriately." Given that I had disagreed with several senior faculty about their treatment of Asian foreign students, which I considered discriminatory, it was clear that she meant I was not to argue or challenge other faculty, especially as I was a junior member of the department. Of course, such constant directions to me resulted in constant fighting, as I very much resented being patronized.

During one of these arguments, the chair suggested I ought to be "grateful" to the faculty for hiring me. This kind of liberal paternalism infuriated me, for obvious reasons. It implied that I was not the most qualified person for the job, despite surviving a national search. It also meant that I was somehow to be her apprentice, that is, to occupy the inferior place white racists habitually reserve for their "dark" friends. Part of this status was evident on one occasion when I was introduced to some visiting faculty as "our little Hawaiian." Of course, it had never entered my mind to introduce the chair to visiting Hawaiians as "our little *haole.*"

Beyond these very telling incidents were larger controversies about my political analysis of historical events. The best case involved student complaints (all by *haole* students) about statements I made regarding genocide against American Indians as comparable to Nazi genocide against Jews. Using the complaints as an excuse, the chair tried to have me formally censured by the department. Despite support from my students disputing what the first set of students, who were not registered in my class, had alleged, the chair asked the personnel committee to censure me. I was not asked for my version of what had taken place. Moreover, the chair argued that by entering a formal complaint in my personnel file, evidence would be available later when I came up for tenure consideration. Finally, our faculty union was consulted, at my insistence. They told the committee, in writing, that neither the chair nor the committee had the power of censure, which was held by the administration. They also urged that a more informal settling of disagreements be attempted.

All except one member of the personnel committee supported the chair in her censuring effort. When they finally agreed to meet with me, the assumption was that I was guilty of unprofessional conduct and deserved a reprimand. Neither the supporting evidence of my students nor my own explanations were allowed into the discussion. Predictably, we never broached the subject of whether Americans *had* committed genocide against Indians, nor whether Hitler *had* used the example of U.S. treatment of Indians in his planning of the extermination of the Jews (which I had said, and which the students had complained about).[3]

To me, this case in particular seems so egregiously a violation of every tenet of university life: the right to teach certain analyses, the right to defend what is taught, the right to confront and wrangle over disagreement, the right to be free of harassment because of what is taught. And yet, such are the contours of racism, of the disgusting detail upon which the small freedom to teach a critical perspective is made to depend.

Finally, the chair had said that university rules prohibited me from teaching graduate courses (a requirement for tenure) until I was formally made a member of the graduate faculty. At the time, I accepted the statement as fact, but later it would prove to be false and thus part of my grievance argument that I had suffered discrimination.

By 1984 and the change in chairs, my relationship with the department was strained almost beyond repair. I had increased my public criticism of the treatment of Hawaiians, the failure of the state of Hawai'i to enforce our Native trusts and place Hawaiians on the land, the historic and contemporary power of white people in Hawai'i, and of the exploitative, prostituting effects of mass-based corporate tourism. I had criticized America and the state of Hawai'i in two national magazines, one national radio show, and in a BBC film about the Pacific. I had also traveled to the United Nations in Geneva to testify about America's overthrow of our government, illegal annexation of our islands, and continued abuse of our trust lands. This testimony was subsequently published in one of our local dailies.

Every occasion on which I made a public lecture or speech that was covered in the local press or, worse, in the national or international press created a flurry of discussion about the damaging reputation—that is, the reputation of a critical voice in a status profession—I was giving the department. As one letter writer to the local newspaper put it, there seemed to be a "department of un-American Studies at the University."

None of this is meant to convey some extraordinary level of activism on my part. In fact, there were other Hawaiians more publicly active, but they were not on the faculty. And that, more than anything, was the crucial line I had crossed. I was a public person in a little colonial university where public dissent, especially on the side of Natives, is perceived as outrageous and threatening. Hawai'i is not California, nor even Wisconsin. We have no "liberal" wing in our state government and certainly not in the university. There are no critical news stations or radical magazines in Hawai'i, and there is definitely no unified opposition. In short, there is widespread censorship, some of it self-induced, most of it institutionally enforced. Thus, my kind of public criticism habitually results in extreme overreactions on the part of the state government, the tourist industry, and American chauvinists (like American Studies faculty) in the islands. Because there is so little dissent, there is no tolerance of what little there is.

Act Three: The Pitched Battle

The next chair had been a member of the personnel committee that had tried to censure me. I had no doubts about the nature of his feelings or the style of his chairmanship. Like his predecessors, he was authoritarian, elitist, occasionally racist, and always hostile to any changes I suggested or privileges I desired.

The deterioration of working conditions made me rethink my whole strategy. Up until 1985, I had been operating defensively. Every little struggle began with my reaction to some policy on the part of the chairs. Despite worsening relations, and increasingly damaging yearly evaluations, I kept performing in the hope that my record of scholarship, teaching, and service, if excellent, would force the faculty to vote for tenure.

But a combination of factors shifted me into an offensive strategy. The first was the constant reference in discussions with the chairs and in my yearly evaluations to my "straining collegiality" in the department. Since "collegiality" was a requirement for tenure (a requirement, by the way, that had been added to departmental criteria only *after* I was hired), I sensed that "collegiality" would be the reason given for my eventual firing. The second factor was the impossible trap of being required to teach a graduate course for tenure consideration at the same time the chairs denied me an opportunity to do so.

Finally, when the department hired a white male assistant professor with a brand new Ph.D. and no publications or teaching experience and gave him a graduate course in his first year, I filed a sex and race discrimination grievance with our union. Before the filing, I tried one last time to talk the chair into allowing me to teach a required graduate course in my field. His answer, without explanation, was no.

The grievance forced the battle into the jarring light of public scrutiny. It took over a year and a half to come to completion during which time my relations with the past two chairs collapsed into near war. Since they were both named in the grievance, they both felt under attack. I alleged that I had been deceived, discriminated against, and obstructed in my professional duties—for example, teaching a graduate course—because of my race, my politics, and my gender. Because I was very critical of the United States, and because I was Hawaiian, I was being denied what noncritical white men, some of whom were less published than I, were being allowed as a matter of course. The whole episode smelled of white male privilege.

Our faculty union supported my efforts and greatly strengthened my arguments. Their presence forced the conflict out of an individual arena into an institutional one. The chairs now had to respond, even if perfunctorily, to an interested party outside the department.

As the grievance made its way through layers of administrative bureaucracy, it was interesting to analyze the responses. At the first two stages, the administration (in the person of a hearing officer) found for the department. This was not surprising, given that chairs are considered to be representatives of the administration in the departments. The basic finding had been that denying me a graduate course was a chair's managerial prerogative. On this reasoning, anyone could be denied all sorts of rights of employment. The principle of "fair rules fairly applied" would never make headway when chairs had such power.

At the third stage of the grievance, however, things began to change. The issue went to the union grievance committee and then to the full union board for a vote. This stage was crucial because my perceptions and arguments would be examined by other, noninvolved faculty. If the grievance committee recommended to the board, which subsequently voted to seek arbitration, then my peers saw merit in my case. Although this was not a judgment of the issue, it did give me an enormous boost of confidence when the Union moved quickly to the arbitration stage.

While both chairs had an opportunity to respond to my charges of sex and race discrimination at the first two stages of the grievance, they took a nonchalant attitude to the entire process. But when the union voted favorably, they began to harass board members, badgering them by phone about the alleged unfairness of the grievance committee procedures. Although the female chair had never complained about the procedures when she was on the Union Board, she found them suddenly biased. Finally, a long letter from both chairs to the union president emphasized that if my allegations were found to have merit by an outside arbitrator, the university could be in violation of federal civil rights laws.

The chairs' letter was intended to frighten the board, possibly even to force them to retract their support of my grievance. But it had the opposite effect. Board members were shocked at the crude efforts to influence them; eventually, the union president directed them to maintain confidentiality.

For me, the chairs' letter gave proof to my argument that every attempt I had made to discuss my situation resulted in being treated ever more like a pariah. The Union Board was now being harassed as I had been, and they did not like it. Unwittingly, the chairs illustrated the very conduct I had deplored.

By the time the university, the union, and I had agreed to an arbitrator, a change in personnel in the upper reaches of the administration had occurred. Drawn from the faculty, these new people dealt with grievances in a less adversarial manner, seeking negotiation rather than arbitration. Again, the public nature of arbitration gave the university pause. For the sake of image and for the well-being of faculty-administration relationships, in-house resolutions of conflict were preferred.

After three months of serious discussion, a satisfactory agreement was achieved. I was transferred to the Hawaiian Studies program and became the first full-time faculty member there. Given that I had been working with faculty across the campus on a Hawaiian Studies Task Force and had published in that area as well, it was a near perfect choice. For me, no other move could have been better.

My position was also transferred, which infuriated the powers at American studies. Since they were scheduled for a gradual loss of four positions through retirement, however, my unexpected departure actually helped them. They also did not have to worry about losing a grievance on sex and race discrimination. I had won, but I had also spent nearly five years under terrible employment conditions because I was both a Hawaiian nationalist and a critic of the United States. No victory, no matter how sweet, could repay those lost five years.

Conclusions: Simple Truths and Strategies

I applied for tenure in Hawaiian Studies in the fall of 1986. With a book, seven articles, and a good teaching record, I felt able to withstand scrutiny from anyone. An ad hoc committee unanimously recommended for tenure and promotion, which was granted by the Board of Regents in July of 1987.

As I look back at my long struggle, some basic truths emerge. The most important truth, I think, is that institutional racism and sexism cannot be fought alone. In my case, lack of tenure, indigenous status, and female gender placed me in a profoundly powerless situation. My politics exacerbated what, in any white department, would have been a disadvantaged position at the start. But a determined public posture as a Native nationalist in a colony guarantees repression. In this situation, it is a truism that the more besieged the activist, the greater the need for support.

A coalition of supporters must be formed for daily strategizing and as a core to organize a larger community group. For faculty who have attentive publics, like feminists, environmentalists, and African American, Asian, Chicano, and Native activists, this organizing effort will prove crucial when negotiations finally occur. And the group will remind both victim *and* institution that the politics of the issue encompass more than just the person involved.

In terms of strategy, the struggle must not bog down on individual players. For example, all three chairs in American Studies were discriminatory, but the first chair acted in such a freakish manner that it seemed for a while the problem was his alone. The behavior of the chairs over the next four and half years proved this wrong. But even if it were otherwise, the tendency to see events as individual acts must be countered by a smart political sense that tells us as people of color when institutional racism is operating. Political analysis must always be primary when formulating strategy.

Tactically, public exposure is the best weapon in fighting an institution whose actions depend on secrecy. In Hawai'i, the myth of racial harmony, indeed, of a veritable racial paradise has so thoroughly obscured the existence of racism against Native Hawaiians that any charge of such is considered false on its face. Beyond our specific problems, universities in general are nervous about racism because they purport to uphold principles long since negated by the rest of the business world. It is always wise to hold the university to its professed ideals because the potential for embarrassment is large.

Other tactical lessons are less central but good to know, such as the fact that liberal supporters who have no professed ideology or analysis and are just "nice people" will be duly shocked by racism, and will offer private expressions of sympathy, but will refuse to join a support committee. They suffer from the fear of public activity that afflicts so many academics. Of course, in my case, such people had nothing to lose, while most of the Hawaiians who supported me had much to lose—a day's pay or other difficulties with work or even families—but felt the injustice so keenly they were willing to take some risks. Professors, especially white men, were generally unwilling to take risks.

In addition, a few supporters were able to go part of the way but gave up at some point because the struggle dragged on and on. This kind of attrition is predictable but must not be allowed to affect the issues or the strategies. Still, more than any other obstacle, this depletion of forces depresses the group. In my case, the Union filled a big gap here because their staff were both paid and emotionally distant.

And as far as unions go, it is my absolute belief that people of color need unions (even mediocre ones) because having *some* institutional voice is better than having *no* institutional voice. The "white male boy's club" is for white males, and on occasion, for compliant white females. But it is no protection for activist faculty of color.

The most obvious conclusion is that racism and sexism are the evil within. Nothing—not the sixties, not Third World wars of liberation, not a minuscule middle class of people of color—has changed any of that. Everywhere in the academy racism and sexism and a host of other oppressive creatures are festering and growing.

While speaking out on controversial issues is apparently protected at universities, there are countless stories of denied tenure that tell a different truth, thus, the struggle for faculty of color who are also activists includes free speech, not only academic freedom. In my case, references to the confusion between my roles as "citizen" and "professor" appeared in my yearly job renewals as causes of collegial "strain." I had replied that no distinction exists between the categories. The chair, however, argued that political speech *by* a *professor* is inappropriate *in the public realm*. Of course, they meant *critical* political speech. Professors who supported the status quo never had the problems I did. Given that political speech is absolutely protected speech, it is not difficult to see why the chairs attempted such stupid distinctions.

This denial to faculty of the role of "public intellectuals" is one of the most serious abridgements now taking place in universities. Of all the institutions in society, the university is the one that has an obligation to analyze, criticize, and provoke in the public realm. Without this, the role of "public intellectual" will be filled by gadflies, entrepreneurs, or publicity hounds. And the function of public criticism will pass from the university altogether.

This brings me to a last point, which is, as well, a beginning: resistance. More than verbal disagreement, resistance takes organization, planning, and a tenacity that develops and sustains individual and group capacities. For women of color, especially those who are very public in their positions as intellectuals and as activists, there is no other alternative but vigilance and struggle. Without it, institutions wear us down by petty bureaucratic procedures and the force of inertia.

As someone who has persevered over the years, I can truthfully say that resistance is its own reward.

Notes

1. See an incisive article by Ralph Steuber, "Twentieth-Century Educational Reform in Hawai'i," *Journal of the College of Education* (University of Hawai'i at Mānoa) 20 (1981). Steuber writes that schooling in Hawai'i is "a tiny but significant part of the total impact of western and American imperialism in the Pacific." According to the University of Hawai'i Equal Employment Opportunity (EEO) office, there were thirteen tenured Hawaiian faculty and 660 tenured *haole* faculty in 1989. The underrepresentation of Hawaiians on the faculty has remained the same for twenty years.

2. Frantz Fanon, to me, has much to say about the effects of colonial education. He writes, "Colonialism is not satisfied with merely holding a people in its grip and emptying the native's brain of all form and content. By a kind of perverted logic, it turns to the past of the oppressed people, and distorts, disfigures, and destroys it. This work of devaluing pre-colonial history takes on a dialectical significance today." From *The Wretched of the Earth* (New York: Grove Press, 1968), p. 210.

3. See John Toland's account of what Hitler thought of America's extermination of the "red savages" in *Adolf Hitler* (New York: Doubleday, 1976), p. 702.

The Politics of Academic Freedom as the Politics of White Racism

In 1990 and 1991, a huge controversy erupted in Hawai'i over my letter to a student newspaper chiding a white male student for complaining about our word for white people, haole. *The details of the controversy are clear in this speech, which was delivered at a panel on academic freedom called by the Peace Institute on the University of Hawai'i campus. Eventually, the institute published an entire book on the controversy. But what is most amazing is the worldwide coverage of the effort by the university to sanction me for my written speech: articles appeared in various newspapers on the American continent, including the* Los Angeles Times *and the* New York Times; *in Europe and Japan, Australia and New Zealand; and even in places such as Sri Lanka and India. My own opinion about this coverage is that Hawai'i's global reputation as a "paradise" of racial relations made my statement shocking. After all, lots of Natives tell white Americans where to go, but not in Hawai'i.*

Tonight, I am going to relate a story that begins with the genocide of a Native people and ends with an attempt to silence one of their survivors and fiercest defenders. It is a story of white cultural and economic imperialism in its broadest outlines and of white hegemony and white racism on this campus. Specifically, it is a story of the politics of academic freedom as the politics of white racism.

For Hawaiians, American colonialism has been a violent process: the violence of mass death, the violence of American missionizing, the violence of cultural destruction, the violence of the American military. Once the United States annexed my homeland, a new kind of violence took root: the violence of educational colonialism, where foreign *haole* values replace Native Hawaiian values; where schools, such as the University of Hawai'i, ridicule Hawaiian culture and praise American culture, and where white men assume the mantle of authority, deciding what is taught, who can teach, even what can be said, written, and published.

In colony Hawai'i, the University of Hawai'i stands atop the educational pyramid of the state. Like the military, the university is a guardian of white cultural dominance. The standard American university curriculum, bureaucratic structure, and white male faculty characterize the institution. People of color comprise over 75 percent of the student body, while the faculty is over 75 percent *haole*. For Hawaiians, the situation is even worse: thirteen tenured Hawaiian faculty compare with nearly 660 white faculty. This situation constitutes institutional racism, the institutional dominance of white people over people of color.

Enter into this white male university a white male student named Joey Carter, lately come from the American South, where whites are not only dominant but where white supremacist organizations are on the rise. Complaining in a public letter to the student paper, *Ka Leo*, Carter mistakenly says that words like "*haole*-dominated" society and "puppet-*haole* governments" are racist; that "*haole*" is like the word "nigger"; that white repression, persecution, and domination of nonwhites is "supposed" (as opposed to actual); that he was chased and beaten by locals because of his skin and eye color; and finally ending his complaint by asserting that people are individuals (as opposed to members of historical groups) who "classify" themselves as they like.

Clearly, Mr. Carter was feeling uncomfortable in Hawai'i, where white people do not have the usual majority status nor the unquestioned ability to categorize others as they do on the American continent.

Quickly following this letter came dozens of replies in *Ka Leo*, including my own, in which Carter was instructed about his place, history, and role in Hawai'i.[1] Educating Carter about the history of white Americans, I explained that "*haole*" is in fact one of the few surviving Hawaiian language descriptions in common use in Hawai'i. I went on to say that Carter's appeal to "individual" exemption from the power and privilege of white hegemony is itself a typical American ploy to avoid responsibility for an ugly and vicious history that visited genocide on American Indians, slavery on Africans, peonage on Asians, and dispossession of both lands and self-government on Native Hawaiians. I informed Carter that he is a direct beneficiary, as are all white people, of racism, of a system of power in which one racially identified group dominates and exploits another racially identified group for the benefit of the exploiting group. In the United States people of color do *not* have the power to practice racism against white people. The same is true in Hawai'i, particularly in regard to Native Hawaiians who, contrary to Carter's beliefs, are not free to classify themselves but are legally classified under American law by blood quantum. Hawaiians of 50 percent blood quantum are Native; those with less blood quantum are not Native.

Finally, I argued that the hatred and fear people of color have of white people is born of experience, the experience of white violence. Therefore, it is for self-protection and in self-defense that people of color feel hostility toward the *haole*. This hostility, I went on, is not "*haole*-bashing" but a smart political sense of survival. There is no reason why people who have suffered genocide and land dispossession and who continue to be dominated by white people should like or trust them. It is our prerogative, as the Native people of Hawai'i, to decide whether, if at all, we should extend our trust and friendship to any *haole*. I closed my statement by suggesting that if Mr. Carter did not like Hawai'i, our language, or our ways of doing things, he could leave, since Hawaiians would certainly benefit from one less *haole* in our homeland.

My article was published on September 19, 1990. Five days later, on September 24, Larry Laudan, chair of the philosophy department and himself a recently arrived *haole* in Hawai'i, wrote a letter to the vice-president for academic affairs, Paul Yuen, demanding my public reprimand for voicing such views and arguing that I was an administrator and therefore a spokesperson for the university. His request was followed by a philosophy department resolution, called a "Statement on Racism in Academe," alleging that my public reply to Carter was "racist," condoned "violence against a member of the university community solely because of his social identity and opinions," and consequently betrayed a "most basic professional responsibility," which they defined as a "special duty to protect and sustain the fragile atmosphere within which ideas can be assessed on their merits."[2] Specifically, the philosophy department alleged that my invitation to Carter to leave Hawai'i was similar to a white professor declaring black students unwelcome and proposing that they return to Africa. This resolution was sent by Laudan to Yuen on October 15, 1990, requesting that I be removed from my position as director of the Center for Hawaiian Studies, which they alleged was a position of administrative authority.

This resolution was distributed widely to the press by Larry Laudan and others and was answered by President Albert J. Simone on November 2, 1990. Simone assured his good friend "Larry" that "administrators may not speak for the University of Hawai'i without appropriate consultation with senior officers of the University." The president ended his letter by saying that his administration does not condone creating an "unfriendly, intimidating, and non-supportive environment for faculty and students.[3]

On November 3, 1990, the faculty union of the University of Hawai'i reaffirmed academic freedom at the university "for the expression of all points of view regarding the racial issues recently raised on the Mānoa campus," and endorsing fair and open debate about race, colonialism, and any other related issues in Hawai'i. The union went on to reaffirm its position that chairs and directors are not administrators but faculty included in the collective bargaining unit and as such are free to speak their minds without fear of sanction by the university administration.[4]

On November 8, 1990, President Simone announced his intention to conduct an investigation into my statements, thus violating all semblance of confidentiality, something he prizes for white men. Simone told *The Honolulu Advertiser* (9 November 1990) by phone from Japan that he believed I was an administrator and that administrators must accept "the principle that some things are better off not said publicly." I think it is clear that Simone had made up his mind by this point: my public statements were *not* protected by academic freedom or free speech.

While Simone conducted his investigation, the faculty senate began their own, triggered by the same philosophy department resolution. For the first time in its history, the senate, another white male bastion, decided to investigate a fellow faculty member for written public statements. Without precedent and procedures, the senate moved ahead on the basis of the philosophy department resolution alone. Thus, by the middle of November a "witch hunt" had begun in earnest, and the white male "boy's club" was hysterical with venom. Indeed, white men led the charge, with people like Gary Fuller of the geography department comparing me to Hitler and Sadaam Hussein, and Dick Miller of the William S. Richardson School of Law telling the faculty senate that my thinking was similar to that which led to the rise of Nazi Germany and resulted in the internment of Japanese Americans. Ken Kipnis, of the philosophy department, meanwhile, told one of my faculty supporters that the Hawaiian Movement was like the Ku Klux Klan and that I would have to decide whether I wanted to be a professor or a member of the movement. Charges of impending violence against white people surfaced everywhere, with the most virulent being made by Larry Laudan himself, proclaiming that I was giving "hunting licenses" to my students and other Hawaiians to beat up *haole*. This is the same Larry Laudan who told KHON news that my "brand of radicalism" did not belong in a university, while attacking a rally in my defense as a form of "terrorism" on campus.

Despite my numerous calls, and those of my supporters, for Laudan and others who disagreed with me to come forward and debate the issues, I was charged and condemned in the media and in the faculty senate as a racist. The phenomenon known as McCarthyism—where individuals are accused falsely, and never given an opportunity to confront or disprove their accusers—began to characterize the campus atmosphere. Hate calls and mail began to surface in the Hawaiian Studies office, *Ka Leo* ran a poll asking if students thought I was a racist, and stickers began to appear on campus, attacking me personally and raising the specter of violence by white supremacist groups. Meanwhile, the faculty senate proceeded, as did President Simone, both determined to condemn me without once speaking with me. Indeed, most of my accusers had never read or thought seriously about my statement. They were content to read the philosophy department summary or the ellipses in the Honolulu dailies. The implication seemed to be that white men do not lie, so why read what the Native said, just trust the interpretation of her statements by knowledgeable white men.

And of course this is where the problem began. The philosophy department, like Joey Carter, is ignorant of scholarly and novelistic studies and portrayals of racism. Thinking that racism is a matter of color and not of history and power, the philosophy department intentionally misread my statements, which Larry Laudan then viciously recast, saying I was justifying violence against Carter. However, I never justified violence against Carter, only our rights as Native and oppressed people to feel hostility toward the *haole.* Just as Palestinians are justified in their hostility toward Israelis, just as Jews are justified in their hostility toward Germans, just as the Northern Irish are justified in their hostility toward the British, just as all exploited peoples are justified in feeling hostile and resentful toward those who exploit them, so we Hawaiians are justified in such feelings toward the *haole.* This is the legacy of racism, of colonialism.

I explained the long history of white violence against people of color precisely to educate Joey Carter about his place and history. For it is white people and *not* people of color who have a history of violence against others. In Hawai'i, it is the *haole* who stole our land, took our government, destroyed our nationhood, and suppressed our culture. It is white people who created laws to divide Hawaiians by blood quantum; it is white people who created institutions foreign to our ways of life; it is white people who brought capitalism to Hawai'i. In other words, it is white people who, for their own benefit, have exploited and oppressed Hawaiians. Carter, like most white people, did not know or want to learn any of this. But if I did not argue for violence against *haole,* then why did the philosophy department and their vicious chairman say that I did?

The answer I believe lies in the fears and resentments of the *haole* themselves. Here in Hawai'i *haole* have grown accustomed to the myth of racial harmony created and reinforced by the politicians and the tourist industry. *Haole* live in predominantly white or Asian neighborhoods, and if they know anything at all about Hawaiians, it is that we have a funny unpronounceable language, we appear on television as activists or other lawbreakers trying to stop development, and we have a deep wound, called the *overthrow,* when the all-white American government took our sovereignty. Yes, *haole* in Hawai'i are nervous because they know wrongs were committed in their names and for their benefit.

So, when an uppity Native woman educates one of their own about his white history and his obligations to Natives, their fears and angers spill over into crazy accusations that, if examined, reflect back on their own sick history of violence. As Frantz Fanon has taught us, dark skin and dark people are the classic bogeyman of the *haole.* White people know that all over the world people of color have been brutally and unjustly treated by white imperialism. White people know how violent they have been to each other and to us and they know our grievances are real; and thus they imagine how much more violent we would be to them, with our *real* history of violations. This is why every demand for respect and recognition of dignity on our part is read as a sign of violence. This is why white people so fear black people in the United States, despite the fact that it is white people who have a history of violence against black people and not the other way around. White violence, then, has a long and sick history—in the world, in the Americas, in the Pacific, and right here in Hawai'i. And this continues to be denied. The denial is evident in the philosophy department resolution.

For white male power and white racism are alive and well on this campus. Where else but in a colony would a Native woman be investigated by three committees for exercising her right as a Native and a citizen to publicly criticize a white man? Where else but in a colony would white administrators talk babble about "responsible" speech? Do they mean the "responsible" speech of Larry Laudan defending certain forms of sexual harassment in a student publication called *Voices*? Or the "responsible" speech of Ian Reid, another white man and faculty member, arguing the mental inferiority of women in the same student magazine? Or the "responsible" speech of Dick Miller accusing me of creating an atmosphere similar to the one that led to Nazi Germany and the internment of the Japanese? Or the "responsible" speech of Ken Kipnis comparing the Hawaiian Movement to the KKK, when our movement has never been violent? Is this speech "responsible" because it was spoken by white men in support of continued white male power?

Indeed, in the long history of Hawai'i, it is white people who killed Hawaiians, beat Filipinos and Japanese on the plantations, and lynched and shot workers and denied them decent wages. It is white people who wanted statehood and who continue to deny us sovereignty. It is white people who continue to live on stolen Hawaiian land and thereby benefit from our dispossession.

Thus, "responsible" speech, as it is defined by white men, creates the parameters of academic freedom. White men can say all manner of dangerous, violent, and false things—and tell absolute lies, in fact, like the lies of Miller, Kipnis, Laudan, and the rest—and their speech is acceptable. But when an articulate Native woman speaks the truth about the *haole,* she must be reprimanded, removed, and shut up. No academic freedom for her, nor free speech either, because by definition, dissenting speech, speech that criticizes and opposes the prevailing system of colonial domination, cannot be "responsible."

Why? Because such speech is dangerous. It is the voice of political analysis and of a critical, alternative intellectual tradition. In my specific case, what I wrote in my newspaper article was the truth, the unalloyed, ugly truth about *haole* power in the United States and in Hawai'i. This truth has anchored a great tradition of resistance created by Black and American Indian and Palestinian and Asian and Pacific Islander peoples. Further, this tradition is unknown and untaught by most *haole* in this university, which means by nearly 80 percent of the faculty. Native people *do* have a claim to feel hostility toward their oppressors, and Hawaiians *would* benefit from one less *haole* in Hawai'i. In fact, we would benefit from thousands less, beginning with the military. Indeed, Native people all over the world would benefit if their colonizers went home.

So we come to the last McCarthy-like accusation by the philosophy department: I am guilty of racial harassment because my public statement created a "climate of intimidation" for Joey Carter.[5]

First, let us be clear about what Joey Carter did. He wrote a public statement in a public forum, stating a position for which he alone is responsible. Part of that responsibility is that he must answer for his argument and for the reactions it provokes, both favorable and unfavorable, just as I am responsible for my public statements. But when Carter received unfavorable responses, from myself and others, he chose to blame his personal misfortunes on me and then to run away from the controversy. This in itself is irresponsible. In other words, Carter wanted to dish out nasty remarks, but he did not want to be responsible for them.

Let us pursue the question of a "climate" of racial intimidation. How did I intimidate Carter when I have never met, seen, or spoken with him? Indeed, to my knowledge, I have never even been near him. Am I, then, one of those primitive Natives with all sorts of "black magic" at my disposal, who conjures up climate systems, say rain or snow or in this case racial intimidation, at the scribble of my pen? Apparently I am, or so think Larry Laudan, Ken Kipnis, Dick Miller, and a host of other white men.

To discover whether I created a "climate of intimidation," Tom Gething, the university's dean of students, investigated Joey Carter's allegations against me. After several months of inquiry, he released his report. The following is a direct quote from Dean Gething's findings:

> I have found no evidence that Dr. Trask, who has never met or spoken with Mr. Carter, discriminated against him in regard to his race or color. . . . I have found considerable evidence that a hostile environment in regard to race or color exists at the University of Hawai'i–Mānoa. This condition existed prior to Mr. Carter's column and Dr. Trask's response. It is clear, moreover, that the existence of this hostile environment was brought to the attention of the community and was highlighted by the two columns and the ensuing events. . . . However, I have been unable to determine a cause-and-effect relationship between either Mr. Carter or Dr. Trask and the existence of this condition.[6]

Dean Gething says nothing in his report about the racist historical antecedents of this "hostile environment." I have suggested that they are to be found, for anyone interested in searching them out, in the colonization of Hawai'i.

A hostile climate *does* exist at the University of Hawai'i, and the best evidence of it lies strewn all over the campus in hate flyers calling for the physical dismemberment of an Asian woman who is an antiwar protester and supporter of mine, describing a black student from Nigeria who had the courage to support me as a "nigger" and a "dumb black boy," and calling me a "dominating lesbian sex offender."

But these are only flyers, you say. Well then, let us turn to white men in their classes, such as Mark Merlin of the department of general science, who my students have complained about to the administration because he teaches that the royal insignia of our *ali'i,* called *lei palaoa,* are made out of female pubic hair. Or let us take Gary Fuller, who compared me to Hitler and whom my students also complained about because he says Hawaiian language is dead and not worth learning. Or a number of political science and history professors who say that Hawaiians practiced infanticide when no credible evidence exists that we did. Or all the snide, off-the-cuff remarks that tell Hawaiian students their culture is primitive, undeveloped, or inauthentic. Does this create a hostile racial environment? Is this a form of racial intimidation? Or is this just history—white colonial history—that no one, not the philosophy department, not the administration, and certainly not the white press, is about to protest or investigate or condemn?

Yes, there certainly is a hostile environment on this campus, an environment that is similar to colonial environments in occupied countries all over the world, an environment that is Native-hating, that keeps power in the hands of the colonizers, and that attacks any dissenting voice, any political alternative. Intimidation on this campus is enforced by white racist ideology that praises and reproduces white racist culture and ensures the dominance of white faculty, white administrators, and white curriculum. This situation constitutes "intimidation" and worse.

This situation constitutes racism—the racism of white men with access to power, of Larry Laudan and the philosophy department, of certain members of the faculty senate, and of President Al Simone and his administration, the racism of members of one racially identified group—the *haole*—who oppress and subordinate another racially identified group—Hawaiians and other people of color—for the benefit of the exploiting group. For who benefits if Hawaiians are degraded, if they are kept to a small population on campus, if one of their number is publicly investigated and removed? Who benefits? White power benefits, and white men benefit. Hawaiians, of course, lose. They lose a voice, they lose a fighter, they lose a place where defiance is taught and encouraged. And all of us lose the richness of critical ideas, cultures, and people.

Academic freedom, then—the freedom to learn, to teach, to argue, and above all, to dissent—is determined by white men. If they do not like what you say, they will try to shut you up by punitive actions and public vilification.

Let me just end by way of an update. All three investigations triggered by my column have been concluded in my favor: nothing I did was worthy of reprimand or removal. But the message of all this investigating is simply this: if, in a public forum, faculty members of color exercise the right to argue a position that is contrary to, and critical of, white ideology, they will be investigated. Moves by white faculty or white students against people of color will be protected, however. The fact that President Al Simone has said to the *Honolulu Star-Bulletin* that publishing flyers calling for the physical dismemberment of an Asian woman who is an antiwar protester is the same as my supporters holding a rally and my Hawaiian Studies program publishing a newsletter reveals that the president has lost all sense of proportion. In particular, the Nazi-like quality of the flyer against Mari Matsuoka, calling for her "sterilization" and the "fumigation" of this "vermin" from the campus is shocking. The combination of superpatriotic militaristic ideology in the flyer with this call for physical harm against Mari is a clear sign of the vicious intent of these racists. How President Simone can compare this to public statements in support of my position, although dissenting from his own, is remarkable. It seems that the president cannot distinguish between signed public disagreement that is in opposition to white ideology and anonymous death threats. Even the police consider such threats to be criminal and a violation of state law. But we have a president who thinks such behavior is only "deplorable" and not criminal and who thinks that dissent equals physical harm.

To me, this state of affairs proves what I have been saying, as a Hawaiian and an intellectual, all along. White men protect white men, this university protects white hegemony. If any of you had doubts about this, the latest response from President Simone equating public dissent with death threats proves my point. I am certain the president would not think the same about death threats to white men.

Please think about the comparisons I have drawn. When dark people are treated with less dignity than white people, that is, when Hawaiians and Asians and other people of color suffer racism, and when threats against their safety are considered unimportant, indeed frivolous, we are living in dangerous times.

Postscript: The controversy was actually more physically threatening than I explained in my speech. I received five hours of taped hate calls, including death threats, at my home. My Hawaiian female students received rape threats from white male students. My staff at the Center for Hawaiian Studies received threatening phone calls at work, and an assistant professor and I were physically threatened by a white man, age 56, at my office. Although most of this was known to the president or his staff, none of it was considered as dangerous as my letter to the student paper. It is obvious that in Hawai'i, where Hawaiians fill up the prisons, harassing and threatening us is keeping the peace. But criticizing white men is perceived as a danger to the entire social order.

Notes

1. Letter by Haunani-Kay Trask, "Caucasians are haole," *Ka Leo o Hawai'i* (September 19, 1990), p. 5.

2. Faculty of the Philosophy Department, University of Hawai'i–Mānoa, "A Statement on Racism in Academe," in *Restructuring for Ethnic Peace: A Public Debate at the University of Hawai'i*, Majid Tehranian, ed. (Honolulu, University of Hawai'i Institute of Peace, 1991), pp. 180–181. This article was reprinted from the student newspaper of the University of Hawai'i–Mānoa, *Ka Leo o Hawai'i* (October 26, 1990).

3. Letter by President Albert J. Simone, 2 November 1990. See in *Restructuring for Ethnic Peace*, p. 174.

4. Resolution of the Board of the University of Hawai'i Professional Assembly (the faculty union). See in *Restructuring for Ethnic Peace*, p. 174.

5. See in *Restructuring for Ethnic Peace*, p. 180.

6. See Dean Gething's findings in *Restructuring for Ethnic Peace*, p. 19.

During the controversy over the university's racist attempt to censure me because of my speech, President George Bush visited Hawai'i. The *Honolulu Advertiser* cartoonist captured my anti-American sentiment even as he deplored my resistance. The caricature of the nerdy philosophy professor enraged many university faculty who believe college campuses should be serene havens from the rough world of politics. (Reprinted by permission of Dick Adair, *The Honolulu Advertiser*.)

Over 300 students, faculty, and community people rallied in front of the philosophy department to protest a demand that the administration remove Trask as Director of the Center for Hawaiian Studies. This photograph was reprinted in the *Los Angeles Times*, Japanese newspapers, and other media around the Pacific and Asia. My defiance made good copy, but so did my leis and "Native dress." To a world saturated with tourist propaganda about Hawai'i, defiant Hawaiians are news. (Photo by Charles Okamura, reprinted by permission of *The Honolulu Advertiser*.)

Corky Trinidad, cartoonist for the *Honolulu Star-Bulletin*, saw very clearly that the McCarthy-like actions of the philosophy department were motivated by their fear of a Native culture they knew nothing about. He caricatured them as ivory-tower buffoons scared to death by activism and the dreaded "H" word. Because we knew this, the "H" word was used over and over in signs and speeches, making sure they understood that *haole* means white foreigner.

Haunani-Kay Trask at a teach-in at the University of Hawai'i during the free speech controversy. (Photo by Carl Viti, reprinted by permission of *The Honolulu Advertiser*.)

A *haole* woman supporter at the protest rally at the philosophy department summed up our analysis of the politics of their department. (Photo by Ed Greevy.)

Native Student Organizing: The Case of the University of Hawai'i

Like most Native programs in American universities, Hawaiian Studies was founded only after a long struggle, which included endless lobbying of two university administrations and of three state legislative sessions for funding. We had to contend with a lawsuit designed to stop our Hawaiian studies building and with hostile white faculty on the campus who thought, predictably, that Natives should not have five acres to themselves to teach about their culture and people.

Hawaiian Studies, both in theory and in reality, became a site of engagement. This locus of struggle generated enormous public attention and thereby attracted more Hawaiians to our campus and to our center.

Like many such programs on the American continent, Hawaiian studies was born of intense resistance. For ten years prior to our establishment in 1987, Hawaiians throughout our archipelago were engaged in struggles for the land. These included efforts to stop military misuse of lands; to protect our lush natural environment, including wetlands, coastal regions, and agricultural lands; and to prevent urbanization. Eventually, land struggles became part of the push for Hawaiian sovereignty. Given that the United States had invaded Hawai'i in 1893, overthrown our Queen, Lili'uokalani, and put in her place an all-white sugar planter oligarchy, Hawaiians organized to reconstitute our government. Today, some twenty years since the beginning of the sovereignty movement, we are still fighting for reestablishment of our

Native nation, the return of two million acres of Native lands, and inclusion in the federal policy on Native self-determination in the United States.

Hawaiian Studies is part of the larger Hawaiian sovereignty movement. We are part of the struggle for Native control over Native lands and Native communities. We represent Hawaiians in resistance at the University of Hawai'i, and we are consciously focused on training cadres for the nationalist front of our movement. My students come into our center, then, partly because we are engaged in the study of our culture and history but also because we are Native nationalists.

For students, as for any other organic group, organizing occurs at the site of engagement. The campus—where students study, live, and work—is the primary site of their resistance. This is not to say that students do not participate in community efforts, but the main arena of student resistance is the campus. It has to be, since that is where the forces of power penetrate and construct student lives.

Given the campus focus, then, one of the first targets for student engagement is usually the multiple centers of control over student life. Good examples here include the administration of universities, that is, various offices of the president or chancellor, student services, even, at times, the Board of Regents.

These are power centers where policy is made and unmade. Another arena is student government, where the fiction of student empowerment is often invoked to mask the unequal power relationship between students and administration. At the University of Hawai'i, student government for many years was nothing more than a training ground for state politics. Rarely did student government officers represent students. They were usually too busy serving the interests of the university's central administration, making contacts for later use when they would move on to lucrative positions in the state legislature or county government.

But if past individuals used student government only as a stepping stone to electoral politics outside the university, student government as a political entity *itself* is always a potential critical site of resistance. Because the institution of student government commands resources, such as student fees, a physical space, and support staff, it is ripe for takeover by progressive forces. Additionally, university administrators, Boards of Regents, and the press also assume the authority of student government to represent students, thus conveying legitimacy. As a legally created, recognized voice, student government can be captured by progressive forces, just as state governments can be captured by revolutionaries.

Other ready-made campus arenas can also be taken over by progressive forces: for example, official student newspapers, student housing or co-ops, sports facilities, even parking structures. Potential sites of engagement are where students predominate, even if they have no well-defined roles in those institutions or structures, and even if, as students, they do not fully comprehend their own potential. After all, cadre organizing exists precisely to increase consciousness of radical potential.

To say, however, that these areas are sites of engagement does not imply that only campus concerns shape student issues. Far from it. When I was an undergraduate and graduate student at the University of Wisconsin from the late 1960s through the mid-seventies, the Vietnam War focused a great deal of our organizing and protest. The Black Civil Rights Movement came also to define our resistance as did one of its offshoots, the fight for a Black Studies (now African American) studies program. We were so vocal as students that the governor of the state of Wisconsin called in several thousand troops to "maintain order," as he put it. In truth, the naked power of the state was forced into the open by unruly, protesting youth at the university.

Predictably, the very presence of engagement, or political resistance, challenges the ideological and actual power of the state to maintain order. The value of resistance inheres in the challenge to authority. Unmasking state or other institutional power is part of the value of resistance. When governors call out the military to quell civil disturbances on campus or off, the hidden fist of state authority, that is, military power, is made obvious and tangible.

Exposing state power and its mechanism is, in itself, a public good; indeed, it is a revolutionary good. The lines between liberatory practices and oppressive practices are drawn much more clearly when power is exposed. For example, the struggle over affirmative action when taken into public spaces forces the state into conflict with its insurgent citizens. This conflict goes some distance in revealing the extent and nature of state power. Put another way, citizens come to understand the constraints that entangle and disable them when they organize to change the very institutions that possess power over their daily lives.

On campuses, the continuous struggle for affirmative action draws out the racism of a state system of education, and beyond that, the racism of American ideology and politics in general. Without such challenge, the absence of people of color on campuses is naturalized, is made to seem representative of the existing order of things. The presence of so many white people—or in the Hawaiian case, so many non-Natives—on our campuses is made to appear as a kind of Darwinian natural selection instead of the intended result of entrenched systems of class and race and settler discrimination.

The challenge of Hawaiian Studies, indeed our very presence, and my particular relationship to the powers that be, generated so much resistance on the part of the administration and some faculty departments that we were under siege for nearly a decade. First, in 1991, the university tried to remove me as director of Hawaiian studies because I wrote a letter to the campus newspaper chiding a white male student for publicly complaining about our word for white people, that is, *haole*. I said, rather simply, that if he did not like the word or our language and heritage, including our homeland of Hawai'i, then he could leave our beautiful islands, since we would certainly benefit from one less *haole* in Hawai'i.

That letter generated a firestorm of protest, including calls for my removal by the faculty senate, the university president, and a few *haole* male departments like the philosophy department and the law school. For the active Hawaiian Studies students, however, this incident precipitated a historical moment for organizing. Forming themselves as Make'e Pono, the student group took on the university student newspaper, which ran a series of racist cartoons and polls targeting me, Hawaiians in general, and the students in Hawaiian Studies. Make'e Pono was so active that they became, for a time, the focus of political protest by right-wing students and organizations on campus.

But as a result of their involvement in defending me, Make'e Pono students experienced a heightened consciousness regarding the oppression of Hawaiians on campus. Soon, they began to see that student government, as well as the student newspaper, had a certain amount of visibility and power. Alleged "student institutions" controlled budgets, offices, telephones, and, perhaps most critically, they possessed a certain status. To speak as a student senator or better, as student body president, meant that status accrued to that position and thereby to the person who occupied it.

Learning quickly, Make'e Pono organized to field candidates for office. They did not have a slate, but they had a decolonizing consciousness. Although only a few students were elected as senators, Hawaiians realized that capturing student government would only be a matter of time. Moreover, their experience sent a message to other Native students that organizing could bring power.

Subsequent student groups, such as Kūikalāhiki, set their goals at running candidates for each general election. They also became a voice for other arenas of resistance, such as the use and correct spelling of the Hawaiian language. They argued for the hiring of a civil rights counselor in student services, partly to relieve the burden carried by Hawaiian Studies but also as an acknowledgment that student civil rights were under assault and needed an officer outside the faculty to help in protecting students. Through their efforts, the general campus awareness regarding Hawaiians, racism against us, and campus hostility continued to increase.

This consciousness, like that of the general public, was also increased by the larger sovereignty movement in the archipelago. In one sense, organizing around sovereignty in the political realm spilled over into the university. Hawaiian Studies was led by faculty who actively supported sovereignty and were enrolled citizens of the largest sovereignty organization, Ka Lāhui Hawai'i. Public political commentary was offered by the faculty on all Hawaiian matters—from indigenous burials to antieviction struggles, gathering rights, and, of course, sovereignty. Undoubtedly, our students followed the example of their *kumu,* or "teachers": they committed themselves to engagement in the Native issues of the day.

But on another level, our students chose their own path. Their issues reflected their own concerns, and the ground upon which those issues were enacted was the classroom, student government, and the university administration. The sites of student engagement, then, illustrate the concerns of the students more than their teachers. That is as it should be.

Our current student group, Kālai Pō, followed in the footsteps of the trailblazers before them. They, too, resisted racism on the campus. In their case, their group was formed when two sisters, one eight months pregnant, were removed from their "Geography of Hawai'i" class because they challenged the *haole* professor about his racist misrepresentations of Hawaiian history. They were escorted out of class by four campus security guards. The charge was that their questioning disturbed the class, preventing the teacher from continuing. In fact, they disturbed the professor's lies about Hawaiians committing infanticide, demanding that he provide historical evidence to substantiate his claim. He had them removed on no other grounds than that he did not like their criticism of his racist history.

The fact that the sisters were indigenous Hawaiians is central to this case. They had learned that the allegation of Hawaiian infanticide in traditional times was a missionary fabrication when they took my required Hawaiian Studies class on "Myths of Hawaiian History."

Here, we can see how the teaching of Native history becomes a political project: decolonizing Native minds produces a volatile political atmosphere. Of course, the history of *haole* does not generate resistance among *haole* because their history is taught in a celebratory way. Whatever resistance develops in such courses tends to be from individual students. But teaching people of color the prevailing American racist histories of people of color, especially the "savage" Native or "genetically inferior" African American, often generates insurgency by students of color. In this way does the teaching of our history become a much contested arena, one that presents students with an invigorating moment to decolonize their minds.

Resistance in the case of the sisters led, in turn, to the birth of a Hawaiian student group called Kālai Pō. At the forefront of campus activity, Kālai Pō publicly protested the sisters' eviction from class by holding rallies, challenging the racist professor on his evidence, and demanding a civil rights counselor from the administration. As part of their opposition, the group decided to make capturing student government a priority. They contested all positions. When the votes were counted, a Hawaiian woman had won the presidency by four votes, while the rest of the slate had captured the majority of the senate seats.

Once in office, the Kālai Pō students refused to hold an inaugural ball, saving substantial monies for student programs. Because they had organized themselves the summer before classes began, they came to the campus in the fall prepared to do business. They put elections on-line, challenged the university's president to include them on the Governor's Economic Revitalization Task Force, and constantly issued press releases on every concern they felt to be critical. For example, they lobbied the Board of Regents for tuition waivers for Hawaiians. They also took on the effort to rename the social sciences building, which, like most campus buildings at the University of Hawai'i, is named in honor of a racist, one Stanley D. Porteus.

In the case of Kālai Pō, we have a successful example of student organizing by an insurgent, oppressed group. First, they coalesced around a significant issue, one that erupted on campus and concerned the racist depictions of Native people. Second, they demonstrated publicly at rallies, held forums, and called press conferences. Third, they named themselves in their own language, choosing a name with symbolic meaning. And finally, they decided they would seek student government by running a slate calling for student rights. As the Native Hawaiian slate, they fronted their indigenous status in their effort to capture power. Once elected, they rapidly made connections with other ethnic groups and organized their platform accordingly. In fact, Kālai Pō is now part of a Polynesian slate for next year's student government. The Hawaiian students have made a common link with the Samoan students to form an alliance of Polynesians.

For me, personally, Kālai Pō and its victories have been long in coming. After two previous student attempts to capture campus government, Kālai Pō finally attained the presidency. Given that Hawaiians comprise less than 5 percent of a student body of over 40,000 full- and part-time students, their success was substantial, indeed, phenomenal. Kālai Pō's victory illustrated the value of organizing at the most basic, in-the-trenches level. It sent a message that the Hawaiian sovereignty movement had taken up residency on the campus. As in the state, Hawaiians were asserting their claim to self-government, but this time the arena was the campus and the government was student government.

I am also pleased to say that the leadership of Kālai Pō has been predominately female. The Associated Students of the University of Hawai'i (ASUH) President, Mamo Kim, is female and, not inconsequentially, forty-seven years old. Most of the ASUH senators are female. Most of the hardcore organizing has been accomplished by women. And obviously, the major advisor to Kālai Pō is female, namely myself.

Is this accidental? I do not believe so. Women are at the forefront of our sovereignty movement. Women lead our Hawaiian Studies Center. Women represent most of our leadership in established organizations. In brief, women are on the front lines, the battle lines. There are historical and cultural reasons for this, but the history is not as important as the reality. The reality is simply that women are there, where the action is, where the people live, where the nation resides. We are ready to take risks, to dig in for the long haul, to be present and counted. Not only counted as numbers but counted upon, responsible, enduring. This was true of the 1960s Black Civil Rights Movement in the South. Then, women and young people led the organizing efforts.

The same is true for our sovereignty movement today. And the same is true for our campus organizing. Women lead, and in our movement, they have been the finest leaders. Our students have made alliances with Samoan students, with some *haole*, or "white," students; even with the few African-American students on campus who are engaged in student government.

To me, our women's leadership is really quite natural, that is to say, our women's leadership is everywhere, in every field, in every category. The same is true, now, of campus leadership. The presence of our women is partly explained by our sovereignty movement, but it is also explained by our amazing individual and cultural strength. As Hawaiians, we expect leadership among our women. I expect it of myself. This is the way of our people.

Haunani-Kay Trask speaking at the "Stop Racism against Hawaiians" rally held in 1994 to protest racist cartoons and articles by the Asian-dominated student newspaper, *Ka Leo o Hawai'i.* (Photo by Ed Greevy.)

Appendixes

Draft United Nations Declaration on the Rights of Indigenous Peoples*

Affirming that indigenous peoples are equal in dignity and rights to all other peoples, while recognizing the right of all peoples to be different, to consider themselves different, and to be respected as such,

Affirming also that all peoples contribute to the diversity and richness of civilizations and cultures, which constitute the common heritage of humankind,

Affirming further that all doctrines, policies and practices based on or advocating superiority of peoples or individuals on the basis of national origin, racial, religious, ethnic or cultural differences are racist, scientifically false, legally invalid, morally condemnable and socially unjust,

Reaffirming also that indigenous peoples, in the exercise of their rights, should be free from discrimination of any kind,

Concerned that indigenous peoples have been deprived of their human rights and fundamental freedoms, resulting, *inter alia*, in their

*The declaration is a report of the Sub-Commission on Prevention of Discrimination and Protection of Minorities on its Forty-Sixth Session, Geneva, Switzerland, 1–26 August 1994.

colonization and dispossession of their lands, territories and resources, thus preventing them from exercising, in particular, their right to development in accordance with their own needs and interests,

Recognizing the urgent need to respect and promote the inherent rights and characteristics of indigenous peoples, especially their rights to their lands, territories and resources, which derive from their political, economic and social structures and from their cultures, spiritual traditions, histories and philosophies,

Welcoming the fact that indigenous peoples are organizing themselves for political, economic, social and cultural enhancement and in order to bring an end to all forms of discrimination and oppression wherever they occur,

Convinced that control by indigenous peoples over developments affecting them and their lands, territories and resources will enable them to maintain and strengthen their institutions, cultures and traditions, and to promote their development in accordance with their aspirations and needs,

Recognizing also that respect for indigenous knowledge, cultures and traditional practices contributes to sustainable and equitable development and proper management of the environment,

Emphasizing the need for demilitarization of the lands and territories of indigenous peoples, which will contribute to peace, economic and social progress and development, understanding and friendly relations among nations and peoples of the world,

Recognizing in particular the right of indigenous families and communities to retain shared responsibility for the upbringing, training, education and well-being of their children,

Recognizing also that indigenous peoples have the right freely to determine their relationships with States in a spirit of coexistence, mutual benefit and full respect,

Considering that treaties, agreements and other arrangements between States and indigenous peoples are properly matters of international concern and responsibility,

Acknowledging that the Charter of the United Nations, the International Covenant on Economic, Social and Cultural Rights and the International Covenant on Civil and Political Rights affirm the fundamental importance of the right of self-determination of all peoples, by virtue of which they freely determine their political status and freely pursue their economic, social and cultural development,

Bearing in mind that nothing in this Declaration may be used to deny any peoples their right of self-determination,

Encouraging States to comply with and effectively implement all international instruments, in particular those related to human rights, as they apply to indigenous peoples, in consultation and cooperation with the peoples concerned,

Emphasizing that the United Nations has an important and continuing role to play in promoting and protecting the rights of indigenous peoples,

Believing that this Declaration is a further important step forward for the recognition, promotion and protection of the rights and freedoms of indigenous peoples and in the development of relevant activities of the United Nations system in this field,

Solemnly proclaims the following United Nations Declaration on the Rights of Indigenous Peoples:

Part I

Article 1

Indigenous peoples have the right to the full and effective enjoyment of all human rights and fundamental freedoms recognized in the Charter of the United Nations, the Universal Declaration of Human Rights and international human rights law.

Article 2

Indigenous individuals and peoples are free and equal to all other individuals and peoples in dignity and rights, and have the right to be free from any kind of adverse discrimination, in particular that based on their indigenous origin or identity.

Article 3

Indigenous peoples have the right of self-determination. By virtue of that right they freely determine their political status and freely pursue their economic, social and cultural development.

Article 4

Indigenous peoples have the right to maintain and strengthen their distinct political, economic, social and cultural characteristics, as well as their legal systems, while retaining their rights to participate fully, if they so choose, in the political, economic, social and cultural life of the State.

Article 5

Every indigenous individual has the right to a nationality.

Part II

Article 6

Indigenous peoples have the collective right to live in freedom, peace and security as distinct peoples and to full guarantees against genocide or any other act of violence, including the removal of indigenous children from their families and communities under any pretext.

In addition, they have the individual rights to life, physical and mental integrity, liberty and security of person.

Article 7

Indigenous peoples have the collective and individual right not to be subjected to ethnocide and cultural genocide, including prevention of and redress for:

(a) Any action which has the aim or effect of depriving them of their integrity as distinct peoples, or of their cultural values or ethnic identities;

(b) Any action which has the aim or effect of dispossessing them of their lands, territories or resources;

(c) Any form of population transfer which has the aim or effect of violating or undermining any of their rights;

(d) Any form of assimilation or integration by other cultures or ways of life imposed on them by legislative, administrative or other measures;

(e) Any form of propaganda directed against them.

Article 8

Indigenous peoples have the collective and individual right to maintain and develop their distinct identities and characteristics, including the right to identify themselves as indigenous and to be recognized as such.

Article 9

Indigenous peoples and individuals have the right to belong to an indigenous community or nation, in accordance with the traditions and customs of the community or nation concerned. No disadvantage of any kind may arise from the exercise of such a right.

Article 10

Indigenous peoples shall not be forcibly removed from their lands or territories. No relocation shall take place without the free and informed consent of the indigenous peoples concerned and after agreement on just and fair compensation and, where possible, with the option of return.

Article 11

Indigenous peoples have the right to special protection and security in periods of armed conflict.

States shall observe international standards, in particular the Fourth Geneva Convention of 1949, for the protection of civilian populations in circumstances of emergency and armed conflict, and shall not:

(a) Recruit indigenous individuals against their will into the armed forces and, in particular, for use against other indigenous peoples;

(b) Recruit indigenous children into the armed forces under any circumstances;

(c) Force indigenous individuals to abandon their lands, territories or means of subsistence, or relocate them in special centres for military purposes;

(d) Force indigenous individuals to work for military purposes under any discriminatory conditions.

Part III

Article 12

Indigenous peoples have the right to practise and revitalize their cultural traditions and customs. This includes the right to maintain, protect and develop the past, present and future manifestations of their cultures, such as archaeological and historical sites, artifacts, designs, ceremonies, technologies and visual and performing arts and literature, as well as the right to the restitution of cultural, intellectual, religious and spiritual property taken without their free and informed consent or in violation of their laws, traditions and customs.

Article 13

Indigenous peoples have the right to manifest, practise, develop and teach their spiritual and religious traditions, customs and ceremonies; the right to maintain, protect, and have access in privacy to their religious and cultural sites; the right to the use and control of ceremonial objects; and the right to the repatriation of human remains.

States shall take effective measures, in conjunction with the indigenous peoples concerned, to ensure that indigenous sacred places, including burial sites, be preserved, respected and protected.

Article 14

Indigenous peoples have the right to revitalize, use, develop and transmit to future generations their histories, languages, oral traditions, philosophies, writing systems and literatures, and to designate and retain their own names for communities, places and persons.

States shall take effective measures, whenever any right of indigenous peoples may be threatened, to ensure this right is protected and also to ensure that they can understand and be understood in political, legal and administrative proceedings, where necessary through the provision of interpretation or by other appropriate means.

Part IV

Article 15

Indigenous children have the right to all levels and forms of education of the State. All indigenous peoples also have this right and the right to establish and control their educational systems and institutions providing education in their own languages, in a manner appropriate to their cultural methods of teaching and learning.

Indigenous children living outside their communities have the right to be provided access to education in their own culture and language.

States shall take effective measures to provide appropriate resources for these purposes.

Article 16

Indigenous peoples have the right to have the dignity and diversity of their cultures, traditions, histories and aspirations appropriately reflected in all forms of education and public information.

States shall take effective measures, in consultation with the indigenous peoples concerned, to eliminate prejudice and discrimination and to promote tolerance, understanding and good relations among indigenous peoples and all segments of society.

Article 17

Indigenous peoples have the right to establish their own media in their own languages. They also have the right to equal access to all forms of non-indigenous media.

States shall take effective measures to ensure that State-owned media duly reflect indigenous cultural diversity.

Article 18

Indigenous peoples have the right to enjoy fully all rights established under international labour law and national labour legislation.

Indigenous individuals have the right not to be subjected to any discriminatory conditions of labour, employment or salary.

Part V

Article 19

Indigenous peoples have the right to participate fully, if they so choose, at all levels of decision-making in matters which may affect their rights, lives and destinies through representatives chosen by themselves in accordance with their own procedures, as well as to maintain and develop their own indigenous decision-making institutions.

Article 20

Indigenous peoples have the right to participate fully, if they so choose, through procedures determined by them, in devising legislative or administrative measures that may affect them.

States shall obtain the free and informed consent of the peoples concerned before adopting and implementing such measures.

Article 21

Indigenous peoples have the right to maintain and develop their political, economic and social systems, to be secure in the enjoyment of their own means of subsistence and development, and to engage freely in all their traditional and other economic activities. Indigenous peoples who have been deprived of their means of subsistence and development are entitled to just and fair compensation.

Article 22

Indigenous peoples have the right to special measures for the immediate, effective and continuing improvement of their economic and social conditions, including in the areas of employment, vocational training and retraining, housing, sanitation, health and social security.

Particular attention shall be paid to the rights and special needs of indigenous elders, women, youth, children and disabled persons.

Article 23

Indigenous peoples have the right to determine and develop priorities and strategies for exercising their right to development. In particular, indigenous peoples have the right to determine and develop all health, housing and other economic and social programmes affecting them and, as far as possible, to administer such programmes through their own institutions.

Article 24

Indigenous peoples have the right to their traditional medicines and health practices, including the right to the protection of vital medicinal plants, animal and minerals.

They also have the right to access, without any discrimination, to all medical institutions, health services and medical care.

Part VI

Article 25

Indigenous peoples have the right to maintain and strengthen their distinctive spiritual and material relationship with the lands, territories, waters and coastal seas and other resources which they have traditionally owned or otherwise occupied or used, and to uphold their responsibilities to future generations in this regard.

Article 26

Indigenous peoples have the right to own, develop, control and use their lands and territories, including the total environment of the lands, air, waters, coastal seas, sea-ice, flora and fauna and other resources which they have traditionally owned or otherwise occupied or used. This includes the right to the full recognition of their laws, traditions and customs, land-tenure systems and institutions for the development and management of resources, and the right to effective measures by States to prevent any interference with, alienation of, or encroachment upon these rights.

Article 27

Indigenous peoples have the right to the restitution of the lands, territories and resources which they have traditionally owned or otherwise occupied or used, and which have been confiscated, occupied, used or damaged without their free and informed consent. Where this is not possible, they have the right to just and fair compensation. Unless otherwise freely agreed upon by the peoples concerned, compensation shall take the form of lands, territories and resources equal in quality, size and legal status.

Article 28

Indigenous peoples have the right to the conservation, restoration and protection of the total environment and the productive capacity of their lands, territories and resources, as well as to assistance for this purpose from States and through international cooperation. Military activities shall not take place in the lands and territories of indigenous peoples, unless otherwise freely agreed upon by the peoples concerned.

States shall take effective measures to ensure that no storage or disposal of hazardous materials shall take place in the lands and territories of indigenous peoples.

States shall also take effective measures to ensure, as needed, that programmes for monitoring, maintaining and restoring the health of indigenous peoples, as developed and implemented by the peoples affected by such materials, are duly implemented.

Article 29

Indigenous peoples are entitled to the recognition of the full ownership, control and protection of their cultural and intellectual property.

They have the right to special measures to control, develop and protect their sciences, technologies and cultural manifestations, including human and other genetic resources, seeds, medicines, knowledge of the properties of fauna and flora, oral traditions, literatures, designs and visual and performing arts.

Article 30

Indigenous peoples have the right to determine and develop priorities and strategies for the development or use of their lands, territories and other resources, including the right to require that States obtain their free and informed consent prior to the approval of any project affecting their lands, territories and other resources, particularly in connection with the development, utilization or exploitation of mineral, water or other resources. Pursuant to agreement with the indigenous peoples concerned, just and fair compensation shall be provided for any such activities and measures taken to mitigate adverse environmental, economic, social, cultural or spiritual impact.

Part VII

Article 31

Indigenous peoples, as a specific form of exercising their right to self-determination, have the right to autonomy or self-government in matters relating to their internal and local affairs, including culture, religion, education, information, media, health, housing, employment, social welfare, economic activities, land and resources management, environment and entry by non-members, as well as ways and means for financing these autonomous functions.

Article 32

Indigenous peoples have the collective right to determine their own citizenship in accordance with their customs and traditions. Indigenous citizenship does not impair the right of indigenous individuals to obtain citizenship of the States in which they live.

Indigenous peoples have the right to determine the structures and to select the membership of their institutions in accordance with their own procedures.

Article 33

Indigenous peoples have the right to promote, develop and maintain their institutional structures and their distinctive juridical customs, traditions, procedures and practices, in accordance with internationally recognized human rights standards.

Article 34

Indigenous peoples have the collective right to determine the responsibilities of individuals to their communities.

Article 35

Indigenous peoples, in particular those divided by international borders, have the right to maintain and develop contacts, relations and cooperation, including activities for spiritual, cultural, political, economic and social purposes, with other peoples across borders.

States shall take effective measures to ensure the exercise and implementation of this right.

Article 36

Indigenous peoples have the right to the recognition, observance and enforcement of treaties, agreements and other constructive arrangements concluded with States or their successors, according to their original spirit and intent, and to have States honour and respect such treaties, agreements and other constructive arrangements. Conflicts and disputes which cannot otherwise be settled should be submitted to competent international bodies agreed to by all parties concerned.

Part VIII

Article 37

States shall take effective and appropriate measures, in consultation with the indigenous peoples concerned, to give full effect to the provisions of this Declaration. The rights recognized herein shall be adopted and included in national legislation in such a manner that indigenous peoples can avail themselves of such rights in practice.

Article 38

Indigenous peoples have the right to have access to adequate financial and technical assistance, from States and through international cooperation, to pursue freely their political, economic, social, cultural and spiritual development and for the enjoyment of the rights and freedoms recognized in this Declaration.

Article 39

Indigenous peoples have the right to have access to and prompt decision through mutually acceptable and fair procedures for the resolution of conflicts and disputes with States, as well as to effective remedies for all infringements of their individual and collective rights. Such a decision shall take into consideration the customs, traditions, rules and legal systems of the indigenous peoples concerned.

Article 40

The organs and specialized agencies of the United Nations system and other intergovernmental organizations shall contribute to the full realization of the provisions of this Declaration through the mobilization, inter alia, of financial cooperation and technical assistance. Ways and means of ensuring participation of indigenous peoples on issues affecting them shall be established.

Article 41

The United Nations shall take the necessary steps to ensure the implementation of this Declaration including the creation of a body at the highest level with special competence in this field and with the direct participation of indigenous peoples. All United Nations bodies shall promote respect for and full application of the provisions of this Declaration.

Part IX

Article 42

The rights recognized herein constitute the minimum standards for the survival, dignity and well-being of the indigenous peoples of the world.

Article 43

All the rights and freedoms recognized herein are equally guaranteed to male and female indigenous individuals.

Article 44

Nothing in this Declaration may be construed as diminishing or extinguishing existing or future rights indigenous peoples may have or acquire.

Article 45

Nothing in this Declaration may be interpreted as implying for any State group or person any right to engage in any activity or to perform any act contrary to the Charter of the United Nations.

Ho'okupu a Ka Lāhui Hawai'i: The Master Plan 1995

I. Endorsement of Fundamental Principles

The Ka Lāhui Hawai'i Master Plan for Hawaiian Self-Government is founded upon a firm belief in and commitment to certain fundamental principles which set international standards for the protection of individual human rights and civil liberties, for maintaining the well-being and peaceful coexistence of our nation with other sovereigns, and for the protection and recognition of collective rights of our citizenry.

These Fundamental Principles include the following:

A. Commitment to Peace, Disarmament, and Non-Violence

The practice of peace requires that we resolve conflict in a non-violent manner. This commitment to non-violence relates not only to our undertakings in the political arena, but involves the seeking of non-violent solutions to family, personal, and community problems. Violence in all forms including spouse and child abuse, elderly abuse and neglect is rejected.

Disarmament means that the Hawaiian Nation shall not engage in acts of militarism, nor shall it endorse military undertakings on its land or territories.

Civil disobedience is the use of non-violent means to oppose injustice, to stop violations of human rights, and to stop the degradation of our trust assets. Civil disobedience should be utilized only after good faith efforts to resolve conflict have failed. Where civil disobedience is contemplated, the community impacted should be supportive of the event and fully informed of the reasons for the event.

B. Recognition of the Inherent Dignity and of the Equal and Inalienable Rights of Native Hawaiians and their Descendants Under International Legal Standards

Considering the obligation of States, including the United States, under the Charter of the United Nations to promote universal respect for and observance of human rights and freedoms of all peoples, Native Hawaiians and their descendants endorse and assert the rights and principles contained in the following international covenants, declarations, and agreements:

1. The Charter of the United Nations (done at San Francisco, June 26, 1945. [entered into force for the United States, October 24, 1945. 59 Stat. 1031, T.S. No. 993]);

2. The Draft United Nations Declaration on the Rights of Indigenous Peoples (E/CN.4Sub.2/1993/29);

3. The International Covenant on Civil and Political Rights (999 UN Treaty Series 171, I-14668, 19 December 1966);

4. The International Covenant on Social, Economic and Cultural Rights (993 UN Treaty Series 3, I-14531, 16 December 1966).

C. The Right to Self-Determination

Native Hawaiians and our descendants have the right of self-determination. By virtue of that right, we are entitled to freely determine our political status and freely pursue our economic, social and cultural development (International Covenant on Civil and Political Rights, Section 1.1, 999 UN Treaty Series 171).

D. The Right to Self-Development

Native Hawaiians and our descendants have the right to determine and set priorities and choose strategies for development. This right includes the development and administration of programs relating to land, housing, economic and social needs.

Native Hawaiians and our descendants have the right to maintain and develop our own political, economic, and social systems; to be secure in the enjoyment of our own means of subsistence and development; and to engage freely in all traditional and other economic activities (UN Draft Declaration of the Rights of Indigenous Peoples, Articles 21 and 23, E/CN.4Sub.2/1993/29).

E. Termination of Wardship

The imposition of the Western Doctrine of Manifest Destiny and the Tyler Doctrine in the Pacific Region resulted in the colonization of the Hawaiian Archipelago. The consequences of Hawai'i's unique legal and historical experience are:

1. The current political status of Native Hawaiians and their descendants as wards of the State of Hawai'i; and

2. The usurpation of our people's collective rights to land and to political and social power by state agencies and instrumentalities; and

3. The violation of the human and civil rights of Native Hawaiians and their descendants by the United States of America and its agent, the State of Hawai'i.

The policy of wardship imposed by the United States and State of Hawai'i is explicitly rejected as a fundamental violation of Native Hawaiians' right to self-determination. The Ka Lāhui Hawai'i Master Plan seeks to establish a new relationship between the Hawaiian people and other sovereigns, including the United States of America and its agent, the State of Hawai'i.

F. Establishment Jurisdiction, and Recognition of Ka Lāhui Hawai'i

The inherent right of self-determination provides for the establishment of an indigenous sovereign nation by processes determined and created by Native Hawaiians and their descendants without interference from other sovereigns. The Nation, as the collective representative of Native Hawaiians and their descendants, shall have jurisdiction over its lands, territories, internal and external relationships, including, but not limited to the following powers:

1. The power to determine its membership;
2. Police powers;
3. The power to administer justice;
4. The power to exclude persons from National Territory;
5. The power to charter business organizations;
6. Sovereign immunity;
7. The power to regulate trade and enter into trade agreements;
8. The power to tax;
9. The power to legislate and regulate all activities on its land base, including natural resources and water management, activities and economic enterprises.

II. Consensus Building

Ho'okupu a Ka Lāhui Hawai'i—The Hawaiian Initiative for Self-Government

The legislature of Ka Lāhui Hawai'i has fashioned our Nation as a Ho'okupu (offering) to future generations and to the 'Aumākua. We believe that we have provided a strong vehicle for the indigenous peoples of Hawai'i—to express self-determination. We offer our Ho'okupu to all of the people of Hawai'i, indigenous and non-indigenous.

Consensus can be achieved by building upon what has been established and agreeing to abide by and support determinations endorsed by the collective whole.

A. Building Upon What We Have Established

Ka Lāhui Hawai'i is a political expression of self-determination. Ka Lāhui Hawai'i was created by Native Hawaiians and their descendants. Our Constitution is a reflection of what we believe about ourselves, our culture, traditions and political rights, and other inalienable human rights. Ka Lāhui Hawai'i was created without interference or financial support from the United States of America or its agent, the State of Hawai'i.

Ka Lāhui Hawai'i is the evolutionary product of several generations of Hawaiians who sought to address past and present injustices arising from the subversion of our indigenous culture and political system and the overthrow and annexation of our territories by the United States of America.

Ka Lāhui Hawai'i has been endorsed by thousands of Native Hawaiians and their descendants. Our accomplishments include:

1. The formation of a strong, democratic, and elective nation whose indigenous citizens, by virtue of their individual vote (regardless of wealth, genealogy or sex) exercise self-determination;

2. The drafting of a constitution which incorporates traditional, cultural and spiritual values and practices with current processes and which can be altered to accommodate the need of the indigenous people to change;

3. Establishing a respected international reputation including membership in U.N.P.O. (Unrepresented Nations and Peoples Organizations—The Hague); acknowledgment and inclusion in the U.N. Working Group Treaty Study; participation in International Consultation with the World Council of Churches in Geneva; and participation with other indigenous collectives in international consultations in Vienna,

Austria; Geneva, Switzerland; Cairo, Egypt; Rio de Janeiro, Brazil; Darwin, Australia; and elsewhere;

4. A long track record on issues relating to human rights violations and the mismanagement of Native trust assets and other entitlements by the United States government and the State of Hawai'i.

No other Hawaiian group or purported Hawai'i sovereign has such a record of accomplishments. These and many other achievements of Ka Lāhui Hawai'i can be shared with all those who endorse this initiative and choose to participate as citizens or legislators of the Nation.

B. Accepting the Challenge of Change

In order to safeguard the right of self-determination for future generations, Ka Lāhui Hawai'i's Constitution provides the opportunity for its citizens to change the nation's governmental structure, its processes, policies, and land base. Acknowledging that all things change, we accept that the Nation we have built may need to be changed to meet the needs of our peoples and of our *'āina.* We believe that the process for change is what makes change possible.

All citizens of Ka Lāhui Hawai'i are empowered with the ability to create political change or to completely restructure the Nation if we can work collectively and gain the support of and the consensus of our own people.

Persons or groups who may favor other structures of government, for example: monarchical, traditional, free-association, or commonwealth status can change Ka Lāhui Hawai'i's structure if they win the support of the Nation's citizens and elected leaders. Ka Lāhui Hawai'i has the process for change, but it can only work if people choose to use it.

III. Dealing with the United States

A. The Evolution of United States Policy Relating to Hawai'i and Its Indigenous People

1. The Policy of Perpetual Peace and Friendship—1826–1842

The United States recognized the sovereignty of the Hawaiian Nation and pledged perpetual "peace and friendship" between the United States and the "people and subjects" of the "Sandwich Islands" in the first United States/Hawai'i Convention dated December 23, 1826. Subsequent Conventions reiterated this pledge of mutual respect. (See *Treaty of Friendship, Commerce and Navigation*, December 1849; *Convention of Reciprocity*, June 1876.)

2. The Policy of United States Colonial Domination—The Tyler Doctrine, 1842

On December 30, 1842 the United States Secretary of State Daniel Webster delivered to Hawaiian envoys a document which stated that the United States had a special interest in Hawai'i. This document, which was sent by the United States to England and France, stated, "no power ought either to take possession of the islands as a conquest, or for the purpose of colonization and that no power ought to seek for any undue control over the existing government." This document became known as the Tyler Doctrine after then United States President, John Tyler.

By imposing the Tyler Doctrine on Hawai'i, the United States was asserting that Hawai'i was within the United States sphere of influence and was to be subjected to United States colonial domination. All treaties and conventions between the Hawaiian Nation and the United States negotiated subsequent to 1842 favored United States' interests over those of the Nation.

3. The Policy of Armed Intervention—The Overthrow of 1893 and Annexation of 1898

In 1872 the United States War Department dispatched a secret military mission to Hawai'i "for the purpose of ascertaining the defense capabilities of the different ports . . . in order to collect all information that would be of service to the Country [United States] in the event of war. . . ." This military mission also mapped and surveyed Pearl Harbor, Schofield Barracks, Fort Armstrong, and other staging areas of the islands. This mission and its report were kept secret until 1897, when they were released to the Congressional Committee considering Annexation. (See Volume II, *Native Hawaiians Study Commission*, June 23, 1994, page 39.)

The United States Congressional Record of the United States Senate (S.6956), June 23, 1969 reveals the following:

a) In February 1874 United States armed forces landed in Hawai'i "to preserve order and protect American lives and interests during the inauguration of a new King";

b) In July 1889 United States armed forces landed in Hawai'i "to protect American interests at Honolulu during a revolution"; and

c) From January 16 to April 1, 1893, United States armed forces occupied Hawai'i "ostensibly to protect American lives and property: in actuality to promote a provisional government under Sanford B. Dole. This action was disavowed by the United States."

4. The Policy of the "Sacred Trust": 1946–1959

Following the annexation of Hawai'i in 1898, Hawai'i was held by the United States as a territory. In 1946 when the United Nations was created, the United Nations listed Hawai'i as a Non-Self-Governing Territory under United States Administration. Pursuant to Chapter XI of the United Nations Charter, the United States had a "sacred trust" obligation to promote the political aspirations of the peoples of the territory and to assist them in developing self-government (see Section VIII herein - International Issues).

The United States never fulfilled its "sacred obligation," nor did it comply with the international standards requiring that the peoples of the "territory" be provided with several options for self-government. In 1959 when the United States imposed statehood on Hawai'i, the United Nations without inquiry or investigation and at the United States' request, removed Hawai'i from the United Nations List of Non-Self-Governing Territories.

B. The Current Policy of the United States Towards Hawaiians: The Policy of Non-Recognition, Denial, and State Wardship

1. State Wardship

In 1959 the United States created a policy of "State Wardship" which it imposed on Hawaiians and the State in the Admissions Act. Under this policy a small portion of vast traditional archipelagic territories were identified for "Native Hawaiians." (Those Hawaiians who could not prove they were "Natives" of 50% blood were excluded.) These lands were given by the United States to the State of Hawai'i in trust for "Native Hawaiians" for homelands and other uses, but they were never inventoried or mapped. Instead, these lands were combined with other public lands and transferred to the State of Hawai'i, thus commingling them with the remaining stolen Ceded Lands of the Kingdom. The United States retained and continues to use a significant portion of Hawaiian Lands.

Under the United States policy of State Wardship, Hawaiians are denied:

a) Our collective right to self-determination;

b) The power to collectively receive, develop, and utilize our lands and natural resources, fisheries, and cultural properties; and

c) The ability to preserve and protect our entitlements for future generations.

2. Non-Recognition

Since 1959 the United States has maintained a policy of non-recognition of the indigenous peoples of Hawai'i and has consistently dealt with the State of Hawai'i despite an extensive record of State neglect and mismanagement of the Native trusts. The record reveals that the United States itself by acting in collusion with the State has illegally acquired for its own use trust lands set aside by the U.S. Congress for homesteading. For over 73 years, the United States has failed to protect the Civil Rights of Hawaiians (see *A Broken Trust,* Report of the Hawai'i Advisory Committee to the United States Commission on Civil Rights, December 1991.)

3. Reagan, Bush, and Clinton Administrative Policy: Abandonment

In 1979 the Deputy Solicitor of the United States Department of Interior in a letter to the Director of the United States Commission on Civil Rights (Western Division) wrote, ". . . it is the Department's position that the role of the United States under Section 5(f) of the Admissions Act is essentially that of a trustee. . . . The responsibilities of the Federal Government are more than merely supervisory and the United States can be said to have retained its role as trustee under the Act while making the State its instrument for carrying out the trust." (*A Broken Trust,* ID at page 9)

The Reagan Administration began to disavow its responsibilities over the Native trusts in 1986. (See Presidential Statement H.J.R. Res. 17, Public Law No. 99-557, October 27, 1986) On August 2, 1990, Tim Glidden, the Secretary of Interior under George Bush, notified the U.S. Commission on Civil Rights that the Interior Department "disclaimed any trusteeship role in the administration of the [Admissions] Act." On January 19, 1993, the Solicitor of the Department of Interior issued a lengthy legal memo entitled "The Scope of Federal Responsibility for Native Hawaiians under the Hawaiian Homes Commission Act." The memo set forth the following conclusion, "We conclude that the United States had no trust responsibilities to the Native Hawaiians either before Statehood or after." (See Memo of Solicitor to

Counselor to the Secretary of Interior and Secretary Designate, January 19, 1993.)

On November 15, 1993 the new Clinton Administration's Solicitor, John D. Leshy, issued a statement withdrawing the Bush policy of January 19, 1993, and indicating that although the Bush policy (no trust obligation) was withdrawn, *the Clinton Administration would continue to assert there was no trust obligation in Federal Court!* Since this time the Administration has continued to deny its legal trust obligation to Hawaiians and has undertaken closed negotiations with the State of Hawai'i intended to limit United States and State liability. The Hawaiian people have been completely ignored in the process.

4. The Apology Bill

In 1993 the United States Congress passed the Apology Bill (Act of Nov. 23, 1993, Pub. L. No. 103-150, 103d Congress, 107 STAT. 1510), acknowledging its role in the illegal overthrow of the Hawaiian Nation in 1893 and calling for "Reconciliation." The law does not provide for a process for "reconciliation," nor does it define "reconciliation."

The Apology Bill states ". . . the indigenous Hawaiian people never directly relinquished their claims to their inherent sovereignty as a people or over their national lands to the United States, either through their monarchy or through a plebiscite or referendum."

C. Ka Lāhui Hawai'i's Position Regarding United States Policy

1. Ka Lāhui Hawai'i rejects the United States Policy of State Wardship and calls for the immediate termination of this policy by the United States and the State of Hawai'i.

2. The United States accepted a "sacred trust" obligation over Hawai'i under the United Nations Charter and has admitted to its role as a Trustee of the Native Hawaiian trusts. In both

instances, the United States has violated its trust obligations and is obligated to restore the rights and entitlements of the indigenous people of Hawai'i to self-determination and to our lands, assets, and natural resources under the United Nations Charter and other international covenants, and pursuant to its own laws.

3. By adoption of the Apology Bill, the United States has acknowledged that "the indigenous Hawaiian people have never directly relinquished their inherent sovereignty as a people or over their national lands to the United States, either through their monarchy or through a plebiscite or referendum." Therefore under international law, the American government is engaged in an illegal occupation of Hawai'i.

4. As an act of our collective right to self-determination and to self-governance, Ka Lāhui Hawai'i accepts the United States Apology and proposes the following process for "reconciliation" under Public Law 103-150.

D. The Ka Lāhui Hawai'i Initiative for "Reconciliation" with the United States Pursuant to U.S. Public Law 103-150 (The Apology Bill)

1. The goals of "Reconciliation" are:

   a) The final resolution of historic claims relating to

      i. the overthrow;

      ii. State and Federal misuse of Native trust lands and resources;

      iii. violations of human and civil rights; and

      iv. Federally held Lands and resources;

b) The structuring of a new relationship between Ka Lāhui Hawai'i and the United States which acknowledges the rights of Native Hawaiians and their descendants, including our right to self-determination.

2. The Essential Elements of "Reconciliation" with the United States shall include but not be limited to the following:

   a) Express termination of the United States policy of non-recognition of Native Hawaiian self-determination. Repudiation of United States policy of State Wardship.

   b) Federal recognition of Ka Lāhui Hawai'i as the indigenous sovereign Hawaiian Nation and Federal recognition of the jurisdiction of Ka Lāhui Hawai'i over its national assets, lands, and natural resources.

   c) Federal programs, legal and fiscal entitlements, tax benefits, and other obligations to be negotiated.

   d) Recognition of Hawaiian sovereign rights to trade and commercial activities based on treaties between the Hawaiian Nations and other sovereigns—before and after the overthrow.

   e) A commitment to decolonize Hawai'i through the United Nations process for non-self-governing territories.

3. Provision for Land, Natural Resources, and Cultural Resources include:

   a) Restoration of traditional lands, natural resources, ocean and energy resources to the Ka Lāhui National Land Trust:

      i. The United States and the State of Hawai'i shall inventory and restore the lands of the Native trusts (State controlled Hawaiian Home Lands and Ceded Lands) and Federally held Lands, and the United States shall remedy all Federal and State breaches of trust relating to these assets.

ii. The United States and the State of Hawai'i shall segregate the Hawaiian National Trust Lands from other public and private lands.

iii. The United States and the State of Hawai'i shall allocate not less than two (2) million acres of land drawn from State-controlled Ceded Lands, State-controlled Hawaiian Homes Lands, and Federally-controlled Lands to the National Land Trust.

iv. The Base Closure Act and Federal Surplus Property Act shall be amended to allow for land banking of these lands for the National Land Trust.

b) Cultural, traditional, religious, and economic rights:

The United States shall recognize individual and collective Hawaiian rights to cultural and religious properties, marine resources (to the 200-mile limit established under International Law) and cultural ecosystems. These entitlements and economic entitlements should be recognized as the jurisdiction of Ka Lāhui Hawai'i, the indigenous Hawaiian Nation.

IV. Terminating Wardship under the State

Native Hawaiians and their descendants have not benefited from the illegal United States imposed policy of State Wardship which was created in 1959 as part of Statehood. On the other hand, the State of Hawai'i has benefited by utilizing its power as a Trustee to diminish, transfer, encumber, and toxify our Native trust lands and resources. By failing to settle Hawaiians and Native Hawaiians on 5(f) Ceded and Hawaiian Home Lands, the State withheld from Native peoples their land entitlements, while Hawaiian "beneficiaries" died in poverty and destitution. The State acted in collusion with the Federal Government to violate the human and civil rights of Hawai'i's indigenous people, and participated in denying the Hawaiian people their collective rights to self-determination and self-government.

A. Ka Lāhui Hawai'i's Position on State Issues (Generally)

1. Self-Determination:

   The State of Hawai'i by legislation shall agree to repudiate the United States imposed policy of State Wardship and recognize Ka Lāhui Hawai'i as a sovereign government with all of its rightful power and jurisdiction over its lands and resources.

2. Native Trust Lands, Assets, and Resources:

   The State of Hawai'i shall cease the sale, transfer, lease, or encumbrance of Hawaiian Homes and State Ceded Lands to non-Hawaiians and shall work collectively with Ka Lāhui Hawai'i and the United States to segregate traditional lands and natural resources for the National Land Trust (see Sec. V herein—Establishment of a National Land Trust). The State shall segregate the financial resources of Native Hawaiians and their descendants and transfer these fiscal resources to the Hawaiian Nation. (The State shall repeal any legislation that provides for the sale of ceded lands.)

3. Hawaiian Home Lands and Natural Resources:

   a) Hawaiian Homes residential, pastoral, and agricultural Lessees shall be given a choice of remaining lessees of the State of Hawai'i or becoming lessees of the Hawaiian Nation. No Native Hawaiian or Hawaiian leases shall be canceled. All of the above leases shall be continued; all residential leases shall be renewable, 99 year leases.

b) All other encumbered Hawaiian Home Lands and all commercial and industrial Hawaiian Homes leases shall be transferred to the National Land Trust.

c) The State of Hawai'i shall assume liability for illegal transfers of these lands and for pollution and waste of these trust assets. If such issues cannot be resolved through negotiation, the State shall consent to be sued for its breaches of trust.

d) The State of Hawai'i shall work cooperatively with Ka Lāhui Hawai'i to obtain redress from the United States for all actions of the United States which have diminished the Hawaiian Home Lands Trust or the Ceded Land Trust.

4. State Controlled 5(f) Lands and Natural Resources:

a) The State of Hawai'i, including the Office of Hawaiian Affairs, shall work cooperatively with Ka Lāhui Hawai'i and the United States to finalize *one* accurate inventory of the Ceded Lands, and the segregation of not less than one-half of these lands for the National Land Trust. The State of Hawai'i, including the Office of Hawaiian Affairs, shall work cooperatively with Ka Lāhui Hawai'i to inventory the financial resources of the Native Hawaiians and their descendants and transfer these fiscal resources to the Nation.

b) The State of Hawai'i shall acknowledge the jurisdiction of Ka Lāhui Hawai'i over its lands and natural resources, including but not limited to:

i. the total environment of the lands, air, water, coastal seas, submerged lands, flora and fauna, and other resources which we have traditionally owned or otherwise occupied or used, and

ii. surface and ground water, and energy resources.

The State of Hawai'i shall agree that National Land Trusts are not subject to State or County Taxation, legislation, or control or jurisdiction. Ka Lāhui Hawai'i believes that the management of natural resources will involve working collectively with all those who use these resources.

c) The State of Hawai'i shall assume liability for illegal transfer of these lands and for pollution and waste of these trust assets. If such issues cannot be resolved through negotiation, the State will consent to be sued for its breaches of trust.

V. Establishment of a National Land Trust

A. The Need

The survival of Native Hawaiians, our ancestors, and descendants is rooted deeply in the land. The life of the land is the spiritual and cultural foundation of Native Hawaiians and our children. Therefore, Ka Lāhui Hawai'i, like all other sovereign nations, needs to reclaim and recover its land base. Land is one of the fundamental elements of sovereignty. The Hawaiian people's loss of their traditional lands has resulted in genocide and diaspora. In order to care for its people and to ensure their survival, Ka Lāhui Hawai'i seeks to establish a National Land Trust to develop housing, medical and educational facilities, and business enterprises. Lands and natural resources also include the cultural properties, sacred sites, traditional fisheries, and other resources of the Hawaiian nation which are necessary to maintain and preserve the spiritual and economic foundation of the indigenous culture for future generations.

B. The Entitlement

Ka Lāhui Hawai'i's Constitution identifies the land and natural resource entitlements of indigenous Hawaiians within the archipelagic boundaries of our traditional territories because we assert that our collective rights to land and natural resources preceded the illegal overthrow of 1893.

Ka Lāhui Hawai'i's Constitution sets forth an expansive view of these entitlements, including, but not limited to, the following:

1. State held trust lands: Hawaiian Homes and ceded lands;

2. Marine Resources and Fisheries to the 200-mile limit recognized under international law;

3. Surface and ground water rights and submerged lands (i.e. shoals, reefs, atolls, estuaries, and marshes to the 200-mile limit);

4. Lands and natural resources under the Federal Government of the United States;

5. Energy resources: Ocean thermal and geothermal resources;

6. Minerals and other metallic substances;

7. Airspace above the land and marine resources;

8. The trust assets of the Private Trusts (see Section VI herein—The Private Land Trusts).

C. The Commitment

Ka Lāhui Hawai'i asserts that the Hawaiian Nation has an obligation to maintain, protect, and preserve the lands and the resources of the Hawaiian people for future generations. The following are the basic components which comprise Ka Lāhui Hawai'i's Land Management and development strategy:

1. The lands and natural resources of the Hawaiian Nation shall be held for future generations. The lands and natural resources of the Hawaiian Nation are inalienable.

2. Maintenance and development of the national land base shall be guided by the traditional concept of Mālama 'Āina, which includes sound principles of Natural Resource Management based on the carrying capacity of the land or the resource.

3. Cultural and historic properties, sacred sites, and other ecosystems of religious or archeological significance shall be inventoried, managed, and preserved.

4. National lands and resources shall be allocated not only for the collective needs of the citizenry (national undertakings), but for the individual private uses of the citizens which are licensed or permitted by the Hawaiian Nation.

D. The Establishment of a National Land Trust

The preservation and management of our Traditional lands and natural resources require the establishment of a National Land Trust under the control and management of the Hawaiian nation. Hawaiian lands and resources are currently under the control of state and federal agencies, private trusts, corporations, and individuals.

The termination of the United States imposed policy of wardship shall require that Hawaiians devise a new way to:

1. Marshal our lands and resources, and

2. Collectively manage our lands and resources in order to ensure their appropriate use for future generations, and

3. Most importantly to prevent other sovereigns and private corporations who may attempt to deplete, encumber, tax, or otherwise utilize and diminish our resources.

To this end, Ka Lāhui Hawai'i asserts that a National Land Trust should be established immediately as a preliminary primary undertaking. This undertaking should precede any formal negotiation or claims settlement with the United States or the State of Hawai'i. The criteria used above should be utilized in the process of amassing the lands of the Hawaiian nation.

Land and water resources which have been toxified, polluted, or rendered dangerous by virtue of military, state, commercial, or industrialized uses should not be automatically transferred to the Hawaiian Nation. Rather, the Hawaiian Nation and its citizens shall establish a method to secure lands and resources which *can* be used or need to be preserved for future uses.

The National Land Trust shall be comprised of lands currently called:

1. Hawaiian Home Lands;

2. State Ceded Lands;

3. Federally held lands; and

4. Private Land Trusts (see Sec. VI herein—The Private Land Trusts).

Ka Lāhui Hawai'i asserts that the current and immediate needs of the Hawaiian people for economic development, housing, education, health, and for the protection of cultural ecosystems and historic and sacred properties requires not less than two (2) million land acres. It is Ka Lāhui Hawai'i's position that the National Land Trust of the Hawaiian Nation should eventually encompass all of the traditional lands of the Native Hawaiians and their descendants.

VI. The Private Land Trusts

The Hawaiian Monarchy provided for future generations by bequeathing their personal entitlements to land in trust for the Hawaiian people. These include:

1. The Kamehameha Schools / Bishop Estate;

2. The Queen Emma Foundation, Queen's Medical Center and Health Care System;

3. The Lunalilo Trust;

4. The Queen Lili'uokalani Trust;

5. The Queen Kapi'olani Women's and Children's Medical Center.

These private trusts were created to provide for education, medical assistance and assistance for elderly and orphaned children. These private trust lands and assets are currently managed pursuant to State and Federal law, despite the fact that they are entitlements of Hawaiians.

Hawaiian beneficiaries have never had any opportunity to set policy for the administrations of these assets, nor have they been able to participate in the selection or appointment of the persons who administer the trusts. The appointment process for trustees and administrators of these trusts has been highly politicized and has resulted in the mismanagement of these trusts.

Some of the Private Trust Lands and assets have been severely diminished by State condemnation. The Bishop Estate lands have been confiscated by State law in order to provide for private home ownership—a State obligation which the State did not address. These lands are not entitled to the tax and other benefits as proposed by the Ka Lāhui Hawai'i National Land Trust.

A. Ka Lāhui Hawai'i's Position Regarding the Private Trusts

1. Ka Lāhui Hawai'i asserts that Native Hawaiians and their descendants are beneficiaries of these trusts, and should be able to participate in their management and in the setting of policies relating to these lands.

2. Ka Lāhui Hawai'i asserts that the lands and assets of the private trusts must be protected from State and Federal actions which diminish their land base or financial resources.

B. Ka Lāhui Hawai'i, as the Native Hawaiian Nation, acknowledges its responsibility and obligation to provide for the health, education, and welfare of its people. To this end, our national objectives and those of the private trusts are common goals.

C. The Private Trusts shall work cooperatively with Ka Lāhui in the following areas:

1. To find ways in which the assets of the Private Trusts can be incorporated into the National Land Trust or otherwise designated "National Lands" in order to shield them from State, Federal, and County actions (including taxation);

2. To devise processes which shall allow Native people and Ka Lāhui Hawai'i to participate in the setting of policies relating to the management of the private trusts and the appointment and employment terms of the trustees and administrators overseeing these trusts;

3. To collectively develop and implement Service Programs so that duplication is avoided and adequate financing is available;

4. The creation of an H.M.O. (Health Maintenance Organization) providing health services and coverage to all citizens of Ka Lāhui Hawai'i who subscribe and which can maximize medical benefits from Medicaid, Medicare, et cetera. Medical and health services should include, but not be limited to: mental health, substance abuse, family and domestic abuse, nutrition and dietary needs, and elderly health services. Medical services shall be provided to all indigent Ka Lāhui Hawai'i citizens.

There are many issues which the Private Trusts and Ka Lāhui Hawai'i need to explore. The Private Trusts cannot avoid Sovereignty or escape the ramifications of Hawaiian self-determination. Working cooperatively with Ka Lāhui Hawai'i towards common goals is an alternative to beneficiary suits.

Our private trusts are being targeted and diminished; we must all work collectively to maintain and maximize these assets for future generations.

VII. Economic Development

Ka Lāhui Hawai'i defines the fifth element of sovereignty as an economic base, the ability of the nation to work on behalf of its citizens to be self-supporting. Ka Lāhui Hawai'i asserts that the goal of nationhood is economic self-sufficiency.

The cornerstones and fundamental building blocks of our sovereign initiative for economic development are the following:

1. The Hawaiian Nation shall establish a National Land Trust and have jurisdiction over its capital assets (revenues) in order to support economic initiatives for housing, employment, education, and the development of its own businesses and those of its citizens;

2. The Hawaiian Nation shall attain international and United States recognition of its sovereignty and shall negotiate economic and tax benefits appropriate for a National Land Trust. This shall not only exempt "national" business from taxation, but it shall provide the private sector (Hawaiian and non-Hawaiian) businesses with the opportunity to share in these benefits if they undertake to joint-venture with the Hawaiian Nation. This approach provides the Hawaiian Nation with the ability to utilize the tax incentive to work with the broader business community in meeting the needs of our citizens while creating more opportunities for affordable products and services.

3. The international trade agreements, covenants, and treaties between the Monarchy and other "foreign" nations are a historic entitlement, the benefits of which are due Native Hawaiians and their descendants. Therefore, the Hawaiian Nation has an established history of international trade agreements which is a basis for seeking such status with other nations, including the United States. It is Ka Lāhui Hawai'i's position that our sovereign nation should be free to enter into international trade agreements and contracts without the burden of United States customs, tariffs, and import and export regulations and costs.

4. Ka Lāhui Hawai'i supports the concept of community-based economic development. Economic self-sufficiency is an achievable goal of our citizens and local communities. Hawaiian small businesses should be given the financial and technical support to create and maintain businesses which

employ citizens and return benefits to the community that supports the business enterprises.

A. Taxation and Regulations

The power to tax and to regulate economic activities on its land base is an essential expression of self-determination of people through their sovereign nation. This power cannot be limited to economic activities of indigenous peoples, but must extend to all economic undertakings pursued within the domain (land, air, and water) of the Hawaiian Nation.

B. The Right to Self-Development and Technology

Ka Lāhui Hawai'i asserts that economic development must be culturally appropriate and environmentally responsible. Technological applications which meet these criteria should be utilized by the Hawaiian Nation. The right to determine whether development occurs and how development proceeds is a sovereign right vested in the Hawaiian Nation.

In keeping with our national commitment to peace and disarmament, Ka Lāhui Hawai'i opposes the use of all trust lands and marine and air resources for military ends.

VIII. International Issues

A. Reinscription

1. History

Hawai'i was part of the United Nations System until 1959 when the United States imposed statehood on the archipelago. Hawai'i was one of several territories on the United Nations list of Non-Self-Governing Territories from 1946 to 1959. During this time the United States was, under international law, the "administering agent" of Hawai'i. Pursuant to Chapter XI, Article 73 of the United Nations Charter, the

United States, as Hawai'i's "administering agent," accepted as a "sacred trust" the obligation to assist the "inhabitants" of the territory "in the progressive development of their free political institutions." In 1953 the Fourth Committee of the United Nations General Assembly passed Resolution 742.* Resolution 742 required that the inhabitants of the territories be given several choices in achieving self-government. These choices included: Free Association, Commonwealth, Integration (Statehood), and Independence or "other separate systems of self-government."

The United States never initiated a program for "decolonization" in Hawai'i under the United Nations process, nor did it allow the inhabitants of the territory their right to choose the options identified in Resolution 742. In 1959 the United States controlled the Statehood Plebiscite; the ballot provided for only one choice—statehood. History reveals that the 1959 Statehood Plebiscite was a violation of international legal standards intended to protect Hawai'i's indigenous people.

2. Position Statement

Ka Lāhui Hawai'i supports the reinscription of Hawai'i on the United Nations list of Non-Self-Governing Territories. *Ka Lāhui Hawai'i in its work to date has chosen to develop a culturally appropriate "separate system of self-government," which incorporates Hawaiian values and traditions and which sets forth the "cultural jurisdiction" of the Hawaiian Nation as provided by Part II of Resolution 742.* The Commonwealth and Free Association options under international law are essentially western forms of government which do not address or protect the rights of the indigenous peoples of the land.

3. By adoption of the Apology Bill, the United States has acknowledged that "the indigenous Hawaiian people have

---

* UN General Assembly Fourth Committee Resolution 742 (VIII), "Factors which should be taken into account in deciding whether a Territory is or is not a Territory whose people have not yet attained a full measure of self-government," 27 November 1953, item 33.

never directly relinquished their inherent sovereignty as a people or over their national lands to the United States, either through their monarchy or through a plebiscite or referendum." Therefore under international law, the indigenous people of Hawai'i are entitled to a separate system of self-government.

B. International Treaties

Prior to the illegal overthrow of the Hawaiian government, the Kingdom had negotiated several international treaties with all the sovereigns of Western Europe, the United States, Japan, and Russia. These treaties were declared by the United States to be null and void upon annexation. Ka Lāhui Hawai'i asserts that these treaties should be honored by the United States and other treaty signatories and that the trade and commercial benefits conferred by these treaties should be recognized.

To date, Ka Lāhui Hawai'i has negotiated and ratified 17 treaties with 85 indigenous nations on the American Continent. Ka Lāhui Hawai'i has also been granted voting membership with U.N.P.O (Unrepresented Nations and Peoples Organizations—the Hague).

C. International Instruments

Ka Lāhui Hawai'i asserts that the indigenous people of Hawai'i are entitled to the full protection of all international instruments, conventions, and treaties. Ka Lāhui Hawai'i is committed to achieving the passage of the *Draft Declaration on the Rights of Indigenous Peoples* in the form in which it was passed by the United Nations Working Group in August 1993.

The Ka Lāhui Hawai'i Platform on the Four Arenas of Sovereignty

Sovereignty as a political concept is applied in four distinct political arenas. It is important to understand these political arenas if you are to understand what the Ka Lāhui Hawai'i Sovereign initiatives are. All indigenous peoples working with sovereignty work in these four arenas.

Political Arena No. 1: Native To Native

All native peoples committed to sovereignty must deal with themselves, their culture, their traditions, lands, and government. Indeed, all indigenous peoples must begin by defining who they are and what they mean when they say they are sovereign.

A. Issues relating to Native Entitlements and National Identity

1. What kind of nation do we Hawaiians want?

2. Do we believe in self-determination?

3. What do we say sovereignty means?

4. What are our cultural traditions? How are they incorporated in our Nation?

5. What is the land base of the Nation?

6. What are our entitlements?

7. How will we govern ourselves and exercise jurisdiction over our lands?

8. What is the goal of our Nation? What principles are we committed to?

B. Issues relating to the obligations and responsibilities of the nation

1. How will the "government" provide for and incorporate the *mana'o* (thoughts) of its citizens in meeting the needs?

2. What national initiatives will be pursued for health, education, welfare, housing, etc., for our citizens and their families?

3. How will the nation train our leaders and acquire the necessary skills for self-governance?

4. How will the nation generate revenue and develop an economic base?

5. How will we provide for land and natural resources management?

C. Ka Lāhui Hawai'i's Agenda in Arena No. 1 (by priority)

1. Create a native initiative for self-governance. Create a real nation which incorporates self-determination into its governing structure. Stop mourning the loss of sovereignty and begin the work of nationhood. Kanaka Maoli must define the terms and powers of government.

2. Develop and implement a mass educational project on our entitlements, land base, status, etc.

3. Seek funding to train Hawaiians in areas needed to strengthen our skills in self-governance (land, education, finance, and health).

4. Obtain resolutions of support from our broader community, especially our churches.

Political Arena No. 2: Native to Nation/State

Many indigenous peoples and nations were taken over or colonized by Western and European powers. These native cultures, when asserting sovereignty, must deal with the nations/states that have control over their traditional lands. Hawaiians, Alaskan Natives, American Indians, Western Samoans, Puerto Ricans, Chamorros (native people of Guam) all deal with the U.S. The Yanonamis deal with Brazil, the Ainu with Japan. Some indigenous peoples deal with many nation/states; e.g., the Sami (Laplanders) deal with Russia, Sweden, Denmark, and Finland.

A. Issues to the U.S. and its agent the State of Hawai'i

1. Why has the U.S. Policy for native self-governance not been extended to Hawaiians? Why are we the only natives residing within a state that are wards of the State?

2. What is the nature of the State-Federal trust obligation to "native Hawaiians" and to "Hawaiians"?

3. Segregation and transfer of trust assets, revenues, and lands to the native nation.

4. Our right to access the federal court system to sue the U.S. and State to protect our land and enforce the State and Federal statutory and trust obligations.

5. Reparations for the illegal overthrow and illegal uses of our trusts and for violations of our human and civil rights.

B. Ka Lāhui Hawai'i's Agenda in Arena No. 2

1. Maintain our commitment to peace and disarmament (we will not declare war or engage in violence).

2. Participate to the greatest extent in all U.S./State legislative processes promoting our national platform. Obtain federal and state recognition of our nation under the U.S. Policy. Termination of the policy of wardship.

3. Obtain segregation of our lands, trust assets, and revenues from the State. Establish jurisdiction to tax and raise revenues and to have tax exemptions for national undertakings.

4. Establish the record of the extensive human and civil rights abuse of Kanaka Maoli. Advocate strenuously for correction of these abuses and for allocation of our lands. Use civil disobedience if necessary.

5. Raise the National (U.S.) consciousness about our status. See National (U.S.) publication of our issues.

6. Oppose and expose the State's ceded land settlement.

Political Arena No. 3: The International Arena

The International Arena is not just limited to the United Nations. It includes the International Labor Organization (ILO), World Council of

Churches (WCC), the International Court, and various international/ regional associations such as the Organization of American States (OAS). Also, it includes associations of people and groups not in the U.N. but in the international arena, such as NGOs (e.g. IITC—The International Indian Treaty Council), international jurists, anti-Slavery Society, etc.

Issues impacting the *global* community of indigenous peoples are addressed in the international arena. Human rights conventions, the Draft Universal Declaration, the Martinez Treaty Inquiry, the Law of the Sea Convention, the International Convenant on Civil and Political Rights, etc., impact the global indigenous community.

A. Political Issues and Agenda in Arena No. 3

1. The listing and removal of Hawai'i from the U.N. list of Non-Self Governing Territories in 1959.

2. The violations of human and civil rights under the Covenant on Civil and Political Rights, OAS, and other documents and conventions.

3. U.S. position at U.N. on Draft Declaration and its recent proposal to redefine the term self-determination.

4. Identification of the Pacific Basin as a toxic and munitions dump site for U.S. and Western ordnance (weapons and chemicals).

5. Position on Nations/States regarding treaties with the Hawaiian government (Kingdom).

B. Ka Lāhui Hawai'i's Agenda in Arena No. 3

1. Establish a presence in the International Arena through our Diplomatic and Foreign Ministry. *Educate internationally.*

2. Attend human rights and working group sessions and file written interventions on the Draft Declaration, Martinez Treaty Study, etc.

3. Counter U.S. positions. Work with NGOs.

4. Initiate an international complaint on human rights violations against the United States.

5. Reinstate Hawai'i on the U.N. list of Non-Self Governing Territories (with Guam and Puerto Rico).

Political Arena No. 4: Nation to Nation

Regardless of whether Nations/States (U.S.) recognize indigenous nations whose lands they have colonized, Native Nations can and must solidify diplomatic relations between themselves and other Nations/States. Indigenous nations face common threats and issues in the international arena. Native nations need to forge unified positions in the global arena for the protection of their lands, territories, and human rights.

A. Issues in Arena No. 4

1. What is the best and strongest position all indigenous nations can take on the Draft Declaration and other international conventions?

2. What is the global indigenous response to the U.S. positions at the U.N. on conventions and Pacific Basin development?

3. GATT [General Agreement on Tariffs and Trade], NAFTA [North American Free-Trade Agreement], etc.—The New World Order and Supra-National Corporate treaties which impact native territories and entitlements.

4. How can we benefit from or help other native nations who are dealing with similar health, housing, educational, etc., problems and issues?

B. Ka Lāhui Hawai'i Agenda in Arena No. 4

1. Network through the World Council of Churches. Attend regional consultations on issues No., 1, 2, and 3 above.

2. Enter into treaty negotiations with other Native nations in the U.S. to mutually benefit our people.

3. Associate with other nations and jointly file interventions at the U.N.

The 1989 Hawai'i Declaration of the Hawai'i Ecumenical Coalition on Tourism

The Hawai'i Ecumenical Coalition on Tourism convened an historic conference on "Tourism in Hawai'i: Its Impact on Native Hawaiians and Its Challenge to the Churches." Over 75 people participated in the conference from August 25–28, 1989, at St. Stephen's Diocesan Center on O'ahu. Nearly half of these were Native Hawaiians from Kaua'i, O'ahu, Moloka'i, Lāna'i, Maui, and Hawai'i, who represented their church, religious, and native organizations. Other representatives of church and religious groups in Hawai'i as well as national and international visitors constituted the rest. For the purpose of this conference, Native Hawaiians were identified as those who trace their ancestry prior to A.D. 1778 in Hawai'i.

The conference was initiated and organized by the Hawai'i Ecumenical Coalition on Tourism, the Hawai'i Council of Churches, American Friends Service Committee, and the Hawai'i Conference of the United Church of Christ in collaboration with the Ecumenical Coalition for Third World Tourism (ECTWT) and the North American Coordinating Center for Responsible Tourism (CRT). The fourteen international participants included representatives from ECTWT, CRT, the Third World Tourism Ecumenical European Net, the World Council of Churches (Program to Combat Racism), the National Council of Churches of Christ in the U.S.A., the Republic of the Marshall Islands, the Republic of Belau, the Republic of Fiji, Japan, the Confederated Tribes of the Warm Springs Reservation of Oregon, and the Haida Nation of North America.

A program of exposure and fieldtrips to see the realities of tourism in Hawai'i was organized for the international participants. At the conference itself, participants heard competent research on tourism in Hawai'i, agonizing testimonies from many Native Hawaiians who have been victimized by tourism as well as stories of successful Native efforts in self-sufficiency and self-determination. The participants divided into seven groups whose discussions were reported back for plenary. Subsequent analysis and careful deliberation led us to the following conclusions:

- Contrary to the claims of its promoters, tourism, the biggest industry in Hawai'i, has not benefited the poor and the oppressed Native Hawaiian people. Tourism is not an indigenous practice, nor has it been initiated by the Native Hawaiian people. Rather, tourism promotion and development have been directed and controlled by those who already control wealth and power, nationally and internationally. Its primary purpose is to make money.

- As such, tourism is a new form of exploitation. As a consequence, the Native Hawaiian people suffer the most; their culture has been increasingly threatened; their beaches and even their sacred sites have been taken over or intruded upon in order to build tourist resorts and related developments.

- Furthermore, tourism brings and expands the evil of an economy that perpetuates the poverty of Native Hawaiian people and that leads to sexual and domestic violence and substance abuse among the Native Hawaiian people. In addition, sexism and racism are closely interlinked with tourism. In short, tourism, as it exists today, is detrimental to the life, well-being, and spiritual health of Native Hawaiian people. If not checked and transformed, it will bring grave harm not only to the Native Hawaiian people but also to all people living in Hawai'i.

The plight of Native Hawaiian people is but one example of the destructive impact that tourism is having on indigenous people in communities around the world. All is not well in "paradise." Indeed,

A STATE OF EMERGENCY EXISTS IN REGARD TO THE SURVIVAL, THE WELL-BEING, AND THE STATUS OF THE NATIVE HAWAIIAN PEOPLE ON THE ONE HAND AND THE NEAR EXTINCTION OF THE PRECIOUS AND FRAGILE NATURAL ENVIRONMENT ON THE OTHER.

CALL TO THE CHURCHES

The churches have a moral obligation and responsibility to raise awareness in their congregations and in the State of Hawai'i about tourism's negative impacts and consequences on Native Hawaiians. The churches are called upon to "wrestle against the principalities and powers" that exploit people.

Furthermore, the churches must examine their history of involvement in Hawai'i's past and recognize their role in the loss of Native Hawaiian control over their land and destiny and in the overthrow of the Hawaiian monarchy. Such a recognition should lead to concrete actions on the part of the churches to rectify the wrongs which have been done.

Given these harsh and continuing realities, we, the participants of the conference, call upon the churches and religious institutions of Hawai'i, in consultation with Native Hawaiians, to initiate a process of reconciliation and reparations, as follows:

- Acknowledge the anger expressed by Native Hawaiian people for the past actions of the missionaries, their descendants, and the churches and institutions they established;

- Recognize that this anger is an expression of the suffering of the Native Hawaiian people; and

- Publicly apologize to the Native Hawaiians within their own congregations and the larger Native Hawaiian community for the churches' involvement and participation in the destruction and erosion of Hawaiian culture, religious practices, land base, and the overthrow of Queen Lili'uokalani and the Hawaiian monarchy.

I. Priority Rectifying Actions

We call upon the churches and religious institutions of Hawai'i to redress these injustices by advocating the following:

A. The return of public and private trust lands to the control of the Native Hawaiian people;

B. An immediate ban on all resort and related developments in those areas designated as sanctuaries by Native Hawaiians and in rural Hawaiian communities such as Leeward and Windward Kaua'i; Leeward and Windward O'ahu; Moloka'i; Lāna'i; East Maui; and the districts of North Kohala, South Kona, and Ka'ū on Hawai'i;

C. Technical, financial, and other support from the State of Hawai'i to Native Hawaiian projects which encourage economic self-sufficiency.

Furthermore, we call upon the churches and religious institutions of Hawai'i to support the political claims of Native Hawaiians to establish a sovereign entity, separate from the existing State and Federal governments, in order that they may achieve self-determination.

II. Public Witness

We call upon the churches and religious institutions of Hawai'i to take a stand for social justice and engage in political action, as follows:

A. Make public an inventory of the holdings and use of all church lands;

B. Return those church lands that justly belong to the Native Hawaiian people;

C. Reexamine the church lands and divest church funds currently being used for tourism purposes that negatively impact Native Hawaiians;

D. Refuse to participate in the public blessing of those projects that adversely impact Native Hawaiians or the environment;

E. Support worker demands for higher wages, a full-time work week with benefits, and better working conditions in the tourist industry;

F. Hold the tourist industry and government accountable for the social problems associated with tourism: increased crime, racism, sexual and domestic violence and disruption, substance abuse, housing costs, and land taxes; and

G. Support policies to reverse current trends of tourist industry growth. The human and natural resources cannot withstand the near doubling of total annual tourists to Hawai'i from its current 6.5 to 11 million over the next two decades, projected by the Hawai'i Visitors Bureau.

III. Education

We call upon the churches and religious institutions of Hawai'i to utilize and distribute educational materials and programs for both clergy and congregations in order to reevaluate misconceptions and dependency on tourism. These materials should:

A. Focus on Native Hawaiian culture;

B. Detail the negative effects of tourism on Native Hawaiian land and water rights, economy, and social life-style;

C. Promote Native Hawaiian self-sufficiency, sanctuaries, and sovereignty; and

D. Present a truthful view of Hawaiian history, including the involvement of the church and the U.S. government in the loss of Native Hawaiian land and power, and the overthrow of the Hawaiian monarchy.

IV. Religious Understanding and Practice

We call upon the churches and religious institutions of Hawai'i to be reminded that in God's house are "many mansions" and that "The earth is the Lord's and the fullness thereof."

We call upon the churches and religious institutions of Hawai'i to acknowledge and respect Native Hawaiian rights to:

A. Practice and participate in traditional ceremonies and rituals with the same protection offered all religions;

B. Determine access to and protection of sacred sites and burial grounds and public lands for ceremonial purposes; and

C. Utilize and access religious symbols for traditional ceremonies and rituals.

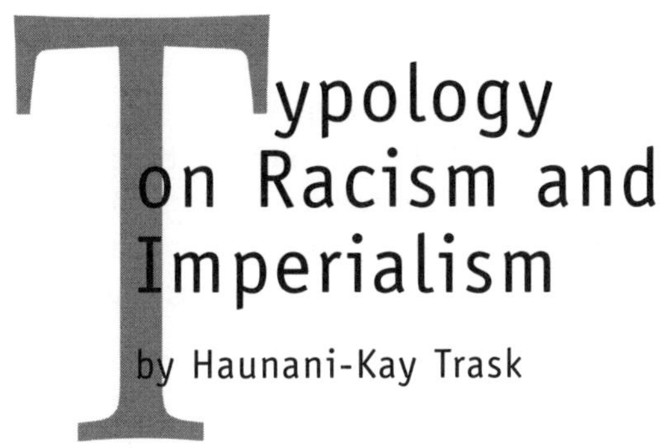

Typology on Racism and Imperialism

by Haunani-Kay Trask

Definitions

Imperialism

A total system of foreign power in which another culture, people, and way of life penetrate, transform, and come to define the colonized society. The function and purpose of imperialism is exploitation of the colony. Using this definition, Hawai'i is a colony of the United States.

Colonialism/Colonialist

Behaviors, ideologies, and economies that enforce the exploitation of Native people in the colonies.

Decolonization

Collective resistance to colonialism, including cultural assertions, efforts toward self-determination, and armed struggle.

Armed Struggle

Collective military resistance to imperialist and racist systems by those exploited by them.

Genocide

The systematic killing of a people identified by ethnic/racial characteristics. The purpose of genocide is extermination.

Distinctions

Racism

A historically created system of power in which one racial/ethnic group dominates another racial/ethnic group for the benefit of the dominating group; economic and cultural domination as well as political power are included in the systemic dominance of the exploiting group; a monopoly of the means of violence is also held by those in the dominating group.

Prejudice

A psychological condition in which individuals/groups are prejudged on the basis of certain characteristics (gender, race, age, etc.) Prejudice is to be distinguished from self-defense actions in the face of individuals and groups representing the dominant culture.

Discrimination

Actions based on prejudicial thinking.

Ethnocentrism

Preference for and belief in the centrality of one's own ethnic/racial group in one's everyday life. Ethnocentrism is not racism.

Righteous Anger

The emotional/psychological response of victims of racism/discrimination to the system of power that dominates/exploits/oppresses them. Righteous anger is *not* racism; rather, it is a defensible response to racism.

Self-Defense

Actions of self-protection taken by victims of racism that may include verbal, physical, and psychological strategies.

Index

About the Author

Haunani-Kay Trask is a member of Ka Lāhui Hawai'i, a Native Hawaiian initiative for self-government. She received her Ph.D. in political science from the University of Wisconsin–Madison. Her publications include numerous articles and a book of political analysis, *Eros and Power: The Promise of Feminist Theory* (1986). An accomplished poet, Trask published the much acclaimed *Light in the Crevice Never Seen* (1994). She served as the executive producer and scriptwriter for the documentary film *Act of War: The Overthrow of the Hawaiian Kingdom*. Currently, she is professor of Hawaiian studies at the University of Hawai'i at Mānoa.